D0742546

80 Years of Best Sellers

80 YEARS OF BEST SELLERS

1895-1975

ALICE PAYNE HACKETT

AND

JAMES HENRY BURKE

R. R. BOWKER COMPANY

NEW YORK · LONDON · 1977

Published by R. R. Bowker Company
1180 Avenue of the Americas, New York, N.Y. 10036
Copyright © 1977 by Xerox Corporation
All rights reserved.
Printed and bound in the United States of America

Library of Congress Cataloging in Publication Data

Hackett, Alice Payne, 1900–
  80 years of best sellers, 1895–1975.

  First published in 1945 under title: Fifty years of
best sellers; in 1956 under title: 60 years of best
sellers; and in 1967 under title: 70 years of best
sellers.
  Includes index.
  1. Best sellers—Bibliography. I. Burke, James
Henry, 1925–   joint author. II. Title.
Z1033.B3H342   011   76-49120
ISBN 0-8352-0908-3

We shall not busy ourselves with what men ought to have admired, what they ought to have written, what they ought to have thought, but with what they did think, write, admire.

—A HISTORY OF CRITICISM

by George Saintsbury

Contents

FOREWORDS by Arnold W. Ehrlich, Mildred C. Smith, and
    Frederic G. Melcher   ix

THE HISTORY OF BEST SELLERS   1

BEST SELLERS, 1895–1975   7

    Combined   9
    Hardbound   21
    Paperbound   32

BEST SELLER SUBJECTS   43

    Children's Books   45
    Cookbooks   47
    Crime and Suspense   49
    Do-It-Yourself and Gardening   52
    Poetry   53
    Reference   54
    Religion   55

BEST SELLERS BY YEARS, 1895–1975   57

EARLY BEST SELLERS   219

BOOKS AND ARTICLES ABOUT BEST SELLERS   225

TITLE AND AUTHOR INDEX   233

FOREWORD
to "80 Years of Best Sellers"

SINCE THE LAST EDITION of this book, the role of best sellers in our professional and cultural life has become more controversial than ever before. Publishers, authors, booksellers, agents, even the general public, recognize their commercial value. Detractors continue to complain that best seller lists represent common and even vulgar popular taste. The argument will rage as long as books are published; so will, as in this book, a civilized attempt to come to terms with a phenomenon of publishing that will long be with us.

The trailblazing innovations of Alice P. Hackett consist not only in establishing the *Publishers Weekly* best seller lists, but also in attempting—through *50, 60, 70,* and now *80 Years of Best Sellers*—to show the cultural and historic background of the making of popular literature.

As a service to the book trade, *Publishers Weekly* continues to make available each week what it believes are the most scientifically accurate lists possible of what is currently selling in the bookstores. Margin for error is unavoidable; perfection is unattainable. Note the plural: in 1976, after considerable reflection and research, *Publishers Weekly* inaugurated paperback mass market and trade best seller lists. These have won a gratifying reception in the trade.

December 1976

ARNOLD W. EHRLICH
Editor-in-Chief
Publishers Weekly

FOREWORD
to "70 Years of Best Sellers"

SOON AFTER Alice Hackett graduated from Wellesley she joined the staff of the *Publishers' Weekly* as an editor. And soon she developed a special interest in the phenomenon of the best seller. She applied her considerable talent for research to the subject and has made *Publishers' Weekly* the prime source of information about best sellers. She also originated the *Publishers' Weekly* Forecasts to which she continues to contribute. She has made of the term best seller at once something glamorous and a practical measure.

The first edition of this book, in 1945, was the first attempt to gather in one place American best seller records. Its scope was much enlarged in the second, 1955, edition. Proliferation of books during the past ten years has necessitated this new edition, which, as it brings the records of seventy years up to date, is most welcome.

August 1967 MILDRED C. SMITH

FOREWORD
to "60 Years of Best Sellers"

THE PROMPT recognition which was accorded ten years ago to Alice Hackett's records and comments on best sellers and the demand which has followed for a continuation of her figures and analysis has shown that such records have an interest to widely different groups of people—to the book trade, of course, but also to reminiscent readers and to students of public taste and social history. This continuation of the yearly lists is now accompanied by an expansion of earlier information which Miss Hackett has gathered by persistent contacts with many sources and to these annual lists has been added a greatly extended group of classified lists which enhance the popular interest and usefulness of the book.

August 1956 FREDERIC G. MELCHER

FOREWORD
to "50 Years of Best Sellers"

THE TERM "BEST SELLER" was coined and came into common use because it filled a need. A term was needed to describe what were not necessarily the best books but the books that people liked best. For a long time people have been interested in what other people read and why. If we are studying what books were popular in any period of our history, it is important to know not only what people could have read, or should have read, but what they did read. The record of what books a great many people have bought and read is a part of the social history of those people.

The books which have been important from a literary standpoint have been recorded in many volumes of literary criticism. Many of those books have had large and continuing sales, though some have only been appreciated years after they were published. These great books are the products in which any country must take great pride. On the other hand the record of best sellers of the hundred or more years during which book publishing has been an active industry in this country has not heretofore been adequately made. The record is only in part literary history. A literary classic is a book which continues to be important to succeeding generations of readers. Some of the best sellers of each decade have done that; many more have not. The lists covering a fifty-year period which this volume includes will make interesting material for study. Whether or not literature of continuing value is to be found among the best sellers, the lists provide significant insight into the thinking and emotions of a people. The trends of such reading may have more significance than a casual glance indicates.

How many copies any book has sold is recorded on the files of its publisher, and business records are not readily unearthed. Fortunately, however, the comparative sales of books year by year for the last half century have been kept systematically. The closing of this fifty year period makes a natural occasion for printing the record. The sales totals of books are more difficult to gather and to verify, but such figures, insofar as they have ever been printed, have become part of the historical files of the *Publishers'* *Weekly* office. Alice Payne Hackett, who has had so much to do with the development and completeness of these files, has pursued for her book every figure that could be verified by the files or records in the publishing offices.

Fifty Years of Best Sellers will open up to the student and bookman new fields for speculation. Perhaps students of literary history will try to chart the evolution of public taste from these records and writers of tomorrow's best sellers find, in these titles of the past, some clue to the perennial elements of popular appeal.

1946   FREDERIC G. MELCHER

80 Years of Best Sellers

The History of Best Sellers

THE HISTORY
OF BEST SELLERS

THE FIRST USE of the words "best sellers" that I have been able to discover appeared in an old copy of *Publishers Weekly*. The article told of a New York bookseller, who, returning to his house on Staten Island, asked a newsstand dealer in the ferryboat terminal what his best-selling books were. Since that long-ago time, "best sellers" have become a universal appellation, not only in reference to books but to all types of merchandise. The words are often misused as far as books are concerned. Publishers, movie producers, and television programers call any popular book a best seller.

Of course, they just may be correct. The term "best seller" is a relative term. A newsstand owner may sell only ten books a week, but they are *his* best sellers. Books may be best sellers in all the big city stores, in only one section of the country, or in a certain state. Most large stores and bookstore chains keep track of their best sellers, weekly or monthly, and often send out lists of them or display the lists in the stores. Most newspapers and some magazines run weekly lists of the best-selling books in their localities. The New York *Times* prints a national list, as do *Publishers Weekly,* the book-trade magazine, and *Time,* the national news magazine.

Best-selling books have often been in disrepute; many groups have tried to abolish the issuance of best seller lists. At present there seems to be less agitation against them. They exist and it is difficult to ignore them. Many readers look to the best seller lists for guidance and the infrequent book buyers, often selecting books as gifts, especially look to the lists for help.

Best-selling books are not always the best in a critical sense, but they do offer what the reading public wants.

The first best seller lists were published in a literary magazine, *The Bookman,* in 1895. *Publishers Weekly* began to run best seller lists in 1912. The 1895–1912 lists in this book are from *The Bookman*. From 1912–1975 they are from *Publishers Weekly*. Readers may be puzzled by the fact that many of the titles on the overall lists do not appear on the yearly lists and vice versa. The reason is that *Publishers Weekly* only includes books distributed through the trade, that is to bookstores and libraries. It does not include titles sold by mail or by book clubs. Incidentally, book clubs have proliferated since the founding of Book-of-the-Month Club in 1926 and Literary Guild in 1928. There are now about 150 adult book clubs covering every conceivable subject plus some 30 or so book clubs for children. In this book sales through all known outlets are included in the overall and special best seller listings.

There are recurrent themes in fiction and nonfiction throughout these 80 years. The historical, romantic adventure story is not as popular as it once was; the religious novel occasionally appears; crime and suspense stories, not usual in the earlier years, are now prevalent; and there are still love stories, although sex is, of course, much more explicit than it was when Elinor Glyn shocked the world with her *Three Weeks*. Once Zane Grey appeared regularly on the lists, now the best-selling western is a rarity. Books concerned with the current social scene, both fiction and nonfiction, have perennially appeared in the listings.

The first best seller lists were confined to fiction only. In 1912 and 1913 lists of ten nonfiction best sellers were compiled; they were then dropped until 1917 when they reappeared as general nonfiction (seven titles) plus a list of ten "war books." In 1919, after World War I, nonfiction lists were reinstated with six titles until 1922 when ten titles were listed. Both fiction and nonfiction lists have carried ten titles ever since. It is interesting to speculate as to why novels were chosen as the only best sellers in the late nineteenth- and early twentieth-century years. Perhaps frivolous romances were more salable—their prices were low at that time. There undoubtedly was an audience for serious nonfiction, but its price was appreciably higher than that of light fiction. Today the nonfiction best sellers outsell the novels by two to one.

During World War I everyone wanted to read about the war whether the medium was poetry or prose. Books by war correspondents and fighting soldiers were particularly popular.

Topical nonfiction whether related to war, assassination, politics, or crime has continued since 1917 to be one of the strongest threads of best-selling nonfiction. Then there are the "how-to" or "self-help" books which have comprised almost half the nonfiction lists from the beginning. The demand for self-development and self-improvement books whether by means of religion, philosophy, diet, exercise, game-playing, or cookery never flags. With the advent of the movies and television, theatrical memoirs have proved popular. Humor and gossip books abound. Too rarely good biographies or autobiographies crop up on the lists.

How these popular books reflect their times and sometimes serve to activate their own times is a fascinating field for the social historian. As James D. Hart said in his *The Popular Book* (Oxford University Press, 1950): "If a student of taste wants to know the thoughts and feelings of the majority who lived during Franklin Pierce's administration, he will find more positive value in Maria Cummins' *The Lamplighter* or T. S. Arthur's *Ten Nights in a Bar-Room* than he will in Thoreau's *Walden*—all books published in 1854."

4

The first edition of this book, *50 Years of Best Sellers,* was published in 1945 in a slim volume of 140 pages. Now it has grown through *60 Years* and *70 Years* to its present size. For purposes of compiling the lists in this book I have arbitrarily set a figure of 750,000 copies as the requirement for listing a hardcover as a best seller and 2,000,000 as the bottom line for a paperback. The requirement for inclusion in the special lists varies.

Finally I offer my most grateful thanks to Jim Burke who undertook the most tedious and difficult work of collecting facts and sales figures from the publishers of the best-selling titles herein.

ALICE PAYNE HACKETT

Best Sellers 1895 - 1975

COMBINED

HARDBOUND

PAPERBOUND

BEST SELLERS

1895 - 1975

COMBINED

THIS OVERALL LIST of best sellers includes books published in the United States from 1895 through 1975 which have, over 80 years, sold at least 2,000,000 copies. Most of them are included in either the hardbound best seller list or the paperbound best seller list. A few titles appear only on the combined list. The books on this list qualified when their hardbound and paperbound sales were combined. New Bible translations are not included but some new dictionaries are. Pamphlets are not included nor are encyclopedias, hymnals, prayer books, textbooks, picture books, and game books.

Publishers' names are not given on this list as they are on succeeding lists because most of the titles have been issued by two or more publishers. The date of original publication in this country follows the author's name. "F" indicates fiction and "J" indicates children's books.

This present list of books contains 366 titles each of which has sold over 2,000,000 copies. There were 307 titles on the combined list in the 1956 edition of this book and 1,000,000 was the qualifying figure then. The enormous increase in both number of best-selling books and in sales is due not only to the accelerated rate in the number of new titles issued in the years since 1945 but in great part to the increase in the production and distribution of paperbound books in the 1950's through 1970's, to the issuance of the Armed Services paperbacks during World War II, and to the big jump in book club sales immediately after that war.

Changes in the composition of the combined best seller list have resulted in the elimination from it of most of the popular books that were published in the years up to 1930, those that sold between 500,000 and 1,000,000. Some of the most popular authors of the early part of this century, like the American novelist Winston Churchill, whose historical tales were the top best sellers of almost every year from 1901 through 1915, and Harold Bell Wright and Gene Stratton Porter whose books predominated on earlier lists, have almost disappeared from this one.

On the following list there are 43 books which have sold more than 6,000,000 copies; only the first eleven on the list of ten years ago had reached that figure.

9

Pocket Book of Baby and Child Care, by Benjamin Spock. 1946   23,285,000

Better Homes and Gardens Cook Book. 1930   18,684,976

Webster's New World Dictionary of the American Language   18,500,000

The Guinness Book of World Records, by Norris and Ross McWhirter. 1962   16,457,000

Betty Crocker's Cookbook. 1950   13,000,000

F The Godfather, by Mario Puzo. 1969   12,140,000

F The Exorcist, by William Blatty. 1971   11,702,097

F To Kill a Mockingbird, by Harper Lee. 1960   11,113,909

Pocket Atlas. 1917 Hammond   11,000,000

F Peyton Place, by Grace Metalious. 1956   10,672,302

English-Spanish, Spanish-English Dictionary, comp. by Carlos Castillo and Otto F. Bond. 1948   10,187,000

F Love Story, by Erich Segal. 1970   9,905,627

F Valley of the Dolls, by Jacqueline Susann. 1966   9,500,000

F Jaws, by Peter Benchley. 1974   9,475,418

F Jonathan Livingston Seagull, by Richard Bach. 1970   9,055,000

The Joy of Cooking, by Irma S. Rombauer and Marion Rombauer Becker. 1931   8,992,700

The Sensuous Woman, by "J." 1969   8,814,662

F Gone with the Wind, by Margaret Mitchell. 1936   8,630,000

New American Roget's College Thesaurus in Dictionary Form   8,442,200

The Dell Crossword Dictionary, ed. by Kathleen Rafferty. 1964   8,292,951

F God's Little Acre, by Erskine Caldwell. 1933   8,258,400

F 1984, by George Orwell. 1949   8,147,629

Everything You Always Wanted to Know about Sex but Were Afraid to Ask, by David Reuben. 1969   8,000,000

F In His Steps, by Charles Monroe Sheldon. 1897   (est) 8,000,000

The American Heritage Dictionary of the English Language. 1969   7,485,207

Larousse French-English, English-French Dictionary. 1961   7,340,000

Mythology, by Edith Hamilton. 1930   7,272,600

F The Carpetbaggers, by Harold Robbins. 1961   7,171,841

F The Happy Hooker, by Xaviera Hollander. 1972   7,141,156

F Animal Farm, by George Orwell. 1946   7,070,892

Roget's Pocket Thesaurus. 1923   7,020,000

The Late Great Planet Earth, by Hal Lindsey and C. C. Carlson. 1970   7,000,000

The New American Webster Handy College Dictionary   6,921,300

How to Win Friends and Influence People, by Dale Carnegie. 1937   6,578,314

F Lady Chatterley's Lover, by D. H. Lawrence. 1932   6,326,470

30 Days to a More Powerful Vocabulary, by Wilfred J. Funk
and Norman Lewis. 1942   6,299,161

Chariots of the Gods?, by Erich Von Daniken. 1970   6,200,000

F Catch-22, by Joseph Heller. 1961   6,113,000

F I, The Jury, by Mickey Spillane. 1947   6,096,700

F The Great Gatsby, by F. Scott Fitzgerald. 1925   6,036,000

I'm O.K., You're O.K., by Thomas Harris. 1969   6,005,000

The Prophet, by Kahlil Gibran. 1923   6,000,000

101 Famous Poems, comp. by R. J. Cook. 1916   (est) 6,000,000

F The Catcher in the Rye, by J. D. Salinger. 1951   5,985,626

J Green Eggs and Ham, by Dr. Seuss. 1960   5,940,776

J One Fish, Two Fish, Red Fish, Blue Fish, by Dr. Seuss. 1960   5,842,024

J Hop on Pop, by Dr. Seuss. 1963   5,814,101

F The Big Kill, by Mickey Spillane. 1951   5,699,000

F Rich Man, Poor Man, by Irwin Shaw. 1970   5,689,545

J Dr. Seuss's ABC, by Dr. Seuss. 1963   5,648,193

Doctor's Quick Weight Loss Diet, by Irving Stillman and S. S.
Baker. 1967   5,608,491

F Airport, by Arthur Hailey. 1968   5,474,949

F Exodus, by Leon Uris. 1958   5,473,710

J The Cat in the Hat, by Dr. Seuss. 1957   5,394,741

F My Gun Is Quick, by Mickey Spillane. 1950   5,296,000

F One Lonely Night, by Mickey Spillane. 1951   5,274,900

F Kiss Me, Deadly, by Mickey Spillane. 1952   5,259,100

F The Long Wait, by Mickey Spillane. 1951   5,245,600

The Diary of a Young Girl, by Anne Frank. 1952   5,213,441

The Power of Positive Thinking, by Norman Vincent Peale. 1952   5,205,000

F Vengeance Is Mine, by Mickey Spillane. 1959   5,176,300

F Fear of Flying, by Erica Jong. 1973   5,072,800

F Doctor Zhivago, by Boris Pasternak. 1958   5,010,520

Modern World Atlas. 1922   5,000,000

J The Wonderful Wizard of Oz, by L. Frank Baum. 1900   (est) 5,000,000

Black Like Me, by John H. Griffin. 1961   4,918,479

F I Never Promised You a Rose Garden, by Joanne Greenberg.
1964   4,913,100

F Mandingo, by Kyle Onstott. 1957   4,905,000

The Pocket Cook Book, by Elizabeth Woody. 1942   4,900,000

F Never Love a Stranger, by Harold Robbins. 1948   4,854,180

F The Adventurers, by Harold Robbins. 1966   4,847,000

F Tragic Ground, by Erskine Caldwell. 1944   4,810,418

F	The Ugly American, by William J. Lederer and Eugene L. Burdick. 1958	4,794,776
	Profiles in Courage, by John F. Kennedy. 1956	4,784,324
F	Once Is Not Enough, by Jacqueline Susann. 1973	4,756,000
J	Charlotte's Web, by E. B. White. 1952	4,670,516
F	The Good Earth, by Pearl S. Buck. 1931	4,635,500
	The Sensuous Man, by "M." 1971	4,572,877
F	The Love Machine, by Jacqueline Susann. 1969	4,493,000
	Folk Medicine, by D. C. Jarvis. 1958	4,488,000
	Let's Eat Right to Keep Fit, by Adelle Davis. 1954	4,446,200
F	Rosemary's Baby, by Ira Levin. 1967	4,411,055
F	Return to Peyton Place, by Grace Metalious. 1959	4,400,000
	Psycho-Cybernetics, by Maxwell Maltz. 1961	4,350,000
	RCAF Exercise Book. 1962	4,330,000
	In Cold Blood, by Truman Capote. 1966	4,243,338
	Future Shock, by Alvin Toffler. 1971	4,213,585
F	Thunderball, by Ian Fleming. 1965	4,211,700
F	79 Park Ave., by Harold Robbins. 1955	4,185,592
F	The Other Side of Midnight, by Sidney Sheldon. 1973	4,134,281
	The Boston Cooking School Cook Book, by Fannie Farmer. 1896	4,100,000
F	The Winthrop Woman, by Anya Seton. 1958	4,080,016
F	Up the Down Staircase, by Bel Kaufman. 1965	4,046,319
	A Message to Garcia, by Elbert Hubbard. 1898	(est)4,000,000
F	Where Love Has Gone, by Harold Robbins. 1962	3,976,000
F	Hawaii, by James A. Michener. 1959	3,913,341
F	Journeyman, by Erskine Caldwell. 1935	3,910,155
	Here Comes Snoopy, by Charles M. Schulz. 1973	3,900,000
F	Portnoy's Complaint, by Philip Roth. 1969	3,866,488
	The Greatest Story Ever Told, by Fulton Oursler. 1949	3,858,948
	Kids Say the Darndest Things!, by Art Linkletter. 1957	3,821,608
F	Christy, by Catherine Marshall. 1967	3,797,732
F	Tobacco Road, by Erskine Caldwell. 1932	3,756,796
F	Goldfinger, by Ian Fleming. 1959	3,747,000
F	The Robe, by Lloyd C. Douglas. 1942	3,724,391
F	Lost Horizon, by James Hilton. 1935	3,714,210
	Good Ol' Snoopy, by Charles M. Schulz. 1973	3,650,000
	Helter Skelter, by Vincent Bugliosi and Curt Gentry. 1974	3,650,000
F	From Here to Eternity, by James Jones. 1951	3,646,004
F	Lolita, by Vladimir Nabokov. 1958	3,633,467

	Love without Fear, by Eustace Chesser. 1949	3,627,900
	Better Homes and Gardens Meat Cook Book. 1959	3,609,105
	All This and Snoopy, Too, by Charles M. Schulz. 1973	3,600,000
F	The Other, by Thomas Tryon. 1971	3,594,693
F	Trouble in July, by Erskine Caldwell. 1940	3,593,268
F	Centennial, by James A. Michener. 1974	3,591,763
F	Butterfield 8, by John O'Hara. 1935	3,577,729
	Xaviera, by Xaviera Hollander. 1973	3,572,000
F	The Case of the Sulky Girl, by Erle Stanley Gardner. 1933	3,564,334
F	Mutiny on the Bounty, by Charles Nordhoff and James Norman Hall. 1932	3,556,694
	The American Woman's Cook Book, ed. by Ruth Berolzheimer. 1939	3,549,276
F	Duel in the Sun, by Niven Busch. 1944	3,501,866
F	Georgia Boy, by Erskine Caldwell. 1943	3,501,281
	Four Days, by American Heritage and U.P.I. 1964	3,500,000
F	The Case of the Lucky Legs, by Erle Stanley Gardner. 1934	3,499,948
F	The Arrangement, by Elia Kazan. 1967	3,485,000
	Sybil, by Flora R. Schreiber. 1973	3,472,000
	Games People Play, by Eric Berne. 1965	3,470,000
F	Pocket Book of Short Stories, ed. by M. E. Speare. 1941	3,445,000
	Langenscheidt's German-English, English-German Dictionary. 1960	3,440,000
F	On Her Majesty's Secret Service, by Ian Fleming. 1963	3,438,700
J	The Cat in the Hat Comes Back, by Dr. Seuss. 1958	3,431,917
F	The Razor's Edge, by W. Somerset Maugham. 1944	3,430,505
F	All Quiet on the Western Front, by Erich Maria Remarque. 1929	3,425,000
F	A Stone for Danny Fisher, by Harold Robbins. 1952	3,409,391
F	A House in the Uplands, by Erskine Caldwell. 1946	3,408,361
F	The Betsy, by Harold Robbins, 1971	3,366,200
F	From Russia with Love, by Ian Fleming. 1957	3,365,100
F	Couples, by John Updike. 1968	3,330,858
F	You Only Live Twice, by Ian Fleming. 1964	3,283,000
	An Analysis of the Kinsey Report, ed. by Donald P. Geddes and Enid Currie. 1954	3,246,300
F	Doctor No, by Ian Fleming. 1958	3,239,500
F	The Group, by Mary McCarthy. 1963	3,230,047
F	The Green Berets, by Robin Moore. 1965	3,200,000
	It's for You, Snoopy, by Charles M. Schulz. 1973	3,200,000

Let's Face It, Charlie Brown, by Charles M. Schulz. 1973		3,200,000
We Love You, Snoopy, by Charles M. Schulz. 1973		3,200,000
Better Homes and Gardens Baby Book. 1943		3,180,808
F The Chinese Room, by Vivian Connell. 1942		3,171,512
F The Vixens, by Frank Yerby. 1947		3,170,056
F The Royal Box, by Frances Parkinson Keyes. 1954		3,156,000
F The Dream Merchants, by Harold Robbins. 1949		3,150,738
F The Case of the Haunted Husband, by Erle Stanley Gardner. 1941		3,127,585
Between Parent and Child, by Haim G. Ginott. 1965		3,108,677
F Captains and the Kings, by Taylor Caldwell. 1972		3,105,045
F Anatomy of a Murder, by Robert Traver. 1958		3,100,000
F The Case of the Curious Bride, by Erle Stanley Gardner. 1934		3,077,368
F Casino Royale, by Ian Fleming. 1953		3,037,253
The Conscience of a Conservative, by Barry Goldwater. 1960		3,007,000
F Tropic of Cancer, by Henry Miller. 1961		3,002,000
Grosset Webster Dictionary. 1956		3,000,000
Halley's Bible Handbook. 1927		3,000,000
The Story of the Bible, by Jesse Lyman Hurlbut. 1904		3,000,000
F The Red Badge of Courage, by Stephen Crane. 1896	(est)	3,000,000
F The Summer of '42, by Herman Raucher. 1971		2,995,291
F Magnificent Obsession, by Lloyd C. Douglas. 1929		2,974,030
F The Cardinal, by Henry Morton Robinson. 1950		2,950,807
Better Homes and Gardens Family Medical Guide. 1964		2,941,443
The I Hate to Cook Book, by Peg Bracken. 1960		2,929,782
F Forever Amber, by Kathleen Winsor. 1944		2,925,268
F The Case of the Velvet Claws, by Erle Stanley Gardner. 1933		2,924,756
F The Sure Hand of God, by Erskine Caldwell. 1947		2,911,666
F The Case of the Rolling Bones, by Erle Stanley Gardner. 1939		2,908,964
F The Fountainhead, by Ayn Rand. 1943		2,905,109
Hey, Peanuts, by Charles M. Schulz. 1973		2,900,000
F The Pirate, by Harold Robbins. 1974		2,900,000
Alive, by Piers Paul Read. 1974		2,884,368
F Live and Let Die, by Ian Fleming. 1954		2,883,400
F Moonraker, by Ian Fleming. 1955		2,877,500
The Rise and Fall of the Third Reich, by William L. Shirer. 1960		2,872,000
The Hidden Persuaders, by Vance Packard. 1957		2,867,523
F The Agony and the Ecstasy, by Irving Stone. 1961		2,866,718
F The Case of the Silent Partner, by Erle Stanley Gardner. 1940		2,850,904

	Fun with Peanuts, by Charles M. Schulz. 1973	2,850,000
	Good Grief, Charlie Brown, by Charles M. Schulz. 1973	2,850,000
F	For Your Eyes Only, by Ian Fleming. 1960	2,848,800
F	The Case of the Counterfeit Eye, by Erle Stanley Gardner. 1935	2,847,765
F	Rebecca, by Daphne du Maurier. 1938	2,820,313
F	Tales of the South Pacific, by James Michener. 1947	2,817,394
	The Total Woman, by Marabel Morgan. 1973	2,817,000
F	The Naked and the Dead, by Norman Mailer. 1948	2,816,662
F	The Chapman Report, by Irving Wallace. 1960	2,812,500
J	The Little Prince, by Antoine de Saint-Exupery. 1943	2,811,478
F	Never Leave Me, by Harold Robbins. 1954	2,802,263
	Very Funny, Charlie Brown, by Charles M. Schulz. 1973	2,800,000
	Let's Get Well, by Adelle Davis. 1954	2,799,110
F	The Spy Who Loved Me, by Ian Fleming. 1962	2,798,400
	See Here, Private Hargrove, by Marion Hargrove. 1942	2,786,223
F	The Case of the Caretaker's Cat, by Erle Stanley Gardner. 1935	2,783,403
	Please Don't Eat the Daisies, by Jean Kerr. 1957	2,778,988
F	The Best of Everything, by Rona Jaffe. 1959	2,760,000
F	The Case of the Substitute Face, by Erle Stanley Gardner. 1938	2,750,710
	The Service Cook Book, by Ida Bailey Allen. 1933	2,750,000
	The Gulag Archipelago, I, by Alexander Solzhenitsyn. 1974	2,742,331
F	The Case of the Baited Hook, by Erle Stanley Gardner. 1940	2,737,397
J	The Little House on the Prairie, by Laura Ingalls Wilder. 1953 ed.	2,732,666
	The Pocket Book of Verse, ed. by M. E. Speare. 1940	2,719,500
F	Around the World with Auntie Mame, by Patrick Dennis. 1958	2,716,816
F	The Foxes of Harrow, by Frank Yerby. 1946	2,702,597
F	The Case of the Stuttering Bishop, by Erle Stanley Gardner. 1936	2,702,363
	Here Comes Charlie Brown, by Charles M. Schulz. 1973	2,700,000
F	The French Lieutenant's Woman, by John Fowles. 1969	2,696,400
F	The Source, by James A. Michener. 1965	2,687,734
F	On the Beach, by Nevil Shute. 1957	2,680,597
F	Brave New World, by Aldous Huxley. 1932	2,672,065
F	Not As a Stranger, by Morton Thompson. 1954	2,667,977
F	Diamonds Are Forever, by Ian Fleming. 1956	2,664,400
F	The Odessa File, by Frederick Forsyth. 1972	2,648,411
F	The Case of the Sleepwalker's Niece, by Erle Stanley Gardner. 1936	2,646,024
	Let's Cook It Right, by Adelle Davis. 1947	2,640,612
	Comparative World Atlas. 1948	2,630,000

F The Inheritors, by Harold Robbins. 1969   2,619,000
  Better Homes and Gardens Casserole Cook Book. 1961   2,613,948
F Battle Cry, by Leon Uris. 1953   2,611,000
F Of Human Bondage, by W. Somerset Maugham. 1915   2,609,236
F Drum, by Kyle Onstott. 1962   2,605,000
F Wheels, by Arthur Hailey. 1971   2,604,614
F The Case of the Half-Wakened Wife, by Erle Stanley Gardner. 1945   2,604,336
  Better Homes and Gardens New Garden Book. 1951   2,601,288
  For the Love of Peanuts, by Charles M. Schulz. 1973   2,600,000
F The Case of the Black-Eyed Blonde, by Erle Stanley Gardner. 1944   2,588,757
  The Weight Watchers Program Cookbook, by Jean Nidetch.   2,575,000
F The Glorious Pool, by Thorne Smith. 1934   2,572,945
  Charlie Brown's All-Stars, by Charles M. Schulz. 1973   2,568,600
  Columbia Viking Desk Encyclopedia. 1953   2,565,899
F Topper, by Thorne Smith. 1926   2,560,806
  What Next, Charlie Brown, by Charles M. Schulz. 1973   2,550,000
F This Very Earth, by Erskine Caldwell. 1948   2,546,252
F The Drifters, by James A. Michener. 1971   2,528,342
  More Dennis the Menace, by Hank Ketcham. 1953   2,527,459
J The Little House in the Big Woods, by Laura Ingalls Wilder. 1953 ed.   2,527,203
  The Nun's Story, by Kathryn Hulme. 1956   2,521,531
  Papillon, by Henri Charrière. 1970   2,510,000
  House Plants, by Sunset Editors. 1968   2,500,000
F Women's Barracks, by Tereska Torres. 1950   2,500,000
F A Tree Grows in Brooklyn, by Betty Smith. 1943   2,487,740
F The Case of the Dangerous Dowager, by Erle Stanley Gardner. 1937   2,485,874
  Better Homes and Gardens Handyman's Book. 1951   2,478,431
F The Case of the Lame Canary, by Erle Stanley Gardner. 1937   2,476,145
  How to Stop Worrying and Start Living, by Dale Carnegie. 1948   2,471,140
  The Greening of America, by Charles A. Reich. 1971   2,462,982
  Honor Thy Father, by Gay Talese. 1971   2,462,000
F Advise and Consent, by Allen Drury. 1959   2,456,718
F Fail-Safe, by Eugene Burdick and Harvey Wheeler. 1962   2,452,000
  You Are Too Much, Charlie Brown, by Charles M. Schulz. 1973   2,450,000

	Dennis the Menace: Household Hurricane, by Hank Ketcham. 1957	2,434,336
F	No Time for Sergeants, by Mac Hyman. 1954	2,433,154
J	My First Atlas. 1959	2,431,000
F	So Well Remembered, by James Hilton. 1945	2,414,460
	The Naked Ape, by Desmond Morris. 1967	2,411,136
	Betty Crocker's Good and Easy Cookbook. 1954	2,400,000
F	The Chosen, by Chaim Potok. 1968	2,400,000
	I'll Cry Tomorrow, by Lillian Roth, Mike Connolly, and Gerold Frank. 1954	2,400,000
	You're a Winner, Charlie Brown, by Charles M. Schulz. 1973	2,400,000
F	The New Centurions, by Joseph Wambaugh. 1970	2,382,316
	English through Pictures (The Pocket Book of Basic English), by I. A. Richards and C. M. Gibson. 1945	2,380,000
	Scholastic World Atlas. 1960	2,370,000
F	The Jungle, by Upton Sinclair. 1906	2,367,600
J	Love and the Facts of Life, by Evelyn Duvall and Sylvanus Duvall. 1950	2,360,000
F	Singing Guns, by Max Brand. 1938	2,360,000
F	The Day of the Jackal, by Frederick Forsyth. 1971	2,357,926
F	Pavilion of Women, by Pearl S. Buck. 1946	2,353,453
	Better Homes and Gardens Salad Book. 1958	2,341,060
F	The Passionate Witch, by Thorne Smith. 1941	2,330,645
F	Cannery Row, by John Steinbeck. 1945	2,330,000
J	Egermeier's Bible Story Book, by Elsie E. Egermeier. 1923	2,326,577
	All the President's Men, by Carl Bernstein and Bob Woodward. 1974	2,320,000
F	Strange Fruit, by Lillian Smith. 1944	2,318,230
F	B. F.'s Daughter, by John P. Marquand. 1946	2,316,989
	Serpico, by Peter Maas. 1973	2,315,000
F	The Crazy Ladies, by Joyce Elbert. 1970	2,313,600
F	The Pearl, by John Steinbeck. 1947	2,310,000
F	The Damned, by John D. MacDonald. 1974	2,300,000
	We're on Your Side, Charlie Brown, by Charles M. Schulz. 1973	2,300,000
	A House Is Not a Home, by Polly Adler. 1953	2,286,000
	The Greatest Book Ever Written, by Fulton Oursler. 1951	2,282,322
F	Kitty, by Rosamond Marshall. 1943	2,273,841
F	The Case of the Empty Tin, by Erle Stanley Gardner. 1941	2,270,297
F	This Is Murder, by Erle Stanley Gardner. 1935	2,266,268
F	The Case of the Careless Kitten, by Erle Stanley Gardner. 1942	2,262,177

F 2001: A Space Odyssey, by Arthur C. Clarke. 1968   2,260,800

    Dennis the Menace Rides Again, by Hank Ketcham. 1955   2,254,960

F Dark Fires, by Rosemary Rogers. 1975   2,250,000

    Family Reference Atlas. 1956   2,250,000

    Gods from Outer Space, by Erich Von Daniken. 1971   2,250,000

    The Wonderful World of Peanuts, by Charles M. Schulz. 1973   2,250,000

F Mr. Roberts, by Thomas Heggen. 1946   2,246,396

J Go Ask Alice, Anonymous. 1971   2,245,605

F The Case of the Cautious Coquette, by Erle Stanley Gardner.
1949   2,244,552

    Kon-Tiki, by Thor Heyerdahl. 1950   2,237,449

F The Silver Chalice, by Thomas B. Costain. 1948   2,236,004

J Benji, by Leonore Fleischer. 1974   2,235,694

    Hiroshima, by John Hersey. 1946   2,230,000

F Pocket Book of Erskine Caldwell Stories, ed. by Henry Seidel
Canby. 1947   2,229,000

    Body Language, by Julius Fast. 1970   2,227,000

    Better Homes and Gardens Sewing Book. 1961   2,225,393

F Pride's Castle, by Frank Yerby. 1949   2,214,669

F The Amboy Dukes, by Irving Shulman. 1947   2,213,167

F The Clue of the Forgotten Murder, by Erle Stanley Gardner.
1935   2,212,271

F Deliverance, by James Dickey. 1970   2,201,244

F The Fan Club, by Irving Wallace. 1974   2,200,000

    How to Be Your Own Best Friend, by Mildred Newman and
Bernard Berkowitz. 1973   2,193,704

    Masters of Deceit, by J. Edgar Hoover. 1958   2,192,133

F The Young Lions, by Irwin Shaw. 1948   2,185,201

F Myra Breckinridge, by Gore Vidal. 1968   2,180,000

J The Little Engine That Could, by Watty Piper. 1926   2,166,000

F The Lord of the Flies, by William Golding. 1962   2,165,000

F National Velvet, by Enid Bagnold. 1935   2,152,210

    According to Hoyle, by Richard L. Frey. 1964   2,150,000

F The Black Rose, by Thomas B. Costain. 1945   2,146,812

F The Seven Minutes, by Irving Wallace. 1969   2,140,000

F The Stranger, by Albert Camus. 1954   2,139,000

F Rally Round the Flag, Boys!, by Max Shulman. 1957   2,134,289

F Prince of Foxes, by Samuel Shellabarger. 1947   2,133,810

J Stuart Little, by E. B. White. 1945   2,129,591

	Soul on Ice, by Eldridge Cleaver. 1968	2,125,335
F	The Deep, by Mickey Spillane. 1961	2,124,418
	Pregnancy, Birth and Family Planning, by Alan F. Guttmacher. 1973	2,122,600
F	The Case of the Golddigger's Purse, by Erle Stanley Gardner. 1945	2,121,708
F	The Man, by Irving Wallace. 1964	2,120,000
F	Topaz, by Leon Uris. 1967	2,105,751
	Wanted: Dennis the Menace, by Hank Ketcham. 1961	2,103,951
	The American College Dictionary, ed. by Clarence L. Barnhart. 1947	2,103,835
	The Song of Our Syrian Guest, by William Allen Knight. 1903	2,103,064
F	The Revolt of Mamie Stover, by William Bradford Huie. 1951	2,102,600
F	The Grapes of Wrath, by John Steinbeck. 1939	2,100,908
	The Pocket Dictionary, by W. J. Pelo. 1941	2,100,000
F	Karen, by Marie Killilea. 1952	2,099,261
	The Boston Strangler, by Gerold Frank. 1967	2,089,800
J	Freckles, by Gene Stratton Porter. 1904	2,089,523
F	Nevada, by Zane Grey. 1928	2,087,837
F	The Caine Mutiny, by Herman Wouk. 1954	2,087,173
F	Sanctuary, by William Faulkner. 1931	2,080,985
F	Seven Days in May, by Fletcher Knebel and Charles W. Bailey, II. 1962	2,073,434
	The Outline of History, by H. G. Wells. 1921	2,070,170
	Harlow, by Irving Shulman. 1964	2,068,000
	Expectant Motherhood, by Nicholson J. Eastman. 1940	2,063,775
F	Another Country, by James Baldwin. 1962	2,054,928
J	The Girl of the Limberlost, by Gene Stratton Porter. 1909	2,053,892
	Bible Readings for the Home Circle. 1914	2,051,488
	Western Garden Book, by Sunset Editors. 1933	2,050,000
	All Things Bright and Beautiful, by James Herriot. 1974	2,044,374
F	Leave Her to Heaven, by Ben Ames Williams. 1944	2,031,210
F	The Case of the Crooked Candle, by Erle Stanley Gardner. 1944	2,029,248
	Listen to the Warm, by Rod McKuen. 1967	2,025,000
	Better Homes and Gardens Fondue and Tabletop Cooking. 1970	2,022,529
F	The Bramble Bush, by Charles Mergendahl. 1958	2,007,000
F	Bridge Over the River Kwai, by Pierre Boulle. 1954	2,007,000

F The Case of the Borrowed Brunette, by Erle Stanley Gardner.
1946   2,006,808

The Elements of Style, by William Strunk, Jr., and E. B. White.
1959   2,000,000

The Feminine Mystique, by Betty Friedan. 1963   2,000,000

How to Prepare Your Income Tax, by David Joseph. 1941 2,000,000

The New Compact Bible Dictionary, by Thomas A. Bryant.
1967   2,000,000

Streams in the Desert, by Mrs. Charles E. Cowman. 1925 2,000,000

F The Tight White Collar, by Grace Metalious. 1960   2,000,000

Webster's New School and Office Dictionary. 1975   2,000,000

BEST SELLERS

1895-1975

HARDBOUND

THESE ARE THE BOOKS, published in the past 80 years, which, in their hardcover editions, have sold 750,000 copies or more. Approximately 60 new titles have been added to the list that was published ten years ago in the previous edition of this volume. In the previous list only seven books had sold 3,000,000 or more copies; the present list has 21 over 3,000,000, eleven of which have sold over 5,000,000. Of these 21 titles, only three are works of adult fiction; seven are cook books; six are juveniles; two deal with the Bible; and there is one book of poetry, one book on child care, and one dictionary.

Of the overall additions to the list, there are about 30 cook books, ten juveniles, and one a children's cook book. Only two are novels in the strict sense of the word. Sinclair Lewis' *Main Street* (1920) and *Babbitt* (1922) have both made the list on the basis of over 50 years cumulative sales.

The day of the big best-selling hardcover novel seems to be waning. The hardcover book that attains best sellerdom today is one that requires a hard cover for practical purposes—a cook book, a juvenile, or a reference book. Undoubtedly there will in the future be isolated instances of hardcover fiction making the list, but the paperbound editions have virtually made enormous sales of hardcover best-selling fiction obsolete.

Members of the publishing industry have held symposia on the fate of the hardcover novel. Although paperback reprints account for the bulk of a novel's sales, the reluctance of the media to review and publicize paperbound books assures the continuing existence of the hardcover novel. Moreover, the author's prestige is involved. Few writers want to be known as merely paperback authors.

Among the books which have gone over the 750,000-mark in the past ten years are *Jonathan Livingston Seagull,* an inspirational work of fiction hardly classifiable as a novel; *The Joy of Sex,* a "how-to-do-it" book; and *I'm O.K., You're O.K.,* psychology and reassurance for the layman. The number-one best seller remains the same. The *Better Homes and Gardens Cook Book,* published in 1930, added 7,359,677 copies to its total in the past ten years and remains in a class by itself.

In view of the developments in publishing since World War II, the time-honored formula for a best seller might now be revised. *Lincoln's Doctor's Dog's Favorite Recipes for Beginners* might just do the trick.

The titles in the following list are arranged by order of sales. The names of the original publishers and the dates of original publication in the United States are included. If the original publisher has gone out of business, but the book is still in print, the name of the present publisher is given. If the book is out of print, the name of the original publisher is stated, whether or not the firm is still in existence. "F" indicates fiction and "J" indicates children's books.

	Better Homes and Gardens Cook Book. 1930 Meredith	18,684,976
	Betty Crocker's New Picture Cookbook. 1950 McGraw-Hill	7,000,000
	The Joy of Cooking, by Irma S. Rombauer and Marion Rombauer Becker. 1931 Bobbs-Merrill	6,800,000
	The Prophet, by Kahlil Gibran. 1923 Knopf	6,000,000
J	Green Eggs and Ham, by Dr. Seuss. 1960 Random House	5,940,776
J	One Fish, Two Fish, Red Fish, Blue Fish, by Dr. Seuss. 1960 Random House	5,842,024
J	Hop on Pop, by Dr. Seuss. 1963 Random House	5,814,101
J	Dr. Seuss's ABC, by Dr. Seuss. 1963 Random House	5,648,193
J	The Cat in the Hat, by Dr. Seuss. 1957 Random House	5,394,741
	The Good Housekeeping Cookbook, ed. by Zoe Coulson. Good Housekeeping Books	5,250,000
F	Gone with the Wind, by Margaret Mitchell. 1936 Macmillan	5,190,004
F	The Winthrop Woman, by Anya Seton. 1958 Houghton Mifflin	4,080,016
	Better Homes and Gardens Meat Cook Book. 1959 Meredith	3,609,105
	The American Woman's Cook Book, ed. by Ruth Berolzheimer. 1939 Doubleday	3,549,276
J	The Cat in the Hat Comes Back, by Dr. Seuss. 1958 Random House	3,431,917
	The Boston Cooking School Cook Book, by Fannie Farmer. 1896 Little, Brown	3,300,744
	Better Homes and Gardens Baby Book. 1943 Meredith	3,180,808
F	The Robe, by Lloyd C. Douglas. 1942 Houghton Mifflin	3,132,288
	Grosset Webster Dictionary. 1956 Grosset & Dunlap	3,000,000
	Halley's Bible Handbook, by Henry H. Halley. 1927 Zondervan	3,000,000
	The Story of the Bible, by Jesse Lyman Hurlbut. 1904 Winston	3,000,000
	Better Homes and Gardens Family Medical Guide. 1964 Meredith	2,941,443
J	The Wonderful Wizard of Oz, by L. Frank Baum. 1900 Bobbs-Merrill	2,834,049

	Better Homes and Gardens Casserole Cook Book. 1961 Meredith	2,613,948
	Better Homes and Gardens New Garden Book. 1951 Meredith	2,601,288
	The Weight Watchers Program Cookbook, by Jean Nidetch. 1972 Hearthside	2,575,000
	Columbia Viking Desk Encyclopedia. 1953 Viking	2,565,899
	The Power of Positive Thinking, by Norman Vincent Peale. 1952 Prentice-Hall	2,505,000
F	A Tree Grows in Brooklyn, by Betty Smith. 1943 Harper	2,487,740
	Better Homes and Gardens Handyman's Book. 1951 Meredith	2,478,431
	The Guinness Book of World Records, by Norris and Ross McWhirter. 1962 Sterling	2,442,000
	Better Homes and Gardens Barbecue Book. 1956 Meredith	2,439,001
	Betty Crocker's Good and Easy Cookbook. 1954 Simon and Schuster	2,400,000
	Jonathan Livingston Seagull, by Richard Bach. 1970 Macmillan	2,355,000
	Better Homes and Gardens Salad Book. 1958 Meredith	2,341,060
	Egermeier's Bible Story Book, by Elsie E. Egermeier. 1923 Warner Press	2,326,577
F	The Silver Chalice, by Thomas B. Costain. 1948 Doubleday	2,236,004
	Better Homes and Gardens Sewing Book. 1961 Meredith	2,225,393
J	The Little Engine That Could, by Watty Piper. 1926 Platt & Munk	2,166,000
F	The Black Rose, by Thomas B. Costain. 1945 Doubleday	2,146,812
	The American College Dictionary, ed. by Clarence L. Barnhart. 1947 Random House	2,103,835
	The Song of Our Syrian Guest, by William Allen Knight. 1903 United Church Press	2,103,064
J	Freckles, by Gene Stratton Porter. 1904 Doubleday	2,089,523
	The Outline of History, by H. G. Wells. 1921 Macmillan	2,070,170
	Expectant Motherhood, by Nicholson J. Eastman. 1940 Little, Brown	2,063,775
J	The Girl of the Limberlost, by Gene Stratton Porter. 1909 Doubleday	2,053,892
F	Leave Her to Heaven, by Ben Ames Williams. 1944 Houghton Mifflin	2,031,210
	Listen to the Warm, by Rod McKuen. 1967 Random House	2,025,000
	Better Homes and Gardens Fondue and Tabletop Cooking. 1970 Meredith	2,022,529

The American Heritage Dictionary of the English Language. 1969 Houghton Mifflin 2,000,000

Streams in the Desert, by Mrs. Charles E. Cowman. 1925 Zondervan 2,000,000

F In His Steps, by Charles Monroe Sheldon. 1897 Grosset & Dunlap et al. .... (est) 2,000,000

F The Razor's Edge, by W. Somerset Maugham. 1944 Doubleday 1,920,505

Better Homes and Gardens Meals in Minutes. 1963 Meredith ... 1,883,866

F The Call of the Wild, by Jack London. 1917 Macmillan ... 1,794,020

30 Days to a More Powerful Vocabulary, by Wilfred J. Funk and Norman Lewis. 1942 Funk & Wagnalls 1,789,161

Federal Aviation Regulations and Flight Standards for Pilots. 1947 Aero Publishers 1,750,000

F Dinner at Antoine's, by Frances Parkinson Keyes. 1948 Messner 1,748,000

The American Everyday Dictionary, ed. by Jess Stein. 1953 Random House 1,710,000

Encyclopedia Cookbook. 1950 Grosset & Dunlap 1,700,000

F Not as a Stranger, by Morton Thompson. 1954 Scribner ... 1,700,000

F The Caine Mutiny, by Herman Wouk. 1952 Doubleday ... 1,696,989

F The Foxes of Harrow, by Frank Yerby. 1946 Dial Press ... 1,671,697

How to Win Friends and Influence People, by Dale Carnegie. 1937 Simon and Schuster 1,664,208

F Forever Amber, by Kathleen Winsor. 1944 Macmillan ... 1,652,837

F The Golden Hawk, by Frank Yerby. 1948 Dial Press ... 1,648,064

F The Virginian, by Owen Wister. 1902 Macmillan 1,636,299

Better Homes and Gardens Holiday Cook Book. 1959 Meredith ... 1,634,809

The Settlement Cook Book, by Mrs. Simon Kander. 1930 Simon and Schuster 1,626,135

F The Harvester, by Gene Stratton Porter. 1911 Doubleday ... 1,611,007

J Laddie, by Gene Stratton Porter. 1913 Doubleday 1,586,529

The Greatest Story Ever Told, by Fulton Oursler. 1949 Doubleday 1,553,988

F Mother, by Kathleen Norris. 1911 Doubleday 1,553,742

F The Vixens, by Frank Yerby. 1947 Dial Press 1,524,123

In Tune with the Infinite, by Ralph Waldo Trine. 1897 Bobbs-Merrill 1,507,502

Better Homes and Gardens Jiffy Cooking. 1967 Meredith ... 1,506,063

Amy Vanderbilt's Complete Book of Etiquette, by Amy Vanderbilt. 1952 Doubleday 1,500,000

J	Big Book of Mother Goose. 1950 Grosset & Dunlap	1,500,000
	Diet Watcher's Guide. 1968 Grosset & Dunlap	1,500,000
	Jogging. 1968 Grosset & Dunlap	1,500,000
	The Specialist, by Chic Sale. 1929 Specialist Publishing Co.	1,500,000
	Stanyan Street and Other Sorrows, by Rod McKuen. 1954 Random House	1,500,000
F	All Quiet on the Western Front, by Erich Maria Remarque. 1929 Little, Brown	1,453,351
F	Strange Woman, by Ben Ames Williams. 1941 Houghton Mifflin	1,443,524
F	Green Dolphin Street, by Elizabeth Goudge. 1944 Coward-McCann	1,425,000
J	A Friend Is Someone Who Likes You, by Joan Walsh Anglund. 1958 Harcourt Brace Jovanovich	1,423,432
F	Lydia Bailey, by Kenneth Roberts. 1947 Doubleday.	1,405,936
	Etiquette, by Emily Post. 1922 Funk & Wagnalls	1,400,000
	Better Homes and Gardens Cooking for Two. 1968 Meredith	1,381,085
	Better Homes and Gardens Dessert Cook Book. 1960 Meredith	1,380,995
	Better Homes and Gardens So Good Meals. 1963 Meredith	1,379,795
	Better Homes and Gardens Eat and Stay Slim. 1968 Meredith	1,371,327
F	The King's General, by Daphne du Maurier. 1946 Doubleday	1,362,045
J	Rebecca of Sunnybrook Farm, by Kate Douglas Wiggin. 1904 Houghton Mifflin	1,357,714
F	Joy Street, by Frances Parkinson Keyes. 1950 Messner	1,349,000
F	Annie Jordan, by Mary Brinker Post. 1948 Doubleday	1,315,551
J	Love Is a Special Way of Feeling, by Joan Walsh Anglund. 1960 Harcourt Brace Jovanovich	1,308,293
	The Worldly Philosophers, by Robert Heilbroner. 1953 Simon and Schuster	1,304,834
	Better Homes and Gardens Lunches and Brunches. 1963 Meredith	1,302,959
	Touch Typing. 1962 Grosset & Dunlap	1,300,000
	Your Dream Home, by Hubbard Cobb. 1950 W. H. Wise	1,300,000
J	The Real Mother Goose. 1915 Rand McNally	1,296,140
F	The Trail of the Lonesome Pine, by John Fox, Jr. 1908 Scribner	1,285,000
F	The Keys of the Kingdom, by A. J. Cronin. 1941 Little, Brown	1,284,198
	Better Homes and Gardens Canning Cook Book. 1973 Meredith	1,280,080
F	Came a Cavalier, by Frances Parkinson Keyes. 1947 Messner	1,279,000
F	This Side of Innocence, by Taylor Caldwell. 1946 Scribner	1,276,000

F Babbitt, by Sinclair Lewis. 1922 Harcourt Brace Jovanovich   1,275,739

Wise Garden Encyclopedia, by E. L. D. Seymour. 1936 W. H. Wise   1,265,000

F Before the Sun Goes Down, by Elizabeth M. Howard. 1946 Doubleday   1,260,725

Better Homes and Gardens Best Buffets. 1963 Meredith   1,252,192

F Desiree, by Annemarie Selinko. 1953 Morrow   1,251,709

A Field Guide to the Birds, by Roger Tory Peterson. 1947 Houghton Mifflin   1,251,184

Modern Encyclopedia, by A. H. McDonnald. 1933 W. H. Wise   1,250,000

F Steamboat Gothic, by Frances Parkinson Keyes. 1952 Messner   1,247,000

Better Homes and Gardens Barbecue and Picnics. 1963 Meredith   1,246,725

F Mutiny on the Bounty, by Charles Nordhoff and James Norman Hall. 1932 Little, Brown   1,246,694

F The Crisis, by Winston Churchill. 1901 Macmillan   1,243,307

Better Homes and Gardens Pies and Cakes. 1966 Meredith   1,242,975

The Greatest Book Ever Written, by Fulton Oursler. 1951 Doubleday   1,237,887

The Egg and I, by Betty MacDonald. 1945 Lippincott   1,228,737

F Gentleman's Agreement, by Laura Z. Hobson. 1947 Simon and Schuster   1,221,986

J Better Homes and Gardens Story Book. 1951 Meredith   1,220,728

F The Riders of the Purple Sage, by Zane Grey. 1912 Harper   1,215,938

Better Homes and 'Gardens Snacks and Refreshments. 1963 Meredith   1,212,090

Daily Strength for Daily Needs, by Mary W. Tileston. 1901 Little, Brown and Revell   1,212,060

Better Homes and Gardens Decorating Book. 1956 Meredith   1,206,278

How to Stop Worrying and Start Living, by Dale Carnegie. 1948 Simon and Schuster   1,203,000

J Charlotte's Web, by E. B. White. 1952 Harper & Row   1,200,000

F David Harum, by Edward Noyes Westcott. 1900 Appleton   1,200,000

The New Century Dictionary of the English Language. 1927 Appleton-Century   1,200,000

Scrabble Word Guide. 1958 Grosset & Dunlap   1,200,000

F The Shepherd of the Hills, by Harold Bell Wright. 1907 Appleton   1,200,000

F Rebecca, by Daphne du Maurier. 1938 Doubleday   1,194,587

F Michael O'Halloran, by Gene Stratton Porter. 1915 Doubleday   1,194,440

F The Sheik, by E. M. Hull. 1921 Dodd, Mead   1,194,000

Better Homes and Gardens Blender Cook Book. 1971 Meredith   1,192,630

	Better Homes and Gardens Favorite Ways with Chicken. 1967 Meredith	1,186,811
F	The River Road, by Frances Parkinson Keyes. 1946 Messner	1,168,000
	Modern Home Medical Advisor, ed. by Morris Fishbein. 1935 Doubleday	1,165,499
F	The Royal Box, by Frances Parkinson Keyes. 1954 Messner	1,156,000
F	Shannon's Way, by A. J. Cronin. 1948 Little, Brown	1,155,018
	Modern Home Physician, by Victor Robinson, M.D. 1934 W. H. Wise	1,150,000
F	The Good Earth, by Pearl S. Buck. 1931 John Day	1,115,500
F	Light of Western Stars, by Zane Grey. 1914 Harper	1,112,697
F	Wildfire, by Zane Grey. 1917 Harper	1,107,754
	Kids Say the Darndest Things!, by Art Linkletter. 1957 Prentice-Hall	1,107,318
	Peace of Mind, by Joshua L. Liebman. 1946 Simon and Schuster	1,107,064
J	Better Homes and Gardens Junior Cook Book. 1955 Meredith	1,100,182
	Appleton's English-Spanish, Spanish-English Dictionary, by Arturo Cuyas. 1903 Appleton-Century	1,100,000
	I'm O.K., You're O.K., by Thomas Harris. 1969 Harper & Row	1,100,000
F	The Little Shepherd of Kingdom Come, by John Fox, Jr. 1903 Scribner	1,100,000
	Rand McNally Dollar World Atlas. 1949 Rand McNally	1,100,000
	The Random House College Dictionary, ed. by Lawrence Urdang and Jess Stein. 1968 Random House	1,100,000
F	The Rosary, by Florence Barclay. 1910 Putnam	1,099,000
	Complete Home Handyman's Guide, by Hubbard Cobb. 1948 W. H. Wise	1,095,000
F	Love Is Eternal, by Irving Stone. 1954 Doubleday	1,093,330
F	My Cousin Rachel, by Daphne du Maurier. 1952 Doubleday	1,093,230
	Better Homes and Gardens Flower Arranging. 1957 Meredith	1,091,287
F	So Well Remembered, by James Hilton. 1945 Little, Brown	1,083,409
	Crusade in Europe, by Dwight D. Eisenhower. 1948 Doubleday	1,076,380
F	Pride's Castle, by Frank Yerby, 1949 Dial Press	1,073,679
F	Hungry Hill, by Daphne du Maurier. 1943 Doubleday	1,068,004
J	Pollyanna, by Eleanor H. Porter. 1913 Page	1,059,000
	Strength for Service to God and Country, by Norman F. Nygaard. 1942 Abingdon Press	1,050,000
F	Lusty Wind for Carolina, by Inglis Fletcher. 1944 Bobbs-Merrill	1,048,247

Five Acres and Independence, by M. G. Kains. 1935 Greenberg 1,044,000

F Doctor Zhivago, by Boris Pasternak. 1958 Pantheon Books 1,042,520

Their Finest Hour, by Sir Winston Churchill. 1949 Houghton Mifflin 1,032,681

Calories Don't Count, by Dr. Herman Taller. 1961. Simon and Schuster 1,025,000

Kon-Tiki, by Thor Heyerdahl. 1950 Rand McNally 1,022,949

F High Towers, by Thomas B. Costain. 1949 Doubleday 1,021,233

F Topper, by Thorne Smith. 1926 Doubleday 1,018,806

F B. F.'s Daughter, by John P. Marquand. 1946 Little, Brown 1,013,977

The Day Christ Died, by Jim Bishop. 1957 Harper 1,012,677

F The Sun Is My Undoing, by Marguerite Steen. 1941 Viking 1,010,000

Better Homes and Gardens Calorie Counter's Cook Book, 1970 Meredith 1,008,666

F Scarlet Sister Mary, by Julia Peterkin. 1928 Bobbs-Merrill 1,007,977

Better Homes and Gardens Meals with a Foreign Flair. 1963 Meredith 1,006,162

Great Controversy, by Ellen G. White. 1926 Review & Herald 1,005,381

J Winnie-the-Pooh, by A. A. Milne. 1926 Dutton 1,005,000

Happiness Is a Warm Puppy, by Charles M. Schulz. 1962 Determined Productions 1,000,054

F Anthony Adverse, by Hervey Allen. 1933 Rinehart 1,000,000

Brave Men, by Ernie Pyle. 1944 Holt 1,000,000

A Heap o' Livin', by Edgar Guest. 1916 Reilly & Lee 1,000,000

The Joy of Sex, ed. by Alex Comfort. 1972 Crown 1,000,000

J Little Black Sambo, by Helen Bannerman. 1899 Lippincott (est) 1,000,000

A Message to Garcia, by Elbert Hubbard. 1898 Roycroft (est) 1,000,000

101 Famous Poems, comp. by R. J. Cook. 1916 Regnery (est) 1,000,000

J Pollyanna Grows Up, by Eleanor H. Porter. 1915 Page 1,000,000

Roget's International Thesaurus. 1962 Crowell 1,000,000

The Simple Life, by Charles Wagner. 1901 Doubleday 1,000,000

F The Song of Bernadette, by Franz Werfel. 1942 Viking 1,000,000

F The Web of Days, by Edna L. Lee. 1947 Appleton-Century 1,000,000

Will Rogers, by Patrick J. O'Brien. 1935 Winston 1,000,000

F Yankee Pasha, by Edison Marshall. 1947 Farrar, Straus 1,000,000

A Man Called Peter, by Catherine Marshall. 1951 McGraw-Hill 998,890

F Floodtide, by Frank Yerby. 1950 Dial Press 993,726

The Story of the Other Wise Man, by Henry Van Dyke. 1895 Harper (est) 989,088

	The Culbertson Summary, by Ely Culbertson. 1935 Winston	983,628
	The Story of Philosophy, by Will Durant. 1926 Simon and Schuster	975,109
	Better Homes and Gardens House Plants. 1959 Meredith	970,547
F	The Golden Fury, by Marian Castle. 1949 Morrow	969,499
	Here Is Your War, by Ernie Pyle. 1943 Holt	967,000
F	Lone Star Ranger, by Zane Grey. 1915 Harper	960,482
	History of the World War, by Richard J. Beamish and F. A. March. 1928 Winston	960,000
	Grand Alliance, by Sir Winston Churchill. 1950 Houghton Mifflin	956,579
F	My Friend Flicka, by Mary O'Hara. 1941 Lippincott	955,000
F	The Prince of Foxes, by Samuel Shellabarger. 1947 Little, Brown	954,021
F	Pavilion of Women, by Pearl S. Buck. 1946 John Day	953,500
	Land Birds East of the Rockies, by Chester A. Reed. 1906 Doubleday	953,173
F	Desert Gold, by Zane Grey. 1913 Harper	950,632
	Low Carbohydrate Diet. 1965 Grosset & Dunlap	950,000
	Six Weeks to Words of Power, by Wilfred J. Funk. 1953 Funk & Wagnalls	932,621
F	Main Street, by Sinclair Lewis. 1920 Harcourt Brace Jovanovich	930,929
	Hinge of Fate, by Sir Winston Churchill. 1950 Houghton Mifflin	930,616
	Better Homes and Gardens Good Food on a Budget. 1971 Meredith	927,289
F	The Calling of Dan Matthews, by Harold Bell Wright. 1916 Appleton	925,000
F	The Great Impersonation, by E. Phillips Oppenheim. 1920 Little, Brown	912,782
	Triumph and Tragedy, by Sir Winston Churchill. 1953 Houghton Mifflin	907,413
	Profiles in Courage, by John F. Kennedy. 1956 Harper	904,324
F	The Winning of Barbara Worth, by Harold Bell Wright. 1911 Appleton	900,000
F	The Mysterious Rider, by Zane Grey. 1921 Harper	898,031
	Better Homes and Gardens Cooking with Cheese. 1966 Meredith	889,694
J	The Cat in the Hat Beginner Book Dictionary, by P. D. Eastman. 1964 Random House	889,445

F The Cleft Rock, by Alice Tisdale Hobart. 1948 Bobbs-Merrill   887,200

F Rainbow Trail, by Zane Grey. 1915 Harper   885,563

F Pilgrim's Inn, by Elizabeth Goudge. 1944 Coward-McCann   885,000

Closing the Ring, by Sir Winston Churchill. 1951 Houghton
Mifflin   883,957

F Thunderhead, by Mary O'Hara. 1943 Lippincott   880,000

F The Chain, by Paul Wellman. 1949 Doubleday   878,813

Better Homes and Gardens Bread Cook Book. 1963 Meredith   873,930

Abundant Living, by E. Stanley Jones. 1942 Abingdon Press   873,534

F Heritage of the Desert, by Zane Grey. 1910 Harper   873,400

F The Big Fisherman, by Lloyd C. Douglas. 1948 Houghton
Mifflin   864,273

F Scaramouche, by Rafael Sabatini. 1921 Houghton Mifflin   862,901

F The Moneyman, by Thomas B. Costain. 1947 Doubleday   855,944

F Green Light, by Lloyd C. Douglas. 1935 Houghton Mifflin   854,828

F Bride of Fortune, by Harnett Kane. 1948 Doubleday   853,672

J My First Book about Jesus, by Mary Alice Jones. 1953 Rand
McNally   850,000

J Santa Mouse. 1966 Grosset & Dunlap   850,000

The Gathering Storm, by Sir Winston Churchill. 1948 Houghton Mifflin   849,094

F The Private Life of Helen of Troy, by John Erskine. 1925
Bobbs-Merrill   844,000

F To the Last Man, by Zane Grey. 1922 Harper   842,946

F The Parasites, by Daphne du Maurier. 1950 Doubleday   841,715

Better Homes and Gardens Make-Ahead Cook Book. 1971
Meredith   835,402

F The Chinese Parrot, by Earl Derr Biggers. 1940 Bobbs-Merrill   812,383

Pictorial History World War II. 1944 W. H. Wise   811,000

J Just So Stories, by Rudyard Kipling. 1902 Doubleday   810,788

Amateur Builder's Handbook, by Hubbard Cobb. 1950 W. H.
Wise   810,000

F Penrod, by Booth Tarkington. 1914 Doubleday   808,916

F For Whom the Bell Tolls, by Ernest Hemingway. 1940 Scribner   805,400

F Impatient Virgin, by Donald Henderson Clarke. 1931 Vanguard   802,500

J Animal Friends. 1954 Grosset & Dunlap   800,000

F The Circular Staircase, by Mary Roberts Rinehart. 1908 Rinehart   800,000

Diet and Health, by Lulu Hunt Peters. 1922 Reilly & Lee   800,000

J When We Were Very Young, by A. A. Milne. 1924 Dutton   800,000

The Royal Road to Romance, by Richard Halliburton. 1925
Bobbs-Merrill   795,000

F The Peacock Sheds His Tail, by Alice Tisdale Hobart. 1954
Bobbs-Merrill   (est) 791,000

F The Miracle of the Bells, by Russell Janney. 1946 Prentice-Hall (est) 790,000

F Parris Mitchell of Kings Row, by Katherine Bellamann. 1948
Simon and Schuster   788,634

F Richard Carvel, by Winston Churchill. 1899 Macmillan   780,000

F The Border Legion, by Zane Grey. 1916 Harper   779,854

F The View from Pompey's Head, by Hamilton Basso. 1954 Doubleday   774,533

F The Man of the Forest, by Zane Grey. 1920 Harper   774,500

F The Case of the Cautious Coquette, by Erle Stanley Gardner.
1949 Morrow   770,552

The Gold Cook Book, by Louis P. De Gouy. 1947 Chilton   769,000

The Book of Etiquette, by Lillian Eichler. 1922 Doubleday   756,432

John Brown's Body, by Stephen Vincent Benét. 1928 Holt,
Rinehart & Winston   755,630

Let's Eat Right to Keep Fit, by Adelle Davis. 1954 Harcourt
Brace Jovanovich   753,000

F The U.P. Trail, by Zane Grey. 1918 Harper   751,926

J ABC. 1958 Grosset & Dunlap   750,000

F Eben Holden, by Irving Bacheller. 1900 Lothrop, Lee & Shepard   750,000

Fondue Cookbook. 1969 Grosset & Dunlap   750,000

J My First Dictionary. 1948 Grosset & Dunlap   750,000

F The Re-Creation of Brian Kent, by Harold Bell Wright. 1919
Appleton   750,000

F Tarzan of the Apes, by Edgar Rice Burroughs. 1914 McClurg   750,000

Our Hearts Were Young and Gay, by Cornelia Otis Skinner and
Emily Kimbrough. 1942 Dodd, Mead   (est) 750,000

BEST SELLERS

1895 - 1975

PAPERBOUND

SINCE THE "PAPERBACK REVOLUTION" of the 1940's this list has proliferated enormously. When the first list of best-selling paperbacks was published in *60 Years of Best Sellers,* there were only 41 books whose sales had reached 2,000,000 copies. The list that follows contains 276 titles, all of which have sold over that number. In the early days of paperback publishing the price of most novels was 25 cents. By the time the first best-selling list appeared in 1955, the cost had gone to 50 or 60 cents. Now the usual price of a not-extraordinary novel is $1.95; nonfiction and other "specials" run higher.

There is no doubt that paperbacks have increased the numbers of the American reading public, in general for the better. At first paperbacks were regarded as descendants of the dime novel. A congressional committee even dubbed their content as "the three S's"—sex, sadism, and the smoking gun. Although a few paperback publishers indulge in violence and pornography, the leaders in the field have offered great service particularly with such efforts as the "instant book" of which the *Warren Report* was one of the first and *90 Minutes at Entebbe* the most recent. The so-called "quality" paperbacks include the classics, erudite works of philosophy, sociology, linguistics, and other limited interest fields, and art books. Many of these are reprints of classics in their fields, published in hardcover when costs were lower and now out of print. Paperbacks have introduced new generations of readers to the works of some of the best authors, both of past and present. Lately, "gothics" seem to be the most popular light fiction in paperback rather than westerns and gangster books.

The latest development in the marketing of the paperback rights is the "book auction" whereby hardcover publishers set up a short time period for accepting bids for the paperback publishing rights of an about-to-be published or a just published book. To date the record payment for paperback rights for a fiction title is held by E. L. Doctorow's *Ragtime* which went for $1,850,000. For nonfiction, the rights to *The Final Days* by Carl Bernstein and Robert Woodward sold for $1,550,000, nosing out by $50,000 the record previously held by *The Joy of Cooking.*

It is felt by many that the paperback market has just begun to be explored. To quote Peter Ognibene in "TV Advertising for Books" (*Pub-*

lishers Weekly, April 12, 1976): "A marketing opportunity of tremendous potential exists right now in book publishing. It is the use of large-scale TV advertising for books. TV's potential for hardcover books is so enormous that titles selling 30,000 to 150,000 copies could, with TV advertising behind them, sell as much as 10 times that number. And for paperback publishers the opportunities are equally dramatic."

For the purpose of this book the bottom line for the inclusion on this paperback best seller list was set at 2,000,000 copies. Names of the paperback publishers are given, but not those of the hardbook edition, if the books are reprints. When the title was issued only by the paperback publisher, this is indicated by (orig) after the publisher's name. "F" indicates fiction and "J" indicates children's books.

	Pocket Book of Baby and Child Care, by Benjamin Spock. Pocket Books	23,210,000
	Webster's New World Dictionary of the American Language. Popular Library	18,500,000
	The Guinness Book of World Records, by Norris and Ross McWhirter. Sterling and Bantam	14,015,000
F	The Godfather, by Mario Puzo. Crest	11,750,000
F	The Exorcist, by William Blatty. Bantam	11,500,000
	Pocket Atlas. Hammond	11,000,000
F	To Kill a Mockingbird, by Harper Lee. Popular Library	10,850,000
	English-Spanish, Spanish-English Dictionary, comp. by Carlos Castillo and Otto F. Bond. Pocket Books	10,180,000
F	Peyton Place, by Grace Metalious. Pocket Books	10,070,000
F	Love Story, by Erich Segal. New American Library	9,477,000
F	Jaws, by Peter Benchley. Bantam	9,275,000
F	Valley of the Dolls, by Jacqueline Susann. Bantam	9,145,000
	New American Roget's College Thesaurus in Dictionary Form. New American Library	8,442,200
	The Dell Crossword Dictionary, ed. by Kathleen Rafferty. Dell (orig)	8,292,951
F	God's Little Acre, by Erskine Caldwell. New American Library	8,237,400
	The Sensuous Woman, by "J." Dell	8,164,662
F	1984, by George Orwell. New American Library	7,815,500
	Larousse French-English, English-French Dictionary. Pocket Books	7,340,000
	Mythology, by Edith Hamilton. New American Library	7,222,600
F	The Happy Hooker, by Xaviera Hollander. Dell (orig)	7,141,156
F	The Carpetbaggers, by Harold Robbins. Pocket Books	7,050,000

Roget's Pocket Thesaurus. Pocket Books		7,020,000
Everything You Always Wanted to Know about Sex but Were Afraid to Ask, by David Reuben. Bantam		7,000,000
The Late Great Planet Earth, by Hal Lindsey and C. C. Carlson. Zondervan		7,000,000
The New American Webster Handy College Dictionary. New American Library		6,921,300
F Animal Farm, by George Orwell. New American Library		6,881,200
F Jonathan Livingston Seagull, by Richard Bach. Avon		6,700,000
F Lady Chatterley's Lover, by D. H. Lawrence. New American Library, Grove, and Pocket Books		6,314,580
Chariots of the Gods?, by Erich Von Daniken. Bantam		6,200,000
F I, The Jury, by Mickey Spillane. New American Library		6,089,700
F Catch-22, by Joseph Heller. Dell		6,067,000
F The Great Gatsby, by F. Scott Fitzgerald. Scribner and Bantam		6,000,000
F In His Steps, by Charles Monroe Sheldon. Advance Publishing Co. (orig)	(est)	6,000,000
101 Famous Poems, comp. by R. J. Cook. Regnery	(est)	6,000,000
F The Big Kill, by Mickey Spillane. New American Library		5,691,000
F Rich Man, Poor Man, by Irwin Shaw. Dell		5,589,545
F The Catcher in the Rye, by J. D. Salinger. New American Library and Bantam		5,563,900
The American Heritage Dictionary of the English Language. Dell		5,485,207
Doctor's Quick Weight Loss Diet, by Irving Stillman and S. S. Baker. Dell		5,328,491
F My Gun Is Quick, by Mickey Spillane. New American Library		5,291,000
F One Lonely Night, by Mickey Spillane. New American Library		5,269,900
F The Long Wait, by Mickey Spillane. New American Library		5,234,600
F Airport, by Arthur Hailey. Bantam		5,200,000
F Kiss Me Deadly, by Mickey Spillane. New American Library		5,178,100
F Vengeance Is Mine, by Mickey Spillane. New American Library		5,171,800
The Diary of a Young Girl, by Anne Frank. Pocket Books		5,090,000
Exodus, by Leon Uris. Bantam		5,000,000
Modern World Atlas. Hammond		5,000,000
How to Win Friends and Influence People, by Dale Carnegie. Pocket Books		4,950,803
F I Never Promised You a Rose Garden, by Joanne Greenberg. New American Library		4,913,100
I'm O.K., You're O.K., by Thomas Harris. Avon		4,905,000
F Mandingo, by Kyle Onstott. Crest		4,900,000

The Pocket Cook Book, by Elizabeth Woody. Pocket Books (orig)   4,900,000

Black Like Me, by John H. Griffin. New American Library   4,884,800

F The Adventurers, by Harold Robbins. Pocket Books   4,660,000

30 Days to a More Powerful Vocabulary, by Wilfred J. Funk and Norman Lewis. Pocket Books   4,510,000

Once Is Not Enough, by Jacqueline Susann. Bantam   4,500,000

F Return to Peyton Place, by Grace Metalious. Dell   4,400,000

F The Ugly American, by William J. Lederer and Eugene L. Burdick. Crest   4,400,000

F Tragic Ground, by Erskine Caldwell. New American Library   4,377,600

Psycho-Cybernetics, by Maxwell Maltz. Wilshire (orig) and Pocket Books   4,350,000

RCAF Exercise Plan. Pocket Books   4,330,000

F Rosemary's Baby, by Ira Levin. Dell   4,325,000

F Never Love a Stranger, by Harold Robbins. Pocket Books   4,250,000

The Sensuous Man, by "M." Dell   4,222,877

F Thunderball, by Ian Fleming. New American Library   4,211,700

F The Love Machine, by Jacqueline Susann. Bantam   4,200,000

F 79 Park Ave., by Harold Robbins. Pocket Books   4,150,000

F The Other Side of Midnight, by Sidney Sheldon. Dell   4,091,213

Folk Medicine, by D. C. Jarvis. Crest   4,000,000

Future Shock, by Alvin Toffler. Bantam   4,000,000

F Fear of Flying, by Erica Jong. New American Library   3,968,000

F Where Love Has Gone, by Harold Robbins. Pocket Books   3,920,000

F Journeyman, by Erskine Caldwell. New American Library   3,909,655

In Cold Blood, by Truman Capote. New American Library   3,902,000

Here Comes Snoopy, by Charles M. Schulz. Crest   3,900,000

Profiles in Courage, by John F. Kennedy. Pocket Books   3,880,000

F Up the Down Staircase, by Bel Kaufman. Avon   3,824,000

F Tobacco Road, by Erskine Caldwell. New American Library   3,750,700

F Goldfinger, by Ian Fleming. New American Library   3,737,700

Hawaii, by James A. Michener. Bantam   3,700,000

Let's Eat Right to Keep Fit, by Adelle Davis. New American Library   3,693,200

Good Ol' Snoopy, by Charles M. Schulz. Crest   3,650,000

All This and Snoopy, Too, by Charles M. Schulz. Crest   3,600,000

F Christy, by Catherine Marshall. Avon   3,583,600

F Trouble in July, by Erskine Caldwell. New American Library   3,578,018

Xaviera, by Xaviera Hollander. Warner Paperback   3,572,000

Love without Fear, by Eustace Chesser. New American Library   3,557,900

F	The Good Earth, by Pearl S. Buck. Pocket Books	3,520,000
F	Butterfield 8, by John O'Hara. Bantam	3,500,000
	Helter Skelter, by Vincent Bugliosi and Curt Gentry. Bantam	3,500,000
F	The Other, by Thomas Tryon. Crest	3,500,000
J	Charlotte's Web, by E. B. White. Harper and Dell	3,470,516
	Pocket Book of Short Stories, ed. by M. E. Speare. Pocket Books (orig)	3,445,000
F	Gone with the Wind, by Margaret Mitchell. Pocket Books	3,440,000
	Langenscheidt's German-English, English-German Dictionary. Pocket Books	3,440,000
F	On Her Majesty's Secret Service, by Ian Fleming. New American Library	3,438,700
F	Portnoy's Complaint, by Philip Roth. Bantam	3,419,300
F	Lolita, by Vladimir Nabokov. Crest	3,400,000
F	A Stone for Danny Fisher, by Harold Robbins. Pocket Books	3,390,000
F	From Russia with Love, by Ian Fleming. New American Library	3,355,100
F	From Here to Eternity, by James Jones. New American Library	3,351,400
F	The Case of the Sulky Girl, by Erle Stanley Gardner. Pocket Books	3,310,000
F	Duel in the Sun, by Niven Busch. Popular Library	3,300,000
	Sybil, by Flora R. Schreiber. Warner Paperback	3,300,000
F	The Betsy, by Harold Robbins. Pocket Books	3,250,000
	An Analysis of the Kinsey Report, ed. by Donald P. Geddes and Enid Currie. New American Library	3,243,300
F	Doctor Zhivago, by Boris Pasternak. New American Library	3,225,500
F	Doctor No, by Ian Fleming. New American Library	3,224,500
F	The Arrangement, by Elia Kazan. Avon	3,222,500
F	You Only Live Twice, by Ian Fleming. New American Library	3,204,605
	It's for You, Snoopy, by Charles M. Schulz. Crest	3,200,000
	Let's Face It, Charlie Brown, by Charles M. Schulz. Crest	3,200,000
F	A House in the Uplands, by Erskine Caldwell. New American Library	3,186,195
F	The Dream Merchants, by Harold Robbins. Pocket Books	3,120,000
F	The Chinese Room, by Vivian Connell. Bantam	3,100,000
F	Couples, by John Updike. Crest	3,100,000
F	The Green Berets, by Robin Moore. Avon	3,100,000
F	The Group, by Mary McCarthy. New American Library	3,048,900
F	The Case of the Haunted Husband, by Erle Stanley Gardner. Pocket Books	3,040,000

36

F	Casino Royale, by Ian Fleming. New American Library	3,027,253
F	Georgia Boy, by Erskine Caldwell. New American Library and Avon	3,011,281
F	Anatomy of a Murder, by Robert Traver. Dell	3,000,000
F	Captains and the Kings, by Taylor Caldwell. Crest	3,000,000
F	Centennial, by James A. Michener. Crest	3,000,000
	Four Days, by American Heritage and U.P.I. U.P.I.	3,000,000
	A Message to Garcia, by Elbert Hubbard. Roycroft (orig)	(est) 3,000,000
F	The Summer of '42, by Herman Raucher. Dell	2,985,291
F	All Quiet on the Western Front, by Erich Maria Remarque. Premiere	2,950,000
	Hey, Peanuts, by Charles M. Schulz. Crest	2,900,000
F	The Fountainhead, by Ayn Rand. New American Library	2,891,200
F	The Sure Hand of God, by Erskine Caldwell. New American Library	2,883,700
F	The Case of the Lucky Legs, by Erle Stanley Gardner. Pocket Books	2,880,000
F	Moonraker, by Ian Fleming. New American Library	2,877,500
F	Live and Let Die, by Ian Fleming. New American Library	2,873,400
F	Lost Horizon, by James Hilton. Pocket Books	2,867,000
	Fun with Peanuts, by Charles M. Schulz. Crest	2,850,000
	Good Grief, Charlie Brown, by Charles M. Schulz. Crest	2,850,000
F	For Your Eyes Only, by Ian Fleming. New American Library	2,848,800
F	The Case of the Rolling Bones, by Erle Stanley Gardner. Pocket Books	2,840,000
F	The Case of the Curious Bride, by Erle Stanley Gardner. Pocket Books	2,830,000
	Very Funny, Charlie Brown, by Charles M. Schulz. Crest	2,800,000
F	The Spy Who Loved Me, by Ian Fleming. New American Library	2,798,400
F	Never Leave Me, by Harold Robbins. Avon	2,765,800
F	The Case of the Silent Partner, by Erle Stanley Gardner. Pocket Books	2,750,000
F	The Pirate, by Harold Robbins. Pocket Books	2,750,000
	The Service Cook Book, by Ida Bailey Allen. Service, Inc. (orig)	2,750,000
	The Hidden Persuaders, by Vance Packard. Pocket Books	2,740,000
F	The Chapman Report, by Irving Wallace. New American Library	2,735,500
	Alive, by Piers Paul Read. Avon	2,733,604

F	The Case of the Velvet Claws, by Erle Stanley Gardner. Pocket Books	2,730,000
F	Tales of the South Pacific, by James Michener. Pocket Books	2,720,000
	The Pocket Book of Verse, ed. by M. E. Speare. Pocket Books	2,719,500
	Kids Say the Darndest Things!, by Art Linkletter. Pocket Books	2,714,290
	Here Comes Charlie Brown, by Charles M. Schulz. Crest	2,700,000
	The Power of Positive Thinking, by Norman Vincent Peale. Crest	2,700,000
F	The Best of Everything, by Rona Jaffe. Dell and Pocket Books	2,695,000
F	The Case of the Counterfeit Eye, by Erle Stanley Gardner. Pocket Books	2,690,000
	Between Parent and Child, by Haim G. Ginott. Avon	2,685,000
F	The Case of the Substitute Face, by Erle Stanley Gardner. Pocket Books	2,680,000
F	Diamonds Are Forever, by Ian Fleming. New American Library	2,659,400
F	The Case of the Caretaker's Cat, by Erle Stanley Gardner. Pocket Books	2,640,000
	Comparative World Atlas. Hammond	2,630,000
F	Drum, by Kyle Onstott. Crest	2,600,000
	For the Love of Peanuts, by Charles M. Schulz. Crest	2,600,000
	The Gulag Archipelago, I, by Alexander Solzhenitsyn. Harper & Row	2,600,000
	The I Hate to Cook Book, by Peg Bracken. Crest	2,600,000
F	The French Lieutenant's Woman, by John Fowles. New American Library	2,596,400
	Charlie Brown's All-Stars, by Charles M. Schulz. New American Library	2,568,600
F	On the Beach, by Nevil Shute. New American Library	2,568,455
F	The Case of the Stuttering Bishop, by Erle Stanley Gardner. Pocket Books	2,550,000
	What Next, Charlie Brown, by Charles M. Schulz. Crest	2,550,000
F	This Very Earth, by Erskine Caldwell. New American Library	2,523,600
F	Battle Cry, by Leon Uris. Bantam	2,500,000
F	Brave New World, by Aldous Huxley. Bantam	2,500,000
	The Conscience of a Conservative, by Barry Goldwater. Macfadden-Bartell	2,500,000
	House Plants, by Sunset Editors. Lane Publishing Co.	2,500,000
	Please Don't Eat the Daisies, by Jean Kerr. Crest	2,500,000
F	Tropic of Cancer, by Henry Miller. Grove and Ballantine	2,500,000
F	Women's Barracks, by Tereska Torres. Gold Medal (orig)	2,500,000

F	The Inheritors, by Harold Robbins. Pocket Books	2,460,000
F	The Case of the Sleepwalker's Niece, by Erle Stanley Gardner. Pocket Books	2,450,000
F	The Source, by James A. Michener. Crest	2,450,000
F	The Case of the Baited Hook, by Erle Stanley Gardner. Pocket Books	2,448,000
F	The Naked and the Dead, by Norman Mailer. New American Library	2,443,662
J	My First Atlas. Hammond	2,431,000
	Papillon, by Henri Charrière. Pocket Books	2,410,000
F	The Drifters, by James L. Michener. Crest	2,400,000
	Wheels, by Arthur Hailey. Bantam	2,400,000
	You're a Winner, Charlie Brown, by Charles M. Schulz. Crest	2,400,000
F	The Case of the Half-Wakened Wife, by Erle Stanley Gardner. Pocket Books	2,390,000
	Dennis the Menace: Household Hurricane, by Hank Ketcham. Pocket Books	2,380,000
	English through Pictures (The Pocket Book of Basic English), by I. A. Richards and C. M. Gibson. Pocket Books (orig)	2,380,000
	Scholastic World Atlas. Hammond	2,370,000
J	Love and the Facts of Life, by Evelyn Duvall and Sylvanus Duvall. Association Press	2,360,000
F	Fail-Safe, by Eugene Burdick and Harvey Wheeler. Dell	2,352,000
F	Magnificent Obsession, by Lloyd C. Douglas. Pocket Books	2,335,123
J	The Little House on the Prairie, by Laura Ingalls Wilder. Harper and Scholastic	2,332,666
F	The Case of the Lame Canary, by Erle Stanley Gardner. Pocket Books	2,330,000
J	Egermeier's Bible Story Book, by Elsie E. Egermeier. Warner Press	2,326,577
F	The Odessa File, by Frederick Forsyth. Bantam	2,325,000
F	The Agony and the Ecstasy, by Irving Stone. New American Library	2,320,000
F	The Crazy Ladies, by Joyce Elbert. New American Library	2,313,600
F	Singing Guns, by Max Brand. Pocket Books	2,310,000
	The Greatest Story Ever Told, by Fulton Oursler. Pocket Books	2,304,960
F	The New Centurions, by Joseph Wambaugh. Dell	2,302,316
F	Cannery Row, by John Steinbeck. Bantam	2,300,000
F	The Chosen, by Chaim Potok. Crest	2,300,000
F	The Damned, by John D. MacDonald. Gold Medal (orig)	2,300,000

	Honor Thy Father, by Gay Talese. Crest	2,300,000
F	The Pearl, by John Steinbeck. Bantam	2,300,000
	We're on Your Side, Charlie Brown, by Charles M. Schulz. Crest	2,300,000
	Serpico, by Peter Maas. Bantam	2,275,000
	See Here, Private Hargrove, by Marion Hargrove. Pocket Books	2,260,000
F	2001: A Space Odyssey, by Arthur C. Clarke. New American Library	2,255,800
F	Dark Fires, by Rosemary Rogers. Avon (orig)	2,250,000
	Family Reference Atlas. Hammond	2,250,000
	Gods from Outer Space, by Erich Von Daniken. Bantam	2,250,000
	The Rise and Fall of the Third Reich, by William L. Shirer. Crest	2,250,000
	The Wonderful World of Peanuts, by Charles M. Schulz. Crest	2,250,000
J	Benji, by Leonore Fleischer. Pyramid (orig)	2,235,694
J	Go Ask Alice, by Anonymous. Avon	2,235,605
	The Naked Ape, by Desmond Morris. Dell	2,233,620
F	The Case of the Empty Tin, by Erle Stanley Gardner. Pocket Books	2,230,000
F	Pocket Book of Erskine Caldwell Stories, ed. by Henry Seidel Canby. Pocket Books	2,229,000
	The Greening of America, by Charles A. Reich. Bantam	2,225,000
F	No Time for Sergeants, by Mac Hyman. New American Library	2,221,502
F	The Passionate Witch, by Thorne Smith. Pocket Books	2,210,000
	The Total Woman, by Marabel Morgan. Revell and Pocket Books	2,209,000
	All the President's Men, by Carl Bernstein and Bob Woodward. Warner Paperback	2,020,000
F	The Amboy Dukes, by Irving Shulman. Avon	2,200,000
	A House Is Not a Home, by Polly Adler. Popular Library	2,200,000
	I'll Cry Tomorrow, by Lillian Roth. Popular Library	2,200,000
F	The Little Prince, by Antoine de Saint-Exupery. Harcourt Brace Jovanovich	2,197,203
	The Joy of Cooking, by Irma S. Rombauer and Marion Rombauer Becker. New American Library	2,192,700
	Dennis the Menace Rides Again, by Hank Ketcham. Pocket Books	2,180,000
	The Nun's Story, by Kathryn Hulme. Pocket Books	2,160,000
	According to Hoyle, by Richard L. Frey. Crest (orig)	2,150,000

F The Case of the Careless Kitten, by Erle Stanley Gardner. Pocket Books — 2,150,000

Let's Cook It Right, by Adelle Davis. New American Library — 2,149,700

F The Red Badge of Courage, by Stephen Crane. Pocket Books — 2,147,000

F The Lord of the Flies, by William Golding. Capricorn — 2,140,000

F The Young Lions, by Irwin Shaw. New American Library — 2,139,400

F Mr. Roberts, by Thomas Heggen. Pocket Books — 2,131,000

J The Wonderful Wizard of Oz, by L. Frank Baum. Bobbs-Merrill — 2,130,395

F Deliverance, by James Dickey. Dell — 2,126,244

F The Jungle, by Upton Sinclair. New American Library — 2,117,600

Pregnancy, Birth and Family Planning, by Alan F. Guttmacher. New American Library — 2,112,600

F The Day of the Jackal, by Frederick Forsyth. Bantam — 2,100,000

F The Fan Club, by Irving Wallace. Bantam — 2,100,000

The Pocket Dictionary, by W. J. Pelo. Pocket Books — 2,100,000

F The Deep, by Mickey Spillane. New American Library — 2,099,400

F The Revolt of Mamie Stover, by William Bradford Huie. New American Library — 2,097,600

F The Case of the Dangerous Dowager, by Erle Stanley Gardner. Pocket Books — 2,090,000

F Karen, by Marie Killilea. Dell — 2,089,261

F The Clue of the Forgotten Murder, by Erle Stanley Gardner. Pocket Books — 2,080,000

F Myra Breckinridge, by Gore Vidal. Bantam — 2,080,000

F Sanctuary, by William Faulkner. New American Library — 2,074,985

Let's Get Well, by Adelle Davis. New American Library — 2,061,700

J The Little House in the Big Woods, by Laura Ingalls Wilder. Harper and Scholastic — 2,052,203

Wanted: Dennis the Menace, by Hank Ketcham. Pocket Books — 2,050,000

Western Garden Book, by Sunset Editors. Lane Publishing Co. — 2,050,000

The Boston Strangler, by Gerold Frank. New American Library — 2,049,800

F The Seven Minutes, by Irving Wallace. Pocket Books — 2,040,000

F Advise and Consent, by Allen Drury. Pocket Books — 2,010,000

Body Language, by Julius Fast. Pocket Books — 2,010,000

F This Is Murder, by Erle Stanley Gardner. Pocket Books — 2,001,000

F Another Country, by James Baldwin. Dell — 2,000,000

F The Bramble Bush, by Charles Mergendahl. Bantam — 2,000,000

F Bridge Over the River Kwai, by Pierre Boulle. Bantam — 2,000,000

	Harlow, by Irving Shulman. Dell	2,000,000
	Hiroshima, by John Hersey. Bantam	2,000,000
	How to Prepare Your Income Tax, by David Joseph. Doubleday (orig)	2,000,000
F	Rally Round the Flag, Boys!, by Max Shulman. Bantam	2,000,000
F	The Tight White Collar, by Grace Metalious. Dell	2,000,000
	Webster's New School and Office Dictionary. Crest	2,000,000

Best Seller Subjects

BEST SELLER SUBJECTS

PEOPLE ARE INTERESTED in the best sellers on almost every conceivable subject. What are the best-selling books on ballet? What are the best sellers about ESP? and so on ad infinitum. It is obviously impossible to compile figures in so many categories; however, presented here are the most obvious classifications: children's books, cookbooks, crime and suspense, do-it-yourself and gardening, poetry, reference, and religion.

CHILDREN'S BOOKS

THE FOLLOWING LIST attempts to record individual titles, published in the United States since 1895, that have sold 1,000,000 copies or more. Modern versions of older favorites are not included unless a specific volume, perhaps with a new illustrator, has accurate sales records. *The Real Mother Goose* is an example.

Juvenile fiction has the disconcerting habit of changing its audience. Some of these best sellers like *Freckles* and *Seventeen* began their careers as adult fiction. Others were launched as children's books and have since added an adult audience, like the A. A. Milne books. Milne's *Winnie-the-Pooh,* in Latin as *Winnie Ille Pu,* was one of the ten best sellers in 1961, presumably in the adult field. Young readers have become highly sophisticated since 1895. Many cannot wait until they are allowed to withdraw books from the adult fiction shelves of the public library. Currently, throughout the country, there is much ado about what adult books are suitable for high school libraries. Many trade publishers note in their catalogs that certain titles are for Young Adults.

Series books sell in great quantities to generation after generation of young people. Some of the older series, the many volumes of which total many millions, are the *Frank Merriwell* books by Burt L. Standish which flourished in the early part of this century; the *Doctor Dolittle* books by Hugh L. Lofting; the *Oz* books by L. Frank Baum; the *Raggedy Ann* books; and the *Little Colonel* books by Annie Fellows Johnston. The *Nancy Drew* stories (60,000,000 sold), the *Bobbsey Twins* series (15,000,000 sold), and the *Tom Swift* series (7,000,000 sold) have been read by several generations. The first *Elsie Dinsmore* book, by Martha Finley, was published in 1868, and the first of the *Five Little Peppers* series, by Margaret Sidney, in 1880.

Highly popular newer series are the Dr. Seuss books, many of which appear near the top of the combined best seller list, the Little Golden Books, and the Tolkien books (for both young and adult readers).

There are many standard books for young people that sell year after year in the religious field and many other areas. These include the *Boy Scouts Handbook,* first published in 1910, and the *Girl Scouts Handbook,* first published in 1916, both of which have gone through many revisions.

Although production of new children's books is a phenomenon of publishing today, not too many have achieved the 1,000,000 sales mark. In general children's books which have sold several million copies in hardback are the older books, most of them published in the first quarter of this century.

Green Eggs and Ham, by Dr. Seuss. 1960 Random House	5,940,776
One Fish, Two Fish, Red Fish, Blue Fish, by Dr. Seuss. 1960 Random House	5,842,024
Hop on Pop, by Dr. Seuss. 1963 Random House	5,814,101
Dr. Seuss's ABC, by Dr. Seuss. 1963 Random House	5,648,193
The Cat in the Hat, by Dr. Seuss. 1957 Random House	5,394,741
The Wonderful Wizard of Oz, by L. Frank Baum. 1900 Bobbs-Merrill	(est) 5,000,000
Charlotte's Web, by E. B. White. 1952 Harper & Row	4,670,516
The Cat in the Hat Comes Back, by Dr. Seuss. 1958 Random House	3,431,917
The Little Prince, by Antoine de Saint-Exupery. 1943 Harcourt Brace Jovanovich	2,811,478
The Little House on the Prairie, by Laura Ingalls Wilder. 1953 ed. Harper & Row	2,732,666
The Little House in the Big Woods, by Laura Ingalls Wilder. 1953 ed. Harper & Row	2,527,203
My First Atlas. 1959 Hammond	2,431,000
Love and the Facts of Life, by Evelyn Duvall and Sylvanus Duvall. 1950 Association Press	2,360,000
Egermeier's Bible Story Book, by Elsie E. Egermeier. 1923 Warner Press	2,326,577
Go Ask Alice, Anonymous. 1971 Prentice-Hall	2,245,605
Benji, by Leonore Fleischer. 1974 Pyramid	2,235,694
The Little Engine That Could, by Watty Piper. 1926 Platt & Munk	2,166,000
Stuart Little, by E. B. White. 1945 Harper & Row	2,129,591
Freckles, by Gene Stratton Porter. 1904 Doubleday, Page	2,089,523

The Girl of the Limberlost, by Gene Stratton Porter. 1909 Doubleday, Page   2,053,892

Sounder, by William Armstrong. 1969 Harper & Row   1,815,401

Harry, the Dirty Dog, by Gene Zion. 1956 Harper & Row   1,690,339

Seventeen, by Booth Tarkington. 1916 Harper   (est) 1,682,891

Where the Wild Things Are, by Maurice Sendak. 1963 Harper &
Row   1,632,020

Laddie, by Gene Stratton Porter. 1913 Doubleday, Page   1,586,529

The Big Book of Mother Goose, 1950 Grosset & Dunlap   1,500,000

The Golden Dictionary, by Ellen Wales Walpole. 1944 Golden
Press   1,450,000

A Friend Is Someone Who Likes You, by Joan Walsh Anglund.
1958 Harcourt Brace Jovanovich   1,423,432

Rebecca of Sunnybrook Farm, by Kate Douglas Wiggin. 1904
Houghton Mifflin   1,357,714

Love Is a Special Way of Feeling, by Joan Walsh Anglund. 1960
Harcourt Brace Jovanovich   1,308,293

The Real Mother Goose. 1915 Rand McNally   1,296,140

The Pigman, by Paul Zindel. 1968 Harper & Row   1,265,876

Better Homes and Gardens Story Book. 1951 Meredith   1,220,728

Trouble after School, by Jerrold Beim. 1957 Harcourt Brace
Jovanovich   1,145,570

Better Homes and Gardens Junior Cook Book. 1955 Meredith   1,100,182

Pollyanna, by Eleanor H. Porter. 1913 Page   1,059,000

Le Petit Prince, by Antoine de Saint-Exupery. 1943 Harcourt
Brace Jovanovich   1,018,373

Mary Poppins, by Pamela L. Travers. 1934 Harcourt Brace Jovanovich   1,005,203

Winnie-the Pooh, by A. A. Milne. 1926 Dutton   1,005,000

Pollyanna Grows Up, by Eleanor H. Porter. 1915 Page   1,000,000

Little Black Sambo, by Helen Bannerman. 1899 Lippincott (est) 1,000,000

COOKBOOKS

COOKBOOKS have been the most consistent sellers in nonfiction since 1895
and the number of cookbooks published and their sales have increased
disproportionately since that time. The gradual liberation of women (and
men) over the past 80 years has meant an increased interest by both sexes
in the culinary arts.

For the first half of the twentieth century the emphasis was on cookbooks that made life easier for the woman who had to cope with cooking

for her family. The refrigerator and the gas or electric range were new appliances for the kitchen and new cookbooks were needed that acknowledged their existence. Refrigeration opened up a new world of molds, mousses, and bombes—available in the summer as well as the winter. A dependable oven made baking less of a dark art than it had been when cooks were at the mercy of wood- or coal-burning stoves. The advent of these kitchen aids meant a change in the writing of a cookbook. Bake for 30 minutes in a preheated 350 degree oven became a possibility and left less to the cook's expertise.

The third quarter of this century has seen the birth of a plethora of electric kitchen gadgets—the microwave oven, the Crockpot, and the Cuisinart. With them have come new cookbooks. In the United States, in the last ten years alone, 3,168 cookbooks have been published.

The list that follows cites the most successful cookbooks of the past 80 years. Out-of-print titles have been omitted. *The Boston Cooking School Cook Book* was published in 1896 and is the doyenne of the group. *Better Homes and Gardens Cook Book* leads the list and the list of best-selling hardbound books as well.

Better Homes and Gardens Cook Book. 1930 Meredith	18,684,976
Betty Crocker's Cookbook. 1950 Golden Press	13,000,000
The Joy of Cooking, by Irma S. Rombauer and Marion Rombauer Becker. 1931 Bobbs-Merrill	8,992,700
The Good Housekeeping Cookbook, ed. by Zoe Coulson. Good Housekeeping Books	5,250,000
The Pocket Cook Book, by Elizabeth Woody. 1942 Pocket Books	4,900,000
The Boston Cooking School Cook Book, by Fannie Farmer. 1896 Little, Brown	4,100,000
Better Homes and Gardens Meat Cook Book. 1959 Meredith	3,609,105
The American Woman's Cook Book, ed. by Ruth Berolzheimer. 1939 Doubleday	3,549,276
The I Hate to Cook Book, by Peg Bracken. 1960 Harcourt Brace Jovanovich	2,929,782
Better Homes and Gardens Casserole Cook Book. 1961 Meredith	2,613,948
The Weight Watchers Program Cookbook, by Jean Nidetch. 1973 Hearthside	2,575,000
Better Homes and Gardens Barbecue Book. 1956 Meredith	2,439,001
Betty Crocker's Good and Easy Cookbook. 1954 Simon and Schuster	2,400,000
Better Homes and Gardens Salad Book. 1958 Meredith	2,341,060

Let's Cook It Right, by Adelle Davis. 1947 Harcourt Brace
Jovanovich   2,151,439
Better Homes and Gardens Fondue and Tabletop Cooking. 1970
Meredith   2,022,529

CRIME AND SUSPENSE

THIS IS THE LONGEST LIST in this special subject group among best sellers
of the past 80 years, and their sales figures, mostly in paperback, are in the
high range. Styles in this branch of fiction have changed greatly over the
years, from the time of *The Leavenworth Case* by Anna Katharine Green
published in 1878. Sir Arthur Conan Doyle and Mary Roberts Rinehart
were authors who appeared regularly on all the annual best seller lists after
the turn of the century. Doyle's Sherlock Holmes will never die and the
more romantic Rinehart novels continue selling well in paperback, as do
the celebrated Agatha Christie stories.

Erle Stanley Gardner, with his Perry Mason stories (still seen on television) and Ellery Queen, dominated the detective scene until 1934 when
Dashiell Hammett's *The Thin Man* introduced a new, more realistic, action-
filled school of suspense writing. The day of the "whodunit" was definitely
over, at least in hardcover. Raymond Chandler, Ross MacDonald, John
D. MacDonald, Eric Ambler, and Graham Greene were followers in this
new school of detective fiction. Then came Mickey Spillane, whose violent
action stories predominate in the following list. The phenomenon of the
1960's was Ian Fleming, with his James Bond, Agent 007 espionage
stories. Spy stories continue to replace the older school of detective fiction,
though Helen MacInnes and Mary Stewart still represent the best-selling
more romantic detective fiction. In the paperback field today, the "gothics,"
outstandingly represented by Barbara Cartland, are in the Rinehart and
Daphne du Maurier genre, mainly of interest to the women's market.

In most recent years the hardcover best sellers in suspense have been
those related to world events like Frederick Forsyth's *The Day of the
Jackal* and *The Odessa File,* both new to this list as is the famous *The Godfather* by Mario Puzo. There are innumerable suspense stories on such
subjects as the Arabs, the Israelis, Swiss banks, oil, organized crime, kidnapping, even the occult. Newly added here are two "factfiction" titles,
Truman Capote's *In Cold Blood,* based on a real midwestern family
massacre, and *Helter Skelter,* by Vincent Bugliosi and Curt Gentry, about
the Manson case.

The requirement for inclusion in the following list is a sales figure of
2,000,000 or more. In the last edition 44 titles had attained that figure.
The present list adds eleven new titles one of which is *The Godfather*
which made the top of the list in a period of five years.

The Godfather, by Mario Puzo. 1969 Putnam, Crest   12,140,000

I, the Jury, by Mickey Spillane. 1947 Dutton, New American Library   6,096,700

The Big Kill, by Mickey Spillane, 1951 Dutton, New American Library   5,699,000

My Gun Is Quick, by Mickey Spillane. 1950 Dutton, New American Library   5,296,000

One Lonely Night, by Mickey Spillane. 1951 Dutton, New American Library   5,274,900

Kiss Me, Deadly, by Mickey Spillane. 1952 Dutton, New American Library   5,259,100

The Long Wait, by Mickey Spillane. 1951 Dutton, New American Library   5,245,600

Vengeance Is Mine, by Mickey Spillane. 1950 Dutton, New American Library   5,176,300

In Cold Blood, by Truman Capote. 1966 Random House, New American Library   4,243,338

Thunderball, by Ian Fleming. 1962 New American Library   4,211,700

Goldfinger, by Ian Fleming. 1959 Macmillan, New American Library   3,747,000

Helter Skelter, by Vincent Bugliosi and Curt Gentry. 1974 Norton, Bantam   3,650,000

The Case of the Sulky Girl, by Erle Stanley Gardner. 1933 Morrow, Pocket Books   3,564,334

The Case of the Lucky Legs, by Erle Stanley Gardner. 1934 Morrow, Pocket Books   3,499,948

On Her Majesty's Secret Service, by Ian Fleming. 1963 New American Library   3,438,700

From Russia with Love, by Ian Fleming. 1957 Macmillan, New American Library   3,365,100

You Only Live Twice, by Ian Fleming. 1964 New American Library   3,283,000

Doctor No, by Ian Fleming. 1958 Macmillan, New American Library   3,239,500

The Case of the Haunted Husband, by Erle Stanley Gardner. 1941 Morrow, Pocket Books   3,127,585

Anatomy of a Murder, by Robert Traver. 1958 St. Martin's Press, Dell   3,100,000

The Case of the Curious Bride, by Erle Stanley Gardner. 1934 Morrow, Pocket Books   3,077,368

Casino Royale, by Ian Fleming. 1953 Macmillan, New American Library   3,037,253

The Case of the Velvet Claws, by Erle Stanley Gardner. 1933
Morrow, Pocket Books   2,924,756

The Case of the Rolling Bones, by Erle Stanley Gardner. 1939
Morrow, Pocket Books   2,908,964

Live and Let Die, by Ian Fleming. 1954 Macmillan, New American Library   2,883,400

Moonraker, by Ian Fleming. 1955 Macmillan, New American
Library   2,877,500

The Case of the Silent Partner, by Erle Stanley Gardner. 1940
Morrow, Pocket Books   2,850,904

For Your Eyes Only, by Ian Fleming. 1960 New American
Library   2,848,800

The Case of the Counterfeit Eye, by Erle Stanley Gardner. 1935
Morrow, Pocket Books   2,847,765

The Spy Who Loved Me, by Ian Fleming. 1962 New American
Library   2,798,400

The Case of the Caretaker's Cat, by Erle Stanley Gardner. 1935
Morrow, Pocket Books   2,783,403

The Case of the Substitute Face, by Erle Stanley Gardner. 1938
Morrow, Pocket Books   2,750,710

The Case of the Baited Hook, by Erle Stanley Gardner. 1940
Morrow, Pocket Books   2,737,397

The Case of the Stuttering Bishop, by Erle Stanley Gardner. 1936
Morrow, Pocket Books   2,702,363

Diamonds Are Forever, by Ian Fleming. 1956 Macmillan, New
American Library   2,664,400

The Odessa File, by Frederick Forsyth. 1972 Viking, Bantam   2,648,411

The Case of the Sleepwalker's Niece, by Erle Stanley Gardner.
1936 Morrow, Pocket Books   2,646,024

The Case of the Half-Wakened Wife, by Erle Stanley Gardner.
1945 Morrow, Pocket Books   2,604,336

The Case of the Black-Eyed Blonde, by Erle Stanley Gardner.
1944 Morrow, Pocket Books   2,588,757

The Case of the Dangerous Dowager, by Erle Stanley Gardner.
1937 Morrow, Pocket Books   2,485,874

The Case of the Lame Canary, by Erle Stanley Gardner. 1937
Morrow, Pocket Books   2,476,145

The New Centurions, by Joseph Wambaugh. 1970 Little, Brown,
Dell   2,382,316

The Day of the Jackal, by Frederick Forsyth. 1971 Viking, Bantam   2,357,926

The Damned, by John D. MacDonald. 1974 Gold Medal   2,300,000

The Case of the Empty Tin, by Erle Stanley Gardner. 1941 Morrow, Pocket Books 2,270,297

This Is Murder, by Erle Stanley Gardner. 1935 Morrow, Pocket Books 2,266,268

The Case of the Careless Kitten, by Erle Stanley Gardner. 1942 Morrow, Pocket Books 2,262,177

The Case of the Cautious Coquette, by Erle Stanley Gardner. 1949 Morrow, Pocket Books 2,244,552

The Clue of the Forgotten Murder, by Erle Stanley Gardner. 1935 Morrow, Pocket Books 2,212,271

The Deep, by Mickey Spillane. 1961 Dutton, New American Library 2,124,418

The Case of the Golddigger's Purse, by Erle Stanley Gardner. 1945 Morrow, Pocket Books 2,121,708

Fail-Safe, by Eugene L. Burdick and Harvey Wheeler. 1962 McGraw-Hill, Dell 2,113,897

Seven Days in May, by Fletcher Knebel and Charles S. Bailey, II. 1962 Harper & Row, Bantam 2,073,434

The Case of the Crooked Candle, by Erle Stanley Gardner. 1944 Morrow, Pocket Books 2,029,248

The Case of the Borrowed Brunette, by Erle Stanley Gardner. 1946 Morrow, Pocket Books 2,006,808

DO-IT-YOURSELF AND GARDENING

THE NUMBER of books in this field has burgeoned in the past ten years. Shorter hours, general prosperity, and nostalgia have been contributing factors to the high interest in arts and crafts. Gardening books are also included in this list. There are not too many really outstanding best sellers here. Various celebrities have done needlepoint books but the only name that has sold over 500,000 copies is Erica Wilson who is famous for her needlecraft.

House Plants, by Sunset editors. 1968 Lane 2,500,000
Sunset Western Garden Book, by Sunset editors. 1933 Lane 2,050,000
Macramé, by Sunset editors. 1971 Lane 1,100,000
Gardening in Containers, by Sunset editors. 1952 Lane 1,002,000
Terrariums and Miniature Gardens, by Sunset editors. 1973 Lane 975,000
Furniture You Can Make, by Sunset editors. 1953 Lane 950,000
Bonsai, by Sunset editors. 1965 Lane 780,000
Garden and Patio Building Book, by Sunset editors. 1969 Lane 660,000

Woodcarving Techniques and Projects, by Sunset editors. 1951
Lane   605,000
Furniture Finishing and Refinishing, by Sunset editors. 1969
Lane   600,000
African Violets, by Sunset editors. 1951 Lane   582,000
Crafts for Children, by Sunset editors. 1968 Lane   572,000
Better Homes and Gardens Gifts to Make Yourself. 1972 Mere-
dith   569,500
Basic Carpentry Illustrated, by Sunset editors. 1972 Lane   544,000
Needlepoint, by Sunset editors. 1972 Lane   542,000
Color in Your Garden, by Sunset editors. 1958 Lane   534,000
Woodworking Projects, by Sunset editors. 1968 Lane   530,000
Ceramics, Techniques and Projects, by Sunset editors. 1953 Lane   510,000
Furniture Upholstery and Repair, by Sunset editors. 1970 Lane   508,000
The Complete Book of Interior Decoration, by M. Derieux and
Isabelle Stevenson. 1949 Hawthorn   500,000
The Complete Book of Sewing, by Constance Talbot and Isabelle
Stevenson. 1949 Hawthorn   500,000
Crewel Embroidery, by Erica Wilson. 1962 Scribner   500,000

POETRY

THIS IS THE SHORTEST specialized list, but in some ways the most interesting. Few poets achieve best-sellerdom, and nearly all who do, reflect the
popular rather than the intellectual American taste. Probably the best
seller in poetry is Shakespeare, as is the Bible in the field of religion. War
poetry and poetry anthologies flourished especially at the time of World
War I. More recent additions have been Kahlil Gibran, Ogden Nash,
Robert Frost, Stephen Vincent Benét, and Rod McKuen whose *Listen to
the Warm* and *Stanyan Street and Other Sorrows* have been the big poetry
sellers of this past decade. There were ten titles on this list in the previous
edition (which included one drama, *Death of a Salesman* by Arthur Miller).
Only the McKuen books have been added.

The Prophet, by Kahlil Gibran. 1923 Knopf   6,000,000
101 Famous Poems, comp. by R. J. Cook. 1916 Regnery   (est)6,000,000
The Pocket Book of Verse, ed. by M. E. Speare. 1940 Pocket
Books   2,719,500
Listen to the Warm, by Rod McKuen. 1967 Knopf   2,025,000
Stanyan Street and Other Sorrows, by Rod McKuen. 1967 Knopf   1,500,000
Pocket Book of Ogden Nash. 1955 Pocket Books   1,121,000

Anthology of Robert Frost's Poems, ed. by Louis Untermeyer. 1949 Holt, Rinehart & Winston   1,054,910

Immortal Poems of the English Language, ed. by Oscar Williams. 1952 Pocket Books   1,054,500

A Heap O'Livin', by Edgar Guest. 1916 Regnery   1,000,000

John Brown's Body, by Stephen Vincent Benét. 1928 Holt, Rinehart & Winston   755,630

Best Loved Poems of the American People, ed. by Hazel Felleman. 1936 Doubleday   608,417

REFERENCE

THERE ARE MANY BEST SELLERS in what, for want of a better term, is called here the reference section. It is comprised mainly of dictionaries and encyclopedias, indispensable to all public and private libraries, all best sellers in many editions since publishing began. When people speak of the Bible or the dictionary, they do not realize how many versions of each exist. Noah Webster published the first American dictionary in 1806. It has been published in many versions, large and small, ever since.

Another important reference work is the almanac. The *Old Farmer's Almanac* was founded in 1792 and is still going strong and the *World Almanac* has large sales every year. A notable addition to this section is *The Guinness Book of World Records* with its sales since 1962 amounting to 16,457,000 copies.

Webster's New World Dictionary of the American Language. Popular Library   18,500,000

The Guinness Book of World Records, by Norris and Ross McWhirter. 1962 Sterling   16,457,000

Pocket Atlas. 1917 Hammond   11,000,000

The English-Spanish, Spanish-English Dictionary, comp. by Carlos Castillo and Otto F. Bond. 1948 Pocket Books   10,187,000

New American Roget's College Thesaurus in Dictionary Form. 1957 New American Library   8,442,200

The Dell Crossword Dictionary, ed. by Kathleen Rafferty. 1950 Dell   8,292,951

The American Heritage Dictionary of the English Language. 1969 Dell   7,485,207

Larousse French-English, English-French Dictionary. 1961 Pocket Books   7,340,000

Roget's Pocket Thesaurus. 1923 Pocket Books   7,020,000

The New American Webster Handy College Dictionary. 1956 New American Library	6,921,300
30 Days to a More Powerful Vocabulary, by Wilfred J. Funk and Norman Lewis. 1922 Funk & Wagnalls	6,299,161
Modern World Atlas. 1922 Hammond	5,000,000
Langenscheidt's German-English, English-German Dictionary. 1960 Pocket Books	3,440,000
Grosset Webster Dictionary. 1956 Grosset & Dunlap	3,000,000
Halley's Bible Handbook, by Henry H. Halley. 1927 Zondervan	3,000,000
The Story of the Bible, by Jesse Lyman Hurlbut. 1904 Winston	3,000,000
Comparative World Atlas. 1948 Hammond	2,630,000
Columbia Viking Desk Encyclopedia. 1953 Viking	2,565,899
My First Atlas. 1959 Hammond	2,431,000
English through Pictures (The Pocket Book of Basic English), by I. A. Richards and C. M. Gibson. 1945 Pocket Books	2,380,000
Scholastic World Atlas. 1960 Hammond	2,370,000
Family Reference Atlas. 1956 Hammond	2,250,000
According to Hoyle, by Richard L. Frey. 1964 Crest	2,150,000
The American College Dictionary, ed. by Clarence L. Barnhart. 1947 Random House	2,103,835
The Pocket Dictionary, by W. J. Pelo. 1941 Pocket Books	2,100,000
The New Compact Bible Dictionary, by Thomas A. Bryant. 1967 Zondervan	2,000,000
Webster's New School and Office Dictionary. 1975 Crest	2,000,000

RELIGION

THE BIBLE does not appear on this list of books in the religious field although it is undoubtedly the best seller of them all. Every time a new important translation or new version of the Bible appears, it heads the list of the year in which it appeared as did the *Revised Standard Version* and, in the past two years, *The Living Bible*. It is impossible to collate figures year by year for all the various types of Bibles and portions of the Bible.

Religion in the book field is an ever-more-popular subject. According to the Association of American Publishers the biggest increase in categories of books in 1975 was the 23.6 percent rise in number of religious books for the layman. It is of interest to note that Harper & Row has recently moved its entire trade religious operation to California where, perhaps, the fields are even more fertile than in the traditional "Bible belt" of the Midwest.

The Power of Positive Thinking, by Norman Vincent Peale. 1952 Prentice-Hall   5,205,000

The Greatest Story Ever Told, by Fulton Oursler. 1949 Doubleday   3,858,948

Halley's Bible Handbook, by Henry H. Halley. 1927 Zondervan   3,000,000

The Story of the Bible, by Jesse Lyman Hurlbut. 1904 Winston   3,000,000

The Nun's Story, by Kathryn Hulme. 1956 Little, Brown   2,521,531

Egermeier's Bible Story Book, by Elsie E. Egermeier. 1923 Warner Press   2,326,577

The Greatest Book Ever Written, by Fulton Oursler. 1951 Doubleday   2,282,322

The Song of Our Syrian Guest, by William Allen Knight. 1903 United Church Press   2,103,064

Bible Readings for the Home Circle. 1914 Review & Herald   2,051,448

The New Compact Bible Dictionary, by Thomas A. Bryant. 1967 Zondervan   2,000,000

Peace with God, by Billy Graham. 1954 Doubleday   2,000,000

Streams in the Desert, by Mrs. Charles E. Cowman. 1931 Zondervan   2,000,000

Best Sellers by Years

1895 - 1975

1895

Fiction

1. Beside the Bonnie Brier Bush, by *Ian Maclaren.* Dodd, Mead
2. Trilby, by *George du Maurier.* Harper
3. Adventures of Captain Horn, by *Frank R. Stockton.* Scribner
4. The Manxman, by *Hall Caine.* Appleton
5. Princess Aline, by *Richard Harding Davis.* Harper
6. Days of Auld Lang Syne, by *Ian Maclaren.* Dodd, Mead
7. The Master, by *Israel Zangwill.* Harper
8. The Prisoner of Zenda, by *Anthony Hope.* Holt
9. Regeneration, by *Max Nordau.* Appleton
10. My Lady Nobody, by *Maarten Maartens.* Harper

THE YEAR in which the first American best seller lists were published was in the era of the pompadoured "Gibson girl." It was also the era of bicycles, which were to stage a return nearly 50 years later during the gas rationing days of World War II and again, even more vigorously, in the gas-shortage days of the '70's. In 1895 rural free delivery was established, an event that was to have a notable effect upon merchandising of every kind, including the marketing of books. Romantic novels like *The Prisoner of Zenda* by Anthony Hope and Richard Harding Davis' *Princess Aline,* the latter illustrated by Charles Dana Gibson, suited the mood of the period, though the homely *Beside the Bonnie Brier Bush* and the exotic *Trilby* were the top best sellers. Of all these ten possibly the only ones awakening a flicker of recognition among today's readers are *Trilby* and *The Prisoner of Zenda.* Only two of the books on this first list were written by Americans. The other eight titles, by British and European authors, would have been unprotected by copyright in this country five years earlier, and several publishers or printers could have issued them without any legal arrangement with the rightful publishers. The passage of the international copyright law in 1891 resulted in orderly publication—a fact which helped to make possible the compiling of best seller lists. It is interesting to note that although the publishers of the books on this 1895 list are all still in existence, only two of them remain virtually the same in nomenclature: Scribner and Dodd, Mead.

1896

Fiction

1. Tom Grogan, by *F. Hopkinson Smith*. Houghton Mifflin
2. A Lady of Quality, by *Frances Hodgson Burnett*. Scribner
3. The Seats of the Mighty, by *Gilbert Parker*. Appleton
4. A Singular Life, by *Elizabeth Stuart Phelps Ward*. Houghton Mifflin
5. The Damnation of Theron Ware, by *Harold Frederic*. Stone & Kimball
6. A House-Boat on the Styx, by *John Kendrick Bangs*. Harper
7. Kate Carnegie, by *Ian Maclaren*. Dodd, Mead
8. The Red Badge of Courage, by *Stephen Crane*. Appleton
9. Sentimental Tommy, by *J. M. Barrie*. Scribner
10. Beside the Bonnie Brier Bush, by *Ian Maclaren*. Dodd, Mead

GOLD WAS DISCOVERED in the Klondike. Bryan ran for President. Books on bimetallism and the gold standard were the most widely-read nonfiction. The best-known of them, *Coin's Financial School*, enjoyed a revival. In Boston the *Aeronautical Annual* was, strangely enough, a best seller. 1896 was the year in which the first movies were shown—introducing a new medium of entertainment that was to have noticeable effect upon the business of publishing. The popularity of the historical novel, America's favorite reading all through the 1890's and the early 20th century and revived again and again, was marked by the sales of such books as *A Lady of Quality* and *The Seats of the Mighty*. *Tom Grogan*, heading the 1896 list, is the first appearance on these lists of its author, that long-time favorite, F. Hopkinson Smith. The success of *A Singular Life* and *The Damnation of Theron Ware* illustrates the continuance of interest in religious novels from the previous decade, when *Robert Elsmere*, by Mrs. Humphry Ward, and *John Ward, Preacher*, by Margaret Deland, were high favorites. The list shows an increase in the number of books by American authors. Books by six of these authors—F. Hopkinson Smith, Frances Hodgson Burnett, Gilbert Parker, Harold Frederic, John Kendrick Bangs, and Stephen Crane—have been in demand by collectors of American first editions over the years.

Fiction

1. Quo Vadis, by *Henryk Sienkiewicz.* Little, Brown
2. The Choir Invisible, by *James Lane Allen.* Macmillan
3. Soldiers of Fortune, by *Richard Harding Davis.* Scribner
4. On the Face of the Waters, by *Flora Annie Steel.* Macmillan
5. Phroso, by *Anthony Hope.* Stokes
6. The Christian, by *Hall Caine.* Appleton
7. Margaret Ogilvy, by *J. M. Barrie.* Scribner
8. Sentimental Tommy, by *J. M. Barrie.* Scribner
9. The Pursuit of the House-Boat, by *John Kendrick Bangs.* Harper
10. The Honorable Peter Stirling, by *Paul Leicester Ford.* Holt

WHILE the sophisticated "400" ruled New York society and decreed conventions, the great novel of the day was that famous story of the early Christians, *Quo Vadis.* This year marked the appearance of Little, Brown & Company as a publisher of best sellers. James McIntyre of that firm showed genius in reaching large markets, especially difficult at that period with a book with a Latin title, the author of which had a long Polish name. The semi-religious novels of Hall Caine were coming into prominence too. This year also saw the first appearance among best sellers of Paul Leicester Ford, whose books, together with those of Winston Churchill (the American novelist), Charles Major, Mary Johnston, and others, were the record makers of their day in the field of historical fiction. *The Honorable Peter Stirling* had an interesting publishing history. Its publisher, Henry Holt & Company, was chiefly known for scholarly volumes and textbooks, although in 1895 it had taken a successful fling in trade publishing with *The Prisoner of Zenda. Peter Stirling,* issued in a small first printing, did not sell well until it was bruited about by a San Francisco bookseller that the chief character was modeled upon President Cleveland. Word-of-mouth advertising brought the sales of the book eventually to 228,000 copies.

1898

Fiction

1. Caleb West, by *F. Hopkinson Smith*. Houghton Mifflin
2. Hugh Wynne, by *S. Weir Mitchell*. Century
3. Penelope's Progress, by *Kate Douglas Wiggin*. Houghton Mifflin
4. Helbeck of Bannisdale, by *Mrs. Humphry Ward*. Macmillan
5. Quo Vadis, by *Henryk Sienkiewicz*. Little, Brown
6. The Pride of Jennico, by *Agnes and Egerton Castle*. Macmillan
7. The Day's Work, by *Rudyard Kipling*. Doubleday, McClure
8. Shrewsbury, by *Stanley Weyman*. Longmans, Green
9. Simon Dale, by *Anthony Hope*. Stokes
10. { The Adventures of François, by *S. Weir Mitchell*. Century
   { The Battle of the Strong, by *Gilbert Parker*. Houghton Mifflin

"REMEMBER THE MAINE!" was the slogan that swept the nation following that battleship's destruction by an explosion in Havana Harbor. Spain declared war on the United States on April 24. The Spanish fleet was destroyed in Manila Bay on May 1. The Philippines were annexed by the United States and the peace treaty with Spain was signed on December 10. "The end of the war came at an opportune time for autumn business," says a book trade letter of the period. Several notable authors were included on the best seller list for the first time—Rudyard Kipling, whose books created a furor, Kate Douglas Wiggin, and S. Weir Mitchell. The sale of Mitchell's *Hugh Wynne* was not handicapped by the book's being published in two volumes, nor was that of *Helbeck of Bannisdale,* by Mrs. Humphry Ward, also a two-volume novel. Though Mark Twain was writing at this period, his books never appeared on bookstore best seller lists, for most of them were issued by subscription companies whose house-to-house sales were not recorded in best seller reports from bookstores.

1899

Fiction

1. David Harum, by *Edward Noyes Westcott.* Appleton.
2. When Knighthood Was in Flower, by *Charles Major.* Bowen-Merrill
3. Richard Carvel, by *Winston Churchill.* Macmillan
4. The Day's Work, by *Rudyard Kipling.* Doubleday, McClure
5. Red Rock, by *Thomas Nelson Page.* Scribner
6. Aylwin, by *Theodore Watts-Dunton.* Dodd, Mead
7. Janice Meredith, by *Paul Leicester Ford.* Dodd, Mead
8. Mr. Dooley in Peace and War, by *Finley Peter Dunne.* Small, Maynard
9. No. 5 John Street, by *Richard Whiteing.* Century
10. The Market Place, by *Harold Frederic.* Stokes

AN INTERNATIONAL PEACE CONFERENCE sponsored by the Russian government met at The Hague. Aguinaldo staged an insurrection in the Philippines. The Boer War broke out in South Africa. The great novel of the day, *David Harum,* a novel that became a stage hit and many years later a movie with Will Rogers in the title role, was the story of a down-to-earth countryman of upper New York State. *When Knighthood Was in Flower* was the first best-selling novel to bear the Indianapolis imprint of the Bowen-Merrill Company, later the Bobbs-Merrill Company, a firm which developed a technique of exploiting popular fiction that greatly influenced American publishing. *When Knighthood Was in Flower, Janice Meredith,* and *Richard Carvel* are perhaps the best-remembered of the novels of this great era of historical fiction. *Richard Carvel* introduced Winston Churchill to the best seller lists, an American author who was to attain leading places on many later annual lists and whose name was much better known then in America than that of Winston Spencer Churchill of England. Also on the 1899 list appeared *Mr. Dooley,* Finley Peter Dunne's humorous character who was quoted for many years.

Fiction

1. To Have and to Hold, by *Mary Johnston*. Houghton Mifflin
2. Red Pottage, by *Mary Cholmondeley*. Harper
3. Unleavened Bread, by *Robert Grant*. Scribner
4. The Reign of Law, by *James Lane Allen*. Macmillan
5. Eben Holden, by *Irving Bacheller*. Lothrop
6. Janice Meredith, by *Paul Leicester Ford*. Dodd, Mead
7. The Redemption of David Corson, by *Charles Frederic Goss*. Bowen-Merrill
8. Richard Carvel, by *Winston Churchill*. Macmillan
9. When Knighthood Was in Flower, by *Charles Major*. Bowen-Merrill
10. Alice of Old Vincennes, by *Maurice Thompson*. Bowen-Merrill

1900 WAS THE YEAR of the Boxer Rebellion in China, the great hurricane and flood in Galveston, Texas, and the first excavation for the New York subway. In Kansas, Carry Nation began her hatchet raids on saloons. Four thousand "horseless carriages," most of them powered by electric batteries or steam, were manufactured during the first year of the new century. Historical novels dominated the nation's reading: *To Have and to Hold, Janice Meredith, Alice of Old Vincennes,* and others. *David Harum* had a follower in the field of rural wisdom in *Eben Holden,* which for a short time brought D. Lothrop & Co. (of *Five Little Peppers* fame) into the field of adult publishing. Bowen-Merrill was prominent on the list with three titles, two of them by Hoosier novelists Charles Major and Maurice Thompson.

1901

Fiction

1. The Crisis, by *Winston Churchill*. Macmillan
2. Alice of Old Vincennes, by *Maurice Thompson*. Bowen-Merrill
3. The Helmet of Navarre, by *Bertha Runkle*. Century
4. The Right of Way, by *Gilbert Parker*. Harper
5. Eben Holden, by *Irving Bacheller*. Lothrop
6. The Visits of Elizabeth, by *Elinor Glyn*. John Lane
7. The Puppet Crown, by *Harold MacGrath*. Bowen-Merrill
8. Richard Yea-and-Nay, by *Maurice Hewlett*. Macmillan
9. Graustark, by *George Barr McCutcheon*. Stone & Kimball
10. D'ri and I, by *Irving Bacheller*. Lothrop

PRESIDENT MCKINLEY was shot while attending the Pan-American Exposition, and Theodore Roosevelt took office on September 14. Though this was a year of financial panic, famous novels sold in the hundreds of thousands. The first book of a previously unknown author, *The Helmet of Navarre,* made such a success as a serial in *The Century* magazine that it was published in an unprecedented first printing of 100,000 copies. Turning from the Revolutionary setting of *Richard Carvel* to the Civil War scene for his new book, Winston Churchill established *The Crisis* as the best seller of the year. *Alice of Old Vincennes* climbed from tenth place on the best seller list of the previous year to second place, via national advertising and promotion such as books had seldom before been given. *Graustark,* with the Chicago imprint of Stone & Kimball, established a lasting reputation for George Barr McCutcheon, another of the Hoosier school of writers. Together with Harold MacGrath's *The Puppet Crown,* it marked a new trend in fiction—toward the light romance of intrigue and adventure in high society.

Fiction

1. The Virginian, by *Owen Wister*. Macmillan
2. Mrs. Wiggs of the Cabbage Patch, by *Alice Caldwell Hegan*. Century
3. Dorothy Vernon of Haddon Hall, by *Charles Major*. Macmillan
4. The Mississippi Bubble, by *Emerson Hough*. Bowen-Merrill
5. Audrey, by *Mary Johnston*. Houghton Mifflin
6. The Right of Way, by *Gilbert Parker*. Harper
7. The Hound of the Baskervilles, by *A. Conan Doyle*. McClure, Phillips
8. The Two Vanrevels, by *Booth Tarkington*. McClure, Phillips
9. The Blue Flower, by *Henry van Dyke*. Scribner
10. Sir Richard Calmady, by *Lucas Malet*. Dodd, Mead

WHILE "RAGTIME" swept America, Debussy's *Pélleas et Mélisande* was a popular success in Paris. The first "skyscrapers" were being built. Historical fiction, still riding high, comprised more than half the best seller list. Advance orders for Mary Johnston's *Audrey* exceeded 100,000 copies. Several new writing reputations were established by 1902 sales— those of Owen Wister, Emerson Hough, and Alice Caldwell Hegan (later Mrs. Rice). The book, the play, in which Dustin Farnum acted for ten years, and the movie in which Gary Cooper portrayed "The Virginian" made the hero's famous words "When you call me that, *smile,*" familiar in many an American household. In the sixties *The Virginian* became the basis for a TV serial. Eventually it sold in the millions. Owen Wister dedicated the book to his lifelong friend, Theodore Roosevelt. The Hoosier school added Booth Tarkington to its best-selling membership with his third book, *The Two Vanrevels*. His first novel, *The Gentleman from Indiana,* had been published in 1899. On this list, too, a detective story appeared for the first time. It was *The Hound of the Baskervilles,* by Sir Arthur Conan Doyle, creator of Sherlock Holmes, whose novels and stories have never stopped selling, and who even enjoyed dramatic revival in the '70's.

1903

Fiction

1. Lady Rose's Daughter, by *Mrs. Humphry Ward.* Harper
2. Gordon Keith, by *Thomas Nelson Page.* Scribner
3. The Pit, by *Frank Norris.* Doubleday, Page
4. Lovey Mary, by *Alice Hegan Rice.* Century
5. The Virginian, by *Owen Wister.* Macmillan
6. Mrs. Wiggs of the Cabbage Patch, by *Alice Hegan Rice.* Century
7. The Mettle of the Pasture, by *James Lane Allen.* Macmillan
8. Letters of a Self-Made Merchant to His Son, by *George Horace Lorimer.* Small, Maynard
9. The One Woman, by *Thomas Dixon, Jr.* Doubleday, Page
10. The Little Shepherd of Kingdom Come, by *John Fox, Jr.* Scribner

1903 was the year of the first successful airplane flight, made by the Wright brothers on December 17. The past few years had been a period of financial crisis; now the era of great industrial expansion was beginning. With *Lovey Mary,* Alice Hegan Rice repeated the success of her *Mrs. Wiggs of the Cabbage Patch.* Both were in the Century Company's famous series of short dollar novels, a series which reached its sales climax with *The Lady of the Decoration* in 1907. A new author, John Fox, Jr., appeared with the first of two novels that were to become almost synonymous with the words "best seller." There was only one English author on the list, Mrs. Humphry Ward, but her *Lady Rose's Daughter* was in number one position. Big business as a subject for fiction has cropped up over the years ever since *The Pit* and the famous *Saturday Evening Post* editor's *Letters of a Self-Made Merchant to His Son* became best sellers.

Fiction

1. The Crossing, by *Winston Churchill.* Macmillan
2. The Deliverance, by *Ellen Glasgow.* Doubleday, Page
3. The Masquerader, Anonymous (*Katherine Cecil Thurston*). Harper
4. In the Bishop's Carriage, by *Miriam Michelson.* Bobbs-Merrill
5. Sir Mortimer, by *Mary Johnston.* Harper
6. Beverly of Graustark, by *George Barr McCutcheon.* Dodd, Mead
7. The Little Shepherd of Kingdom Come, by *John Fox, Jr.* Scribner
8. Rebecca of Sunnybrook Farm, by *Kate Douglas Wiggin.* Houghton Mifflin
9. My Friend Prospero, by *Henry Harland.* McClure, Phillips
10. The Silent Places, by *Stewart Edward White.* McClure, Phillips

THE RUSSO-JAPANESE WAR was raging, and Americans were, on the whole, sympathetic to Japan. Advertisements of the year offered new rolls for phonographs, automobile road maps, one-piece collar buttons, and Sapolio. The World's Fair was on in St. Louis, the New York subway was opened, the Panama Canal was begun, and the first successful tunnel under the Hudson River was completed. In the magazines and newspapers the "literature of exposure" was appearing. Lincoln Steffens was writing; Thomas W. Lawson produced *Friday the Thirteenth*; and Ida Tarbell's *History of the Standard Oil Company* was running in *McClure's Magazine*. Among books, historical and romantic fiction dominated the best seller lists. Again Winston Churchill topped all other novelists of the year. An edition of 110,000 copies of Ellen Glasgow's *The Deliverance* was published; like most of these early 20th-century novels, it was priced at $1.50. The famous house of best sellers, Bowen-Merrill, became Bobbs-Merrill.

1905

Fiction

1. The Marriage of William Ashe, by *Mrs. Humphry Ward.* Harper
2. Sandy, by *Alice Hegan Rice.* Century
3. The Garden of Allah, by *Robert Hichens.* Stokes
4. The Clansman, by *Thomas Dixon, Jr.* Doubleday, Page
5. Nedra, by *George Barr McCutcheon.* Dodd, Mead
6. The Gambler, by *Katherine Cecil Thurston.* Harper
7. The Masquerader, Anonymous (*Katherine Cecil Thurston*). Harper
8. The House of Mirth, by *Edith Wharton.* Scribner
9. The Princess Passes, by *C. N.* and *A. M. Williamson.* Holt
10. Rose o' the River, by *Kate Douglas Wiggin.* Houghton Mifflin

NOVELS WERE beginning to utilize motor cars and wireless telegraphy, the new inventions of the period, in their plots. "Realism" was a literary trend. Novels and plays on business themes were popular. One of the year's stage hits was Charles Klein's *The Lion and the Mouse,* a play about a department store. Maxine Elliott and Mrs. Fiske were stars of the period. The first issue of *Variety* was published on December 16. *The Clansman,* Thomas Dixon's novel of the Ku Klux Klan, which was to become, as *The Birth of a Nation,* one of the most famous feature pictures of the silent movies, was well up on this year's best seller list. The Williamsons made the list with one of their first automobile romances. They specialized in the type of story in which the heroine falls in love with her chauffeur, who is actually the scion of a titled British family. "Motormania" hit the nation in a big way and practically all the publicity pictures of authors showed them at the wheels of their 1905 automobiles.

Fiction

1. Coniston, by *Winston Churchill*. Macmillan
2. Lady Baltimore, by *Owen Wister*. Macmillan
3. The Fighting Chance, by *Robert W. Chambers*. Appleton
4. The House of a Thousand Candles, by *Meredith Nicholson*. Bobbs-Merrill
5. Jane Cable, by *George Barr McCutcheon*. Dodd, Mead
6. The Jungle, by *Upton Sinclair*. Doubleday, Page
7. The Awakening of Helena Ritchie, by *Margaret Deland*. Harper
8. The Spoilers, by *Rex Beach*. Harper
9. The House of Mirth, by *Edith Wharton*. Scribner
10. The Wheel of Life, by *Ellen Glasgow*. Doubleday, Page

ONE of the most influential novels ever published in this country, Upton Sinclair's *The Jungle,* awoke the American public to the menace of the "meat trust" and was influential in the passage of the Pure Food and Drugs Act. Theodore Roosevelt, who took the "big stick" to some of the big corporations, championed simplified spelling as well as trust busting. John Philip Sousa was the March King of the nation. 1906 was also the year of the San Francisco earthquake. William Randolph Hearst was defeated for the governorship of New York State. Here for the first time was an all-American best seller list, which Winston Churchill headed for the third time, with another novel which, like *The Crisis* and *The Crossing* made good use of the letter C. Robert W. Chambers' *The Fighting Chance* was published in a first printing of 50,000 copies, in six weeks went to 100,000 and soon to 200,000. One of the first hits in the mystery-adventure field which was not a costume romance was Meredith Nicholson's *House of a Thousand Candles.*

1907

Fiction

1. The Lady of the Decoration, by *Frances Little.* Century
2. The Weavers, by *Gilbert Parker.* Harper
3. The Port of Missing Men, by *Meredith Nicholson.* Bobbs-Merrill
4. The Shuttle, by *Frances Hodgson Burnett.* Stokes
5. The Brass Bowl, by *Louis J. Vance.* Bobbs-Merrill
6. Satan Sanderson, by *Hallie Erminie Rives.* Bobbs-Merrill
7. The Daughter of Anderson Crow, by *George Barr McCutcheon.* Dodd, Mead
8. The Younger Set, by *Robert W. Chambers.* Appleton
9. The Doctor, by *Ralph Connor.* Revell
10. Half a Rogue, by *Harold MacGrath.* Bobbs-Merrill

1907 WAS a year of financial panic. Harrison Fisher was the popular artist of the time, along with Howard Chandler Christy, who illustrated *Beverly of Graustark,* and James Montgomery Flagg. The Harrison Fisher "gift book" annual was called *A Dream of Fair Women,* each colored illustration inspired by a popular poem. Ian Maclaren died in 1907. He was the great popular novelist of the previous decade and author of the first best seller of these yearly lists, *Beside the Bonnie Brier Bush.* Novelist Stewart Edward White was photographed in his two-cylinder Maxwell runabout; Mrs. Pat Campbell arrived to tour the country; Farrar and Chaliapin were singing at the Metropolitan, and Mary Garden at the Manhattan Opera House; the *Lusitania* made its first voyage to New York; and *The Man from Home,* by Booth Tarkington and Harry Leon Wilson, was the theatrical hit of the year. The Century Company's short dollar fiction series, which had started with the publication of *Mrs. Wiggs of the Cabbage Patch,* reached another high with *The Lady of the Decoration.* Robert W. Chambers' new novel, *The Younger Set,* marking the interest in sophisticated society romance, had sales of 200,000 copies, equaling the sale of his *The Fighting Chance* in 1906. Bobbs-Merrill, Indianapolis publishers, had four titles on this list, to the envy of many an eastern publisher.

1908

Fiction

1. Mr. Crewe's Career, by *Winston Churchill*. Macmillan
2. The Barrier, by *Rex Beach*. Harper
3. The Trail of the Lonesome Pine, by *John Fox, Jr.* Scribner
4. The Lure of the Mask, by *Harold MacGrath*. Bobbs-Merrill
5. The Shuttle, by *Frances Hodgson Burnett*. Stokes
6. Peter, by *F. Hopkinson Smith*. Scribner
7. Lewis Rand, by *Mary Johnston*. Houghton Mifflin
8. The Black Bag, by *Louis J. Vance*. Bobbs-Merrill
9. The Man from Brodney's, by *George Barr McCutcheon*. Dodd, Mead
10. The Weavers, by *Gilbert Parker*. Harper

BELGIUM ANNEXED the Congo. Maude Adams was playing in Barrie's *What Every Woman Knows,* and Augustus Thomas' *The Witching Hour* was another theatrical success. Maxine Elliott became the first American actress to own and operate her own theatre. The Harrison Fisher annual was *Bachelor Belles.* Winston Churchill was again first on the best seller list, having deserted his southern historical scenes for a New Hampshire setting. The first printing of *The Trail of the Lonesome Pine,* third on the list, was sold out in a few months. One of the best-known popular songs used the book's title—a songwriting habit that has persisted. Frances Hodgson Burnett was still a best seller twenty-two years after her greatest hit, *Little Lord Fauntleroy.* Nine of the authors were Americans, but all were "repeaters" from previous years, a characteristic of the fiction lists, which report favorite writers year after year.

Fiction

1. The Inner Shrine, Anonymous (*Basil King*). Harper
2. Katrine, by *Elinor Macartney Lane*. Harper
3. The Silver Horde, by *Rex Beach*. Harper
4. The Man in Lower Ten, by *Mary Roberts Rinehart*. Bobbs-Merrill
5. The Trail of the Lonesome Pine, by *John Fox, Jr*. Scribner
6. Truxton King, by *George Barr McCutcheon*. Dodd, Mead
7. 54-40 or Fight, by *Emerson Hough*. Bobbs-Merrill
8. The Goose Girl, by *Harold MacGrath*. Bobbs-Merrill
9. Peter, by *F. Hopkinson Smith*. Scribner
10. Septimus, by *William J. Locke*. John Lane

WILLIAM HOWARD TAFT was inaugurated as President of the United States; the first "Model T" Ford rolled off the assembly line; Peary reached the North Pole; and suffragettes were chaining themselves to London railings in this year 1909. Rube Goldberg's *Foolish Questions* was a regular feature of the New York *Evening Mail*. Frances Starr was appearing in *The Easiest Way,* and Mary Garden triumphed as Salome. "The art of the moving picture is still in its infancy," wrote Frederic Taber Cooper. Dr. Eliot's *Five-Foot Shelf,* its advertising a milestone in merchandising, made its first appearance. In the publication of Basil King's *The Inner Shrine,* best-selling book of 1909, Harper used anonymity to build up curiosity. The same publisher had also employed that method in selling Katherine Cecil Thurston's hit book of 1904 and 1905, *The Masquerader,* and was to use it again in 1910 with Basil King's *The Wild Olive.* This promotion stunt can be used only infrequently or its effect is blunted. Another example of its success, twenty years later, was the publication of Ursula Parrott's *Ex-Wife* in 1929 by Cape & Smith. *The Man in Lower Ten,* by Mary Roberts Rinehart, was the first American detective story to make the annual best seller list. It was illustrated in color by Howard Chandler Christy. William J. Locke, who had long been popular and was best known for his *Beloved Vagabond,* was introduced to the list, in tenth place, with one of his typically whimsical tales.

Fiction

1. The Rosary, by *Florence Barclay*. Putnam
2. A Modern Chronicle, by *Winston Churchill*. Macmillan
3. The Wild Olive, Anonymous (*Basil King*.) Harper
4. Max, by *Katherine Cecil Thurston*. Harper
5. The Kingdom of Slender Swords, by *Hallie Erminie Rives*. Bobbs-Merrill
6. Simon the Jester, by *William J. Locke*. John Lane
7. Lord Loveland Discovers America, by *C. N.* and *A. M. Williamson*. Doubleday, Page
8. The Window at the White Cat, by *Mary Roberts Rinehart*. Bobbs-Merrill
9. Molly Make-Believe, by *Eleanor Abbott*. Century
10. When a Man Marries, by *Mary Roberts Rinehart*. Bobbs-Merrill

THE END OF AN ERA had come with the death of Edward VII of England, whose death notably was the ending of the first television episode of the "Upstairs, Downstairs" series of the 1970's. 1910 was also the year of the death, in her ninety-second year, of Julia Ward Howe, author of *The Battle Hymn of the Republic*. Japan annexed Korea. The *Mauretania* was queen of the Atlantic. Edmond Rostand's *Chantecler* was produced in Paris; and Maeterlinck's *Blue Bird,* in London. Montague Glass' *Potash and Perlmutter* stories were running in the *Saturday Evening Post,* and the newspaper "funnies" of the day were *The Hall Room Boys* and Bud Fisher's *Mutt and Jeff.* Everyone was humming Ethelbert Nevin's song, "The Rosary," which was used in the plot of the year's best-selling novel—the first to take precedence over a new Churchill novel at the top of the list in a number of years. So popular and profitable was the book that its publisher's new building on West 45 Street, in New York, was dubbed "The Rosary." But its author, Florence Barclay, along with such other authors as the Williamsons and Eleanor Abbott, was soon forgotten. On the other hand, Mary Roberts Rinehart, represented by two books on the 1910 list, was a best-selling author for over half a century, and is still going strong in paperback reprints.

Fiction

1. The Broad Highway, by *Jeffrey Farnol*. Little, Brown
2. The Prodigal Judge, by *Vaughan Kester*. Bobbs-Merrill
3. The Winning of Barbara Worth, by *Harold Bell Wright*. Book Supply Co.
4. Queed, by *Henry Sydnor Harrison*. Houghton Mifflin
5. The Harvester, by *Gene Stratton Porter*. Doubleday, Page
6. The Iron Woman, by *Margaret Deland*. Harper
7. The Long Roll, by *Mary Johnston*. Houghton Mifflin
8. Molly Make-Believe, by *Eleanor Abbott*. Century
9. The Rosary, by *Florence Barclay*. Putnam
10. The Common Law, by *Robert W. Chambers*. Appleton

"ALEXANDER'S RAGTIME BAND" was the song of the year. It swept the country in 1911, and staged a return some twenty-seven years later. As a result of the 1938 movie of that title, an additional 1,000,000 copies of the song were sold. Along with ragtime came the first big wave of mechanized music—the player piano and the phonograph, forerunners of radio, talking screen and TV. The New York Public Library at 42nd Street and Fifth Avenue, which, with other libraries, is a final repository for many of the forgotten best sellers of yesterday, was opened on May 23. Top seller of the year, *The Broad Highway,* by the new English writer, Jeffrey Farnol, marked the last high spot of this long era of the historical novel. A total of 305,000 copies were sold in both original and reprint editions. Here was the first appearance of Harold Bell Wright, who built an extraordinary following, perhaps largely among a public not generally buyers of books. Gene Stratton Porter, many of whose books are among the big American best sellers of all time, made her first appearance on these lists with *The Harvester. Freckles* had been published in 1904 but had missed making an annual list largely because its great sale came after it had gone into a 50-cent reprint edition. *The Winning of Barbara Worth* was priced at $1.30 and *Queed,* a first novel that caught the public fancy, at $1.35— both prices typical of their time.

Fiction

1. The Harvester, by *Gene Stratton Porter*. Doubleday, Page
2. The Street Called Straight, by *Basil King*. Harper
3. Their Yesterdays, by *Harold Bell Wright*. Book Supply Co.
4. The Melting of Molly, by *Maria Thompson Daviess*. Bobbs-Merrill
5. A Hoosier Chronicle, by *Meredith Nicholson*. Houghton Mifflin
6. The Winning of Barbara Worth, by *Harold Bell Wright*. Book Supply Co.
7. The Just and the Unjust, by *Vaughan Kester*. Bobbs-Merrill
8. The Net, by *Rex Beach*. Harper
9. Tante, by *Anne Douglas Sedgwick*. Century
10. Fran, by *J. Breckenridge Ellis*. Bobbs-Merrill

Nonfiction

1. The Promised Land, by *Mary Antin*. Houghton Mifflin
2. The Montessori Method, by *Maria Montessori*. Stokes
3. South America, by *James Bryce,* Macmillan
4. A New Conscience and an Ancient Evil, by *Jane Addams*. Macmillan
5. Three Plays, by *Eugène Brieux*. Brentano
6. Your United States, by *Arnold Bennett*. Harper
7. Creative Evolution, by *Henri Bergson*. Holt
8. How to Live on Twenty-Four Hours a Day, by *Arnold Bennett*. Doran
9. Woman and Labor, by *Olive Schreiner*. Stokes
10. Mark Twain, by *Albert Bigelow Paine*. Harper

WOODROW WILSON was elected President of the United States, defeating both William Howard Taft and Theodore Roosevelt: the latter's Bull Moose candidacy split the Republican party. Arizona and New Mexico were admitted to the Union. The dramatic sinking of the great new luxury liner *Titanic,* with many notables on board and with enormous loss of life, stunned two continents. In this year began the heyday of the

Harold Bell Wright-Gene Stratton Porter novels. Both their 1911 best sellers reappeared on the 1912 list, Mrs. Porter's reaching top place. Anne Douglas Sedgwick's *Tante* gave a note of literary distinction to a none too distinguished group of novels. *The Publishers' Weekly* added nonfiction best-selling records this year and again in 1913, then dropped them for three years until the sales of books about World War I made nonfiction titles big sellers again. Previously fiction and nonfiction had been lumped together, with the result that the list consisted almost entirely of fiction and a book of general literature seldom if ever reached a yearly best seller list. Not until the 1920's did nonfiction sales equal those of fiction, when such books as H. G. Wells' *Outline of History* began to come along. Nonfiction best sellers tell more about the subjects in which the public was interested than which authors were their favorites. The first nonfiction best-seller list was no lightweight assembly. It featured "self-help" books, biography, travel, social and economic problems, philosophy—recurring topics through all later years. Notable was the appearance of two books by Arnold Bennett on the list, and one by Jane Addams. There began a revival of interest in the teaching methods of Maria Montessori 50 years after *The Montessori Method* reached second place among nonfiction best sellers.

1913

Fiction

1. The Inside of the Cup, by *Winston Churchill.* Macmillan
2. V.V.'s Eyes, by *Henry Sydnor Harrison,* Houghton Mifflin
3. Laddie, by *Gene Stratton Porter.* Doubleday, Page
4. The Judgment House, by *Sir Gilbert Parker.* Harper
5. Heart of the Hills, by *John Fox, Jr.* Scribner
6. The Amateur Gentleman, by *Jeffrey Farnol.* Little, Brown
7. The Woman Thou Gavest Me, by *Hall Caine.* Lippincott
8. Pollyanna, by *Eleanor H. Porter.* Page
9. The Valiants of Virginia, by *Hallie Erminie Rives.* Bobbs-Merrill
10. T. Tembarom, by *Frances Hodgson Burnett.* Century

Nonfiction

1. Crowds, by *Gerald Stanley Lee.* Doubleday, Page
2. Germany and the Germans, by *Price Collier.* Scribner
3. Zone Policeman 88, by *Harry A. Franck.* Century
4. The New Freedom, by *Woodrow Wilson.* Doubleday, Page
5. South America, by *James Bryce.* Macmillan
6. Your United States, by *Arnold Bennett.* Harper
7. The Promised Land, by *Mary Antin.* Houghton Mifflin
8. Auction Bridge To-Day, by *Milton C. Work.* Houghton Mifflin
9. Three Plays, by *Eugène Brieux.* Brentano
10. Psychology and Industrial Efficiency, by *Hugo Munsterberg.* Houghton Mifflin

In 1901, 1904, 1906, 1908, and again in 1913 a novel by Winston Churchill headed fiction sales. Hall Caine's *The Woman Thou Gavest Me* sold 346,000 in the year. *Pollyanna* made her first appearance, beginning a series that continued to sell over many years, although later on as juvenile reading. Nonfiction included (a year before the outbreak of World War I) a book on Germany, by Price Collier, and President Wilson's statement of his program, *The New Freedom.* Brieux's plays appeared for the second year—one of the few books of drama in all these lists. The discussion of one of the plays, *Damaged Goods,* when performed in New York probably accounted for the book's large sale. It was based on a theme startling for those times, the problem of venereal disease. Milton Work, first bridge authority to achieve a national sale for his instruction books, was succeeded as a best seller many years later by Ely Culbertson and then by Charles Goren. 1913 was the year in which the Secretary of State declared the first federal income tax law in effect, after the 16th Amendment to the Constitution had been ratified by 42 of the 48 states.

1914

Fiction

1. The Eyes of the World, by *Harold Bell Wright*. Book Supply Co.
2. Pollyanna, by *Eleanor H. Porter*. Page
3. The Inside of the Cup, by *Winston Churchill*. Macmillan
4. The Salamander, by *Owen Johnson*. Bobbs-Merrill
5. The Fortunate Youth, by *William J. Locke*. John Lane
6. T. Tembarom, by *Frances Hodgson Burnett*. Century
7. Penrod, by *Booth Tarkington*. Doubleday, Page
8. Diane of the Green Van, by *Leona Dalrymple*. Reilly & Britton
9. The Devil's Garden, by *W. B. Maxwell*. Bobbs-Merrill
10. The Prince of Graustark, by *George Barr McCutcheon*. Dodd, Mead

IN MIDSUMMER an Austrian archduke was murdered in the obscure Balkan town of Sarajevo, and by fall all Europe was at war. The United States had just opened the Panama Canal to the world's seaborne traffic. At home, everyone was singing one of Jerome Kern's first great song hits, "They Didn't Believe Me," from *The Girl from Utah*. Harold Bell Wright attained first place as most popular novelist of the year, closely followed by Eleanor Porter with *Pollyanna* and Winston Churchill with his story of a liberal minister, which had been the 1913 leader. Among the new names was that of Owen Johnson, already known for his appealing stories of Lawrenceville School. It is interesting to note that in this year of 1914 two best sellers were adult novels about boys. Once in a long while such a story hits the hearts of its readers—as did J. D. Salinger's *Catcher in the Rye* many years later. Perhaps the most famous book on this list is that novel of youth, whose hero, Penrod, belongs in the permanent roll of American literature.

1915

Fiction

1. The Turmoil, by *Booth Tarkington*. Harper
2. A Far Country, by *Winston Churchill*. Macmillan
3. Michael O'Halloran, by *Gene Stratton Porter*. Doubleday, Page
4. Pollyanna Grows Up, by *Eleanor H. Porter*. Page
5. K, by *Mary Roberts Rinehart*. Houghton Mifflin
6. Jaffery, by *William J. Locke*. John Lane
7. Felix O'Day, by *F. Hopkinson Smith*. Scribner
8. The Harbor, by *Ernest Poole*. Macmillan
9. The Lone Star Ranger, by *Zane Grey*. Harper
10. Angela's Business, by *Henry Sydnor Harrison*. Houghton Mifflin

U.S. WAR INDUSTRIES were booming. The *Lusitania* was sunk by a German submarine on May 7. "Hello Frisco" was the song of the day, celebrating the opening of the New York-San Francisco telephone line; the first transatlantic speech was given by radio, and the first telephone message sent across the Atlantic. Poison gas made its appearance on Europe's battlefields. Billy Sunday was exhorting a good many Americans into repentance. *The Birth of a Nation,* first great feature film, based upon *The Clansman,* a best seller of 1905, opened in New York. *The Turmoil,* Booth Tarkington's first long serious novel, headed the list of fiction. *K,* by Mary Roberts Rinehart, in fifth place, became her best-known nonmystery novel. Here came the first of the many Zane Grey books to appear on the lists, and another new name was that of Ernest Poole, with his novel about New York harbor.

1916

Fiction

1. Seventeen, by *Booth Tarkington*. Harper
2. When a Man's a Man, by *Harold Bell Wright*. Book Supply Co.
3. Just David, by *Eleanor H. Porter*. Houghton Mifflin
4. Mr. Britling Sees It Through, by *H. G. Wells*. Macmillan
5. Life and Gabriella, by *Ellen Glasgow*. Doubleday, Page
6. The Real Adventure, by *Henry Kitchell Webster*. Bobbs-Merrill
7. Bars of Iron, by *Ethel M. Dell*. Putnam
8. Nan of Music Mountain, by *Frank H. Spearman*. Scribner
9. Dear Enemy, by *Jean Webster*. Century
10. The Heart of Rachael, by *Kathleen Norris*. Doubleday, Page

THE FIRST WORLD WAR was in its third year. The New York-New Jersey area was rocked by the Black Tom explosion, supposedly engineered by German secret agents. Woodrow Wilson was re-elected on the campaign slogan, "He kept us out of war." "Preparedness" became the watchword of the day. For the second year in succession Booth Tarkington headed the list of best sellers, this time with *Seventeen,* novel of adolescence, almost as well known as his famous *Penrod. Seventeen* has sold over one and a half million. In fourth place was *Mr. Britling Sees It Through,* by H. G. Wells, which gave thousands of Americans a better understanding of the war. Here is the first appearance of Kathleen Norris with *The Heart of Rachael. Dear Enemy* was written by the author of the better-remembered *Daddy-Long-Legs,* which, because of its slow but steady sale, did not appear on any annual list. Along with such books as *Penrod, Seventeen,* and the Pollyanna stories, it marks a noticeable trend through this period toward novels about very young people written to entertain adults.

1917

Fiction

1. Mr. Britling Sees It Through, by *H. G. Wells.* Macmillan
2. The Light in the Clearing, by *Irving Bacheller.* Bobbs-Merrill
3. The Red Planet, by *William J. Locke.* John Lane
4. The Road to Understanding, by *Eleanor H. Porter.* Houghton Mifflin
5. Wildfire, by *Zane Grey.* Harper
6. Christine, by *Alice Cholmondeley.* Macmillan
7. In the Wilderness, by *Robert S. Hichens.* Stokes
8. His Family, by *Ernest Poole.* Macmillan
9. The Definite Object, by *Jeffery Farnol.* Little, Brown
10. The Hundredth Chance, by *Ethel M. Dell.* Putnam

General Nonfiction

1. Rhymes of a Red Cross Man, by *Robert W. Service.* Barse & Hopkins
2. The Plattsburg Manual, by *O. O. Ellis* and *E. B. Garey.* Century
3. Raymond, by *Sir Oliver Lodge.* Doran
4. Poems of Alan Seeger. Scribner
5. God the Invisible King, by *H. G. Wells.* Macmillan
6. Laugh and Live, by *Douglas Fairbanks.* Britton Publishing Co.
7. Better Meals for Less Money, by *Mary Green.* Holt

War Books

1. The First Hundred Thousand, by *Ian Hay.* Houghton Mifflin
2. My Home in the Field of Honor, by *Frances W. Huard.* Doran
3. A Student in Arms, by *Donald Hankey.* Dutton
4. Over the Top, by *Arthur Guy Empey.* Putnam
5. Carry On, by *Coningsby Dawson.* John Lane
6. Getting Together, by *Ian Hay.* Houghton Mifflin
7. My Second Year of the War, by *Frederick Palmer.* Dodd, Mead

8. The Land of Deepening Shadow, by *D. Thomas Curtin.* Doran
9. Italy, France and Britain at War, by *H. G. Wells.* Macmillan
10. The Worn Doorstep, by *Margaret Sherwood.* Little, Brown

THE UNITED STATES declared war on Germany on April 6. The first of the A.E.F. landed in France in June. Liberty Loans were launched and Mary Pickford, Douglas Fairbanks, and Charlie Chaplin drew enormous crowds to buy bonds, as they made appearances in such places as the steps of the New York Public Library. Revolution swept Imperial Russia. Jazz was the rage in America. Large hotels and restaurants introduced *thés dansants* featuring fox trots. As Americans donned khaki and rolled puttees, Britain's *Mr. Britling* rose to top place in fiction, selling 350,000 copies in fifteen months. Irving Bacheller reappeared, after sixteen years, with his *Light in the Clearing* in second place, followed by many other familiar names—Locke, Porter, Grey, Hichens, and so on. Although most of the fiction was on the mediocre side, nonfiction and war books (both added classifications in this year) showed what the war-minded American public wanted, for most books on this "general nonfiction" list reflected the emotions and emergencies of wartime America. First was the poetry of Robert W. Service, then *The Plattsburg Manual* for future officers. Sir Oliver Lodge aroused great interest when he, a noted scientist, proclaimed his belief in communion with the dead, in this case with his son, who had been killed in the war. Alan Seeger's poem, *I Have a Rendezvous with Death,* was responsible for the continued sale of his book through the war years. *Over the Top,* best-remembered of World War I accounts, glorified the doughboy and sold 350,000 copies in 1917.

Fiction

1. The U. P. Trail, by *Zane Grey*. Harper
2. The Tree of Heaven, by *May Sinclair*. Macmillan
3. The Amazing Interlude, by *Mary Roberts Rinehart*. Doran
4. Dere Mable, by *Edward Streeter*. Stokes
5. Oh, Money! Money! by *Eleanor H. Porter*. Houghton Mifflin
6. Greatheart, by *Ethel M. Dell*. Putnam
7. The Major, by *Ralph Connor*. Revell
8. The Pawns Count, by *E. Phillips Oppenheim*. Little, Brown
9. A Daughter of the Land, by *Gene Stratton Porter*. Doubleday, Page
10. Sonia, by *Stephen McKenna*. Doran

General Nonfiction

1. Rhymes of a Red Cross Man, *by Robert W. Service*. Barse & Hopkins
2. Treasury of War Poetry, by *G. H. Clark*. Houghton Mifflin
3. With the Colors, by *Everard J. Appleton*. Stewart, Kidd
4. Recollections, by *Viscount Morley*. Macmillan
5. Laugh and Live, by *Douglas Fairbanks*. Britton Publishing Co.
6. Mark Twain's Letters, ed. by *Albert Bigelow Paine*. Harper
7. Adventures and Letters of Richard Harding Davis, by *Richard Harding Davis*. Scribner
8. Over Here, by *Edgar Guest*. Reilly & Lee
9. Diplomatic Days, by *Edith O'Shaughnessy*. Harper
10. Poems of Alan Seeger. Scribner

War Books

1. My Four Years in Germany, by *James W. Gerard*. Doran
2. The Glory of the Trenches, by *Coningsby Dawson*. John Lane
3. Over the Top, by *Arthur Guy Empey*. Putnam
4. A Minstrel in France, by *Harry Lauder*. Hearst's International Library Co.

5. Private Peat, by *Harold R. Peat.* Bobbs-Merrill
6. Outwitting the Hun, by *Lieut. Pat O'Brien.* Harper
7. Face to Face With Kaiserism, by *James W. Gerard.* Doran
8. Carry On, by *Coningsby Dawson.* John Lane
9. Out to Win, by *Coningsby Dawson.* John Lane
10. Under Fire, by *Henri Barbusse.* Dutton

"THE LONG LONG TRAIL" wound on into the last year of war, which began with a great German offensive and ended with dancing in the streets as the first premature Armistice Day was celebrated. Zane Grey's *U. P. Trail* was the most popular novel of the year, firmly establishing his reputation as a writer of western adventure that was to last for decades. *The Tree of Heaven* introduced an English writer of consequence to the American best seller list. *Dere Mable,* considered the prototype of soldier humor, flashed into popularity as did *See Here, Private Hargrove* a quarter of a century later. Edward Streeter's book, which might well have been classed as a war book instead of fiction, quickly sold half a million copies. Not for thirty-one years did Edward Streeter's name reappear on the annual lists. His *Father of the Bride* in 1949 made almost as big a hit. E. Phillips Oppenheim, whose stories of intrigue, mystery, and adventure have been read by more than two generations in England and America, made his first appearance on the list. There are four books of poetry among non-fiction, all with wartime appeal—a type of writing that was noticeably missing among World War II best sellers with one exception. Edgar Guest, through his thirty-five years of writing, had probably the largest popular audience for poetry since James Whitcomb Riley in the 1890's. Two important volumes of memoirs received attention in that war year of 1918 —*Mark Twain's Letters* edited by Albert Bigelow Paine and the *Recollections* of Viscount Morley. Ambassador Gerard's books on Germany had a noticeable influence on American public opinion just as William L. Shirer's *Berlin Diary,* Ambassador Davies' *Mission to Moscow,* and Ambassador Grew's *Ten Years in Japan* were to have in World War II. One of the most widely discussed books from a literary point of view was the French *Under Fire.* Three books by Coningsby Dawson, star reporter of World War I and extremely popular lecturer in the United States, appeared on this list of war books.

1919

Fiction

1. The Four Horsemen of the Apocalypse, by *V. Blasco Ibañez.* Dutton
2. The Arrow of Gold, by *Joseph Conrad.* Doubleday, Page
3. The Desert of Wheat, by *Zane Grey.* Harper
4. Dangerous Days, by *Mary Roberts Rinehart.* Doran
5. The Sky Pilot in No Man's Land, by *Ralph Connor.* Doran
6. The Re-Creation of Brian Kent, by *Harold Bell Wright.* Book Supply Co.
7. Dawn, by *Gene Stratton Porter.* Houghton Mifflin
8. The Tin Soldier, by *Temple Bailey.* Penn Publishing Co.
9. Christopher and Columbus, by *"Elizabeth."* Doubleday, Page
10. In Secret, by *Robert W. Chambers.* Doran

Nonfiction

1. The Education of Henry Adams, by *Henry Adams.* Houghton Mifflin
2. The Years Between, by *Rudyard Kipling.* Doubleday, Page
3. Belgium, by *Brand Whitlock.* Appleton
4. The Seven Purposes, by *Margaret Cameron.* Harper
5. In Flanders Fields, by *John McCrae.* Putnam
6. Bolshevism, by *John Spargo.* Harper

GENERAL JOHN J. PERSHING and his men of the AEF marched up Fifth Avenue in a great Victory Parade. Then the fight for the League of Nations was on, with Henry Cabot Lodge its most vigorous opponent in the Senate. President Wilson, who was awarded the Nobel Peace Prize in 1919, took his dream of world organization to the people in a nation-wide tour. Calvin Coolidge was settling the Boston police strike, an act that was to win him national fame and help to bring him eventually to the White House. There came a resurgence of the Ku Klux Klan not only in the South but in many northern states. The "high cost of living" made the daily headlines even as the flapper era, of rolled stockings (silk now, instead of cotton), of bobbed hair and of knee-length skirts, dawned. Helen Hayes appeared in a flapper role in Booth Tarkington's play

Clarence, which starred Alfred Lunt. The first airplane crossed the Atlantic, a Navy plane that flew from Nova Scotia to Portugal. *The Four Horsemen of the Apocalypse,* an oustanding war novel of more romantic appeal that *Mr. Britling* of 1916-1917, headed 1919 fiction. Dutton used spectacular display advertising to push it. Its price, $1.90, was a new high for a book destined for wide sales. Later, *The Four Horsemen* became one of the first movies to build the great popularity of Rudolph Valentino. With *The Arrow of Gold,* Doubleday, Page succeeded in giving Joseph Conrad the wide audience he deserved. Here is the first appearance of Temple Bailey, whom Charles Shoemaker, of the Penn Publishing Company of Philadelphia, brought to the front and made a competitor of such writers as Kathleen Norris for the great audience of romantic women readers. Nonfiction best seller and war book records were merged in 1919. *The Education of Henry Adams,* which has become a classic of our literature, took top place among nonfiction. Like Alan Seeger's *Poems,* John McCrae's *In Flanders Fields* became a best seller on the strength of a single poem, the title poem in this case. Kipling's *The Years Between* contained some poems about World War I.

1920

Fiction

1. The Man of the Forest, by *Zane Grey*. Harper
2. Kindred of the Dust, by *Peter B. Kyne*. Cosmopolitan Book Co.
3. The Re-Creation of Brian Kent, by *Harold Bell Wright*. Book Supply Co.
4. The River's End, by *James Oliver Curwood*. Cosmopolitan Book Co.
5. A Man for the Ages, by *Irving Bacheller*. Bobbs-Merrill
6. Mary-Marie, by *Eleanor H. Porter*. Houghton Mifflin
7. The Portygee, by *Joseph C. Lincoln*. Appleton
8. The Great Impersonation, by *E. Phillips Oppenheim*. Little, Brown
9. The Lamp in the Desert, by *Ethel M. Dell*. Putnam
10. Harriet and the Piper, by *Kathleen Norris*. Doubleday, Page

Nonfiction

1. Now It Can Be Told, by *Philip Gibbs*. Harper
2. The Economic Consequences of the Peace, by *John M. Keynes*. Harcourt, Brace
3. Roosevelt's Letters to His Children, ed. by *Joseph B. Bishop*. Scribner
4. Theodore Roosevelt, by *William Roscoe Thayer*. Scribner
5. White Shadows in the South Seas, by *Frederick O'Brien*. Century
6. An American Idyll, by *Cornelia Stratton Parker*. Atlantic Monthly Press

THE FIRST ELECTION returns ever broadcast in the United States (by Station KDKA, Pittsburgh) announced the success of Warren G. Harding's campaign for the Presidency. Women voted for the first time in the 1920 election and helped to put across the amendment to the Constitution that ushered in the prohibition era, the era in which such books as *This Side of Paradise, Flaming Youth,* and *The Plastic Age* brought into the limelight the uninhibited "younger generation." Ponzi, bridge expert Joseph Elwell murdered in New York, Big Jim Colosimo awarded an extravagant gangland funeral in Chicago, Fannie Brice singing "My Man," and the many greats of the sports world—Babe Ruth, Red Grange, Jack Dempsey, Gene Tunney, Walter Hagen, Gertrude Ederle, The Four Horsemen, Big Bill Tilden, Helen Wills, Bobby Jones—are names that echo from the decade ushered in by 1920. Zane Grey again topped best-selling fiction with *The Man of the Forest.* William Randolph Hearst was in the book publishing field for a time; his Cosmopolitan Book Company put two favorites—Peter B. Kyne and James Oliver Curwood, both writers of outdoor adventure stories—on the best seller list. Joseph C. Lincoln, teller of homely New England tales, joined the best sellers with *The Portygee.* Heading nonfiction was Philip Gibbs, a favorite reporter of World War I, who found a waiting market for a volume of war episodes, *Now It Can Be Told.* A new publisher, Harcourt, Brace & Company, appeared on the list with a book of historical importance, *The Economic Consequences of the Peace,* by John M. Keynes. Public interest in President Theodore Roosevelt's letters, written with charm and spontaneity, and in the biography of him by William Roscoe Thayer, was highlighted by his recent death. Frederick O'Brien's *White Shadows in the South Seas* started a new vogue in travel literature and aroused the public's interest in exotic lands.

Fiction

1. Main Street, by *Sinclair Lewis*. Harcourt, Brace
2. The Brimming Cup, by *Dorothy Canfield*. Harcourt, Brace
3. The Mysterious Rider, by *Zane Grey*. Harper
4. The Age of Innocence, by *Edith Wharton*. Appleton
5. The Valley of Silent Men, by *James Oliver Curwood*. Cosmopolitan Book Co.
6. The Sheik, by *Edith M. Hull*. Small, Maynard
7. A Poor Wise Man, by *Mary Roberts Rinehart*. Doran
8. Her Father's Daughter, by *Gene Stratton Porter*. Doubleday, Page
9. The Sisters-in-Law, by *Gertrude Atherton*. Stokes
10. The Kingdom Round the Corner, by *Coningsby Dawson*. Cosmopolitan Book Co.

Nonfiction

1. The Outline of History, by *H. G. Wells*. Macmillan
2. White Shadows in the South Seas, by *Frederick O'Brien*. Century
3. The Mirrors of Downing Street, by a Gentleman with a Duster (*Harold Begbie*). Putnam
4. Mystic Isles of the South Seas, by *Frederick O'Brien*. Century
5. The Autobiography of Margot Asquith. Doran
6. Peace Negotiations, by *Robert Lansing*. Houghton Mifflin

WORLD WAR I's Unknown Soldier was enshrined at Arlington Cemetery. Boston banned the movie, "The Birth of a Nation." Caruso died in Naples. Frank Bacon completed a record run on Broadway in "Lightnin'." Albert Einstein was awarded the Nobel Prize in Physics. Emperor Hirohito of Japan went on a world peace tour. "Normalcy" was President Harding's word for the administration he hoped to provide—but the best-selling novel of the year was a "debunker" of normal small-town life, the book that skyrocketed Sinclair Lewis into fame. *Main Street* sold 295,000 copies in 1921 and brought a new realistic vein into American popular literature which had, for many years, been dominated by royal romance and western adventure. Lewis's book was published by the young firm of Harcourt, Brace & Company, which also provided the second novel on the list, *The Brimming Cup,* by Dorothy Canfield, one of the most beloved writers of a quarter century. Edith Wharton, already a literary notable, appeared on the list for the first time since 1906 with her most famous book, *The Age of Innocence.* Here, too, was the first appearance of Gertrude Atherton, and of Coningsby Dawson as a writer of fiction. Next to *Main Street,* the novel that became most famous was *The Sheik,* by Edith M. Hull. The romantic novel sold like wildfire and eventually became the movie vehicle which made Rudolph Valentino the screen idol of his day. A landmark among best sellers headed nonfiction—H. G. Wells' *Outline of History,* which was issued first as a two-volume set at $10.50, was later marketed in one volume at $5.00, and a few years later had an edition of half a million at $1.00. *White Shadows of the South Seas* was even more popular in its second year; a second and similar book by Frederick O'Brien also appeared on this list. One of the first "debunking" biographies was *The Mirrors of Downing Street,* published under a pseudonym. The visit to the U.S.A. of Margot Asquith, wife of a former English Prime Minister, stirred interest in her autobiography, and Wilson's Secretary of State scored a success with his history of World War peace negotiations. This was almost the last of nonfiction best sellers to deal directly with World War I during the three years after its close. In the 1960's, however, World War I again became a subject of importance in nonfiction for the general reader, when such books as Barbara Tuchman's *The Guns of August* achieved high sales.

Fiction

1. If Winter Comes, by *A. S. M. Hutchinson*. Little, Brown
2. The Sheik, by *Edith M. Hull*. Small, Maynard
3. Gentle Julia, by *Booth Tarkington*. Doubleday, Page
4. The Head of the House of Coombe, by *Frances Hodgson Burnett*. Stokes
5. Simon Called Peter, by *Robert Keable*. Dutton
6. The Breaking Point, by *Mary Roberts Rinehart*. Doran
7. This Freedom, by *A. S. M. Hutchinson*. Little, Brown
8. Maria Chapdelaine, by *Louis Hémon*. Macmillan
9. To the Last Man, by *Zane Grey*. Harper
10. {Babbitt, by *Sinclair Lewis*. Harcourt, Brace
{Helen of the Old House, by *Harold Bell Wright*. Appleton

Nonfiction

1. The Outline of History, by *H. G. Wells*. Macmillan
2. The Story of Mankind, by *Hendrik Willem Van Loon*. Boni & Liveright
3. The Americanization of Edward Bok, by *Edward Bok*. Scribner
4. Diet and Health, by *Lulu Hunt Peters*. Reilly & Lee
5. The Mind in the Making, by *James Harvey Robinson*. Harper
6. The Outline of Science, by *J. Arthur Thomson*. Putnam
7. Outwitting Our Nerves, by *Josephine A. Jackson* and *Helen M. Salisbury*. Century
8. Queen Victoria, by *Lytton Strachey*. Harcourt, Brace
9. Mirrors of Washington, Anonymous (*Clinton W. Gilbert*). Putnam
10. Painted Windows, by a Gentleman with a Duster (*Harold Begbie*). Putnam

WAISTLINES at the hips—mah-jongg—Paul Whiteman at the Palais Royale —Rudy Vallee, first of the crooners—the Castles and the Astaires—and *Babbitt,* which introduced a new descriptive word into our language, are all reminders of the twenties. 1922 was the year in which the *Reader's*

Digest was launched. It was to have a definite effect upon the sale of books it "digested" and to start a tremendous wave of magazine book digests. The English writer, A. S. M. Hutchinson, had two novels on the best seller list, with *If Winter Comes,* which sold 350,000 copies in its first ten months, in first place. *The Sheik* carried over into its second year, this time next to the leader. *The Head of the House of Coombe* brought Frances Hodgson Burnett into her fourth decade of best sellerdom. *Simon Called Peter,* a war novel dealing with a religious problem, was a sensation on both sides of the Atlantic and sold 152,000 copies. *Maria Chapdelaine,* with its background the northern Quebec woods, was a critical as well as a popular success. *The Outline of History* in its lower-priced edition made top place in nonfiction for the second year. With Hendrik Willem Van Loon's *Story of Mankind,* James Harvey Robinson's *Mind in the Making,* and J. Arthur Thomson's *Outline of Science,* it ushered in a period of "outline" books on various cultural and scientific subjects that was to reach a climax with the sales of *The Story of Philosophy* four years later. Edward Bok, who had made a reputation as editor of the *Ladies' Home Journal,* provided a new version of the American success story. Two health books achieved big sales. Lytton Strachey's first outstanding biography was his life of Queen Victoria. *Mirrors of Washington* and *Painted Windows* followed in the anonymous steps of *The Mirrors of Downing Street.*

1923

Fiction

1. Black Oxen, by *Gertrude Atherton*. Boni & Liveright
2. His Children's Children, by *Arthur Train*. Scribner
3. The Enchanted April, by *"Elizabeth."* Doubleday, Page
4. Babbitt, by *Sinclair Lewis*. Harcourt, Brace
5. The Dim Lantern, by *Temple Bailey*. Penn Publishing Co.
6. This Freedom, by *A. S. M. Hutchinson*. Little, Brown
7. The Mine with the Iron Door, by *Harold Bell Wright*. Appleton
8. The Wanderer of the Wasteland, by *Zane Grey*. Harper
9. The Sea-Hawk, by *Rafael Sabatini*. Houghton Mifflin
10. The Breaking Point, by *Mary Roberts Rinehart*. Doran

Nonfiction

1. Etiquette, by *Emily Post*. Funk & Wagnalls
2. The Life of Christ, by *Giovanni Papini*. Harcourt, Brace
3. The Life and Letters of Walter H. Page, ed. by *Burton J. Hendrick*. Doubleday, Page
4. The Mind in the Making, by *James Harvey Robinson*. Harper
5. The Outline of History, by *H. G. Wells*. Macmillan
6. Diet and Health, by *Lulu Hunt Peters*. Reilly & Lee
7. Self-Mastery Through Conscious Auto-Suggestion, by *Emile Coué*. American Library Service
8. The Americanization of Edward Bok, by *Edward Bok*. Scribner
9. The Story of Mankind, by *Hendrik Willem Van Loon*. Boni & Liveright
10. A Man from Maine, by *Edward Bok*. Scribner

ALL America was chanting "Yes, We Have No Bananas." Dance marathons were the latest craze. Sarah Bernhardt died in Paris and Eleanora Duse in Pittsburgh during a farewell American tour. Laurette Taylor was starring in "Peg o' My Heart" in New York. In Germany Hitler's beer hall *Putsch* missed fire. President Harding died, and Calvin Coolidge was quietly sworn in as President of the United States by his father in a simple ceremony in his small native Vermont village of Plymouth. All

95

over the country the revived Ku Klux Klan flourished; white-sheeted men marched openly and fiery crosses burned at night. The magazine *Time* was founded in 1923. With *Black Oxen,* based on what was at the time considered the rather sensational theme of physical rejuvenation, Gertrude Atherton achieved the great popular success of her long writing career. *Babbitt* and *This Freedom* held over into a second year on a fiction list of typical wide-audience appeal, marked with first appearances of Arthur Train and Rafael Sabatini. *Etiquette,* by Emily Post, who had previously been known as a novelist, topped nonfiction sales and developed into a staple bookstore item for many years. Papini's *Life of Christ,* a presentation of the life of Jesus in terms of the new psychology, sold well over 100,000 copies in 1923. The Page *Letters* made a new record for a two-volume biography, with 75,000 sold in a year. Mrs. Peters' *Diet and Health,* in its second year on the list, had just about reached 200,000. Robinson and Van Loon in their second years, Wells in his third, and Bok in his second, the latter with another book besides his *Americanization* on the list, gave evidence of the long life of nonfiction. It was in these post-World War I years that nonfiction titles of worth and importance won a separate listing of their own, perhaps spurred on by public interest in "war books." Previously "best sellers" meant novels, and often very frothy novels. Coué became a conversational byword through the ideas expressed in his little self-help book—particularly "Day by day in every way I am getting better and better."

Fiction

1. So Big, by *Edna Ferber*. Doubleday, Page
2. The Plastic Age, by *Percy Marks*. Century
3. The Little French Girl, by *Anne Douglas Sedgwick*. Houghton Mifflin
4. The Heirs Apparent, by *Philip Gibbs*. Doran
5. A Gentleman of Courage, by *James Oliver Curwood*. Cosmopolitan Book Co.
6. The Call of the Canyon, by *Zane Grey*. Harper
7. The Midlander, by *Booth Tarkington*. Doubleday, Page
8. The Coast of Folly, by *Coningsby Dawson*. Cosmopolitan Book Co.
9. Mistress Wilding, by *Rafael Sabatini*. Houghton Mifflin
10. The Homemaker, by *Dorothy Canfield Fisher*. Harcourt, Brace

Nonfiction

1. Diet and Health, by *Lulu Hunt Peters*. Reilly & Lee
2. The Life of Christ, by *Giovanni Papini*. Harcourt, Brace
3. The Boston Cooking School Cook Book; new ed. by *Fannie Farmer*. Little, Brown
4. Etiquette, by *Emily Post*. Funk & Wagnalls
5. Ariel, by *André Maurois*. Appleton
6. The Cross Word Puzzle Books, by *Prosper Buranelli* and others. Simon & Schuster
7. Mark Twain's Autobiography. Harper
8. Saint Joan, by *Bernard Shaw*. Brentano
9. The New Decalogue of Science, by *Albert E. Wiggam*. Bobbs-Merrill
10. The Americanization of Edward Bok, by *Edward Bok*. Scribner

"TWENTY-FOUR votes for Underwood" rang through the nation as the 1924 Democratic Convention in the old Madison Square Garden on New York's Madison Square went on through the hot summer days and nights. At Aeolian Hall, Paul Whiteman brought jazz into the realm of classical music with his introduction of George Gershwin's *Rhapsody in Blue* to the concert stage. *What Price Glory,* realistic war drama, was the theatrical hit of the year. The Teapot Dome scandal thoroughly discredited the Harding regime, and Calvin Coolidge, who had become President upon Harding's death, was re-elected. Edna Ferber was a new name on best seller lists. Her *So Big* skyrocketed. *The Plastic Age,* a revelation of campus life and the "lost generation," achieved the best sellerdom that F. Scott Fitzgerald's *This Side of Paradise* (1920) had not reached. Attempts to suppress Percy Marks' novel only added to the demand for it. Anne Douglas Sedgwick returned to the list for the first time since 1912. In its third year, *Diet and Health* outsold every other nonfiction title. Papini's *Life of Christ,* approaching 200,000, was in second place for the second year. The *Boston Cooking School Cook Book,* which has sold over 3,000,000 copies through its long career from its first publication in 1896, appeared in a new and best-selling edition. *Etiquette* continued to sell. A French writer, André Maurois, found a big American audience for his biography of Shelley. Shaw's *Saint Joan* was one of the few dramas in all these years to make an annual list. The first and highly successful venture of the new publishing house of Simon and Schuster was that of putting cross word puzzles, long a newspaper feature, into book form. The demand was so great that this firm has continued ever since to publish several volumes of cross word puzzles and the later *Double-Crostics* each year. Since 1924 many novelty books of various kinds from *Ask Me Another, Believe It or Not* and *Boners* to the photographic books of Clare Barnes, Jr., have been issued successfully by other publishers in the wake of this first experiment in game books.

Fiction

1. Soundings, by *A. Hamilton Gibbs*. Little, Brown
2. The Constant Nymph, by *Margaret Kennedy*. Doubleday, Page
3. The Keeper of the Bees, by *Gene Stratton Porter*. Doubleday, Page
4. Glorious Apollo, by *E. Barrington*. Dodd, Mead
5. The Green Hat, by *Michael Arlen*. Doran
6. The Little French Girl, by *Anne Douglas Sedgwick*. Houghton Mifflin
7. Arrowsmith, by *Sinclair Lewis*. Harcourt, Brace
8. The Perennial Bachelor, by *Anne Parrish*. Harper
9. The Carolinian, by *Rafael Sabatini*. Houghton Mifflin
10. One Increasing Purpose, by *A. S. M. Hutchinson*. Little, Brown

Nonfiction

1. Diet and Health, by *Lulu Hunt Peters*. Reilly & Lee
2. The Boston Cooking School Cook Book; new ed. by *Fannie Farmer*. Little, Brown
3. When We Were Very Young, by *A. A. Milne*. Dutton
4. The Man Nobody Knows, by *Bruce Barton*. Bobbs-Merrill
5. The Life of Christ, by *Giovanni Papini*. Harcourt, Brace
6. Ariel, by *André Maurois*. Appleton
7. Twice Thirty, by *Edward Bok*. Scribner
8. Twenty-Five Years, by *Lord Grey*. Stokes
9. Anatole France Himself, by *J. J. Brousson*. Lippincott
10. The Cross Word Puzzle Books. by *Prosper Buranelli* and others. 1st—4th series. Simon & Schuster

COOLIDGE prosperity—the Scopes case in Tennessee, in which Clarence Darrow and William Jennings Bryan argued the theory of evolution, basis of the play *Inherit the Wind* in 1955, and the movie of some years afterward—Red Grange—the Florida boom—the crash of the Shenandoah—are all memories of 1925. *Soundings,* first in fiction, sold nearly 100,000 copies. Better remembered is *The Constant Nymph,* made into a stage hit and the basis of both British and American movies. *Glorious Apollo,* woven around the character of Byron, was the start of E. Barrington's (Mrs. L. Adams Beck) extremely successful series of novels about real people of the past. Michael Arlen made a much talked-about hit with what was considered a daring novel, *The Green Hat,* later a highly successful stage play starring Katharine Cornell. Sinclair Lewis' third novel, *Arrowsmith,* confirmed his place in American literature and probably was an important factor in his being awarded the Nobel Prize. *Arrowsmith* dealt with the medical profession as *Babbitt* had with the businessman and as *Elmer Gantry* was to deal, in 1927, with the ministry. Here was the first appearance of Anne Parrish, long a favorite writer. The records of both *Diet and Health* and *The Boston Cooking School Cook Book* gave evidence of the exceptionally energetic distribution of books which gave practical advice on the always popular subject of food. *When We Were Very Young,* permanent contribution to the literature of childhood, by A. A. Milne, previously known chiefly as a playwright, was the first book in the field of semi-juvenile, semi-adult writing to hit the lists in many years. Bruce Barton topped Papini's *Life of Christ,* then in its third year on the best seller lists, with an American businessman's version of Jesus' life. Lord Grey's reminiscences gave a foretaste of the advent of more basic books on World War I than the reporters' narratives published during and immediately after the war years.

1926

Fiction

1. The Private Life of Helen of Troy, by *John Erskine*. Bobbs-Merrill
2. Gentlemen Prefer Blondes, by *Anita Loos*. Boni & Liveright
3. Sorrell and Son, by *Warwick Deeping*. Knopf
4. The Hounds of Spring, by *Sylvia Thompson*. Little, Brown
5. Beau Sabreur, by *P. C. Wren*. Stokes
6. The Silver Spoon, by *John Galsworthy*. Scribner
7. Beau Geste, by *P. C. Wren*. Stokes
8. Show Boat, by *Edna Ferber*. Doubleday, Page
9. After Noon, by *Susan Ertz*. Appleton
10. The Blue Window, by *Temple Bailey*. Penn Publishing Co.

Nonfiction

1. The Man Nobody Knows, by *Bruce Barton*. Bobbs-Merrill
2. Why We Behave Like Human Beings, by *George A. Dorsey*. Harper
3. Diet and Health, by *Lulu Hunt Peters*. Reilly & Lee
4. Our Times, Vol. I, by *Mark Sullivan*. Scribner
5. The Boston Cooking School Cook Book; new ed. by *Fannie Farmer*. Little, Brown
6. Auction Bridge Complete, by *Milton C. Work*. Winston
7. The Book Nobody Knows, by *Bruce Barton*. Bobbs-Merrill
8. The Story of Philosophy, by *Will Durant*. Simon & Schuster
9. The Light of Faith, by *Edgar A. Guest*. Reilly & Lee
10. Jefferson and Hamilton, by *Claude G. Bowers*. Houghton, Mifflin

THE MIDDLE 1920's were the years of pioneering along the air lanes of the world. Admiral Byrd made the first flight over the North Pole in 1926. Babe Ruth became Sultan of Swat. Philadelphia opened the Sesqui-centennial Exhibition. In Germany, Hitler's *Mein Kampf* had been published. The Book-of-the-Month Club, which was to introduce an extremely successful method of marketing books, was founded in 1926.

Its first "selection," *Lolly Willowes,* by Sylvia Townsend Warner was sent to fewer than 5000 charter members. New fiction writers were coming to the fore in America—John Erskine, with his first great hit, *The Private Life of Helen of Troy,* historical fiction written in a new manner; Warwick Deeping, English author, whose *Sorrell and Son* found a responsive note in thousands of American hearts (his book marking the first appearance of the firm of Alfred A. Knopf, Inc., on the annual best seller lists); and P. C. Wren, whose more popular *Beau Geste* was published late in the previous year and did not make the 1925 list, and whose second book, *Beau Sabreur,* also appeared among 1926 best sellers. Galsworthy was at the height of his American sales, with one of the novels in *A Modern Comedy,* companion volume to *The Forsyte Saga.* Edna Ferber followed *So Big* with the perennially famous *Show Boat,* familiar to the world as book, play, movie, and song. With his *Man Nobody Knows* heading non-fiction, Bruce Barton added an interpretation of the Bible in his series of books on practical religion. George Dorsey rode the wave of the new interest in psychology with *Why We Behave Like Human Beings,* and *Diet and Health* continued in its fifth year, the new edition of *The Boston Cooking School Cook Book* in its third. Mark Sullivan's first volume of *Our Times* marked a new interest in our recent past that was continued some years later by such books as Frederick Lewis Allen's *Only Yesterday* and *Since Yesterday.* Evidence of the bridge craze was the pre-publication print order for 65,000 copies of Milton Work's new manual and the sale of over 100,000 copies of Foster's *Simplified Auction Bridge* within ten months after publication. ("Contract" had not yet come along.) Will Durant's *Story of Philosophy,* which had previously appeared in part in the five-cent booklets published as Little Blue Books by the Haldeman-Julius Co. of Wichita, Kansas, marked the peak of the "outline" era, selling 95,000 copies in 1926 alone.

1927

Fiction

1. Elmer Gantry, by *Sinclair Lewis.* Harcourt, Brace
2. The Plutocrat, by *Booth Tarkington.* Doubleday, Page
3. Doomsday, by *Warwick Deeping.* Knopf
4. Sorrell and Son, by *Warwick Deeping.* Knopf
5. Jalna, by *Mazo de la Roche.* Little, Brown
6. Lost Ecstasy, by *Mary Roberts Rinehart.* Doran
7. Twilight Sleep, by *Edith Wharton.* Appleton
8. Tomorrow Morning, by *Anne Parrish.* Harper
9. The Old Countess, by *Anne Douglas Sedgwick.* Houghton Mifflin
10. A Good Woman, by *Louis Bromfield.* Stokes

Nonfiction

1. The Story of Philosophy, by *Will Durant.* Simon & Schuster
2. Napoleon, by *Emil Ludwig.* Boni & Liveright
3. Revolt in the Desert, by *T. E. Lawrence.* Doran
4. Trader Horn, Vol. I, by *Alfred Aloysius Horn* and *Ethelreda Lewis.* Simon & Schuster
5. We, by *Charles A. Lindbergh.* Putnam
6. Ask Me Another, by *Julian Spafford and Lucien Esty.* Viking Press
7. The Royal Road to Romance, by *Richard Halliburton.* Bobbs-Merrill
8. The Glorious Adventure, by *Richard Halliburton.* Bobbs-Merrill
9. Why We Behave Like Human Beings, by *George A. Dorsey.* Harper
10. Mother India, by *Katherine Mayo.* Harcourt, Brace

MECHANICAL and scientific progress continued in 1927, height of the whole period of invention and exploration that followed World War I. Lindbergh made the flight to Paris that thrilled the world, and later in the year wrote about it in a book that became a best seller. Ford produced his new Model A, the first Ford with a gear shift. The Holland Tunnel under the Hudson River was officially opened. The stock market was booming. The disastrous Mississippi floods occurred the same year that the musical play based upon Edna Ferber's novel of Ol' Man River was produced in New York. The Literary Guild, following book marketing methods similar to those of the Book-of-the-Month Club, started to function in 1927, and one of its first selections, *Trader Horn,* made the yearly list. The publication of *Elmer Gantry* with an initial printing of 100,000 copies and sales of over 200,000 in the first ten weeks found Sinclair Lewis at the peak of popularity. Booth Tarkington was high on the list. So was Warwick Deeping, with two books; *Sorrell and Son,* holding over from 1926, sold 133,830 copies in the two years. Mazo de la Roche, a Canadian contributor to American best seller lists, like Gilbert Parker, Ralph Connor, and Louis Hémon of past years, made a great hit with *Jalna,* first book in a notable series about the Whiteoak family of Canada. The ninth volume in the series, but the earliest chronologically, was published seventeen years afterward, in 1944, and there were more Jalna stories up to the '60's. Louis Bromfield made his first appearance on the list with *A Good Woman. The Story of Philosophy* was the outstanding nonfiction title of the year. Emil Ludwig, who was to write so many popular biographies, revived the always latent interest in Napoleon. *Revolt in the Desert* was a book of permanent historical importance by the great English hero of World War I, the mysterious and daring Lawrence of Arabia. Trader Horn came from South Africa to tell tall tales which caught the public's fancy. As Simon and Schuster had done, a new firm, the Viking Press, scored its first best-selling success with a series of novelty books. Its *Ask Me Another* quiz book was an immediate hit, selling 100,000 copies in its first four weeks and becoming the first of a series which made quizzes a popular pastime for years—perhaps germinating radio's "Information Please!" and television's "$64,000 Question." With two best sellers in 1927, Richard Halliburton captured a public which wanted adventure with glamour, a trend in travel and escape reading that had begun with O'Brien's *White Shadows in the South Seas* a number of years before. Dorsey carried on the interest in popular science, and in *Mother India* Katherine Mayo wrote the first book to make a large audience aware of modern India's problems.

Fiction

1. The Bridge of San Luis Rey, by *Thornton Wilder*. A. & C. Boni
2. Wintersmoon, by *Hugh Walpole*. Doubleday, Doran
3. Swan Song, by *John Galsworthy*. Scribner
4. The Greene Murder Case, by *S. S. Van Dine*. Scribner
5. Bad Girl, by *Viña Delmar*. Harcourt, Brace
6. Claire Ambler, by *Booth Tarkington*. Doubleday, Doran
7. Old Pybus, by *Warwick Deeping*. Knopf
8. All Kneeling, by *Anne Parrish*. Harper
9. Jalna, by *Mazo de la Roche*. Little, Brown
10. The Strange Case of Miss Annie Spragg, by *Louis Bromfield*. Stokes

Nonfiction

1. Disraeli, by *André Maurois*. Appleton
2. Mother India, by *Katherine Mayo*. Harcourt, Brace
3. Trader Horn, Vol. I, by *Alfred Aloysius Horn* and *Ethelreda Lewis*. Simon & Schuster
4. Napoleon, by *Emil Ludwig*. Liveright
5. Strange Interlude, by *Eugene O'Neill*. Liveright
6. We, by *Charles A. Lindbergh*. Putnam
7. Count Luckner, the Sea Devil, by *Lowell Thomas*. Doubleday, Doran
8. Goethe, by *Emil Ludwig*. Putnam
9. Skyward, by *Richard E. Byrd*. Putnam
10. The Intelligent Woman's Guide to Socialism and Capitalism, by *George Bernard Shaw*. Brentano

WITH the outward scars of World War I healed, war itself outlawed by the Kellogg-Briand Pact, and the big bull market well under way, Americans were flocking to Europe by every conceivable means of the time, from freighter to mammoth liner. Amelia Earhart was the first woman to fly the Atlantic. At home, gangsters, bootleggers, and racketeers were riding high. The first all-talking movie, *The Lights of New York,* was presented, and

Walt Disney was working on his first Mickey Mouse picture. *The Bridge of San Luis Rey,* a novel that attained such fame that the Pulitzer Prize committee departed from its usual custom of giving its award to a story laid in the United States, was leader of 1928 fiction. This novel with a South American background, Thornton Wilder's first great success, sold 240,000 copies in its first year. English writers with devoted American audiences were next on the list. A new writer of detective stories, S. S. Van Dine (pseudonym of Willard Huntington Wright), flashed into the book world with big sales. *The Greene Murder Case* was one of the first of many novels that made Philo Vance almost as familiar a fictional character as Sherlock Holmes, and the first detective story to appear on an annual list since Mary Roberts Rinehart's *The Window at the White Cat* in 1910. Booth Tarkington's *Claire Ambler* had an added interest because it was the first book to be issued under the new imprint of Doubleday, Doran & Co., a merger of the old firms of Doubleday, Page and George H. Doran. Biography was the subject of about half the nonfiction list. André Maurois followed his successful *Ariel* with the life of Disraeli. Emil Ludwig's *Napoleon* held over into its second year and he added a biography of Goethe to the list. American antipathy to all things German having subsided, readers devoured Lowell Thomas' account of a German war hero's exploits. *Mother India* and *We* were both best sellers for the second year. Eugene O'Neill's play, widely publicized for its feat of holding audiences through five hours, with intermission for dinner, sold well in book form. Admiral Byrd followed Lindbergh's account of sky adventure with his story of his 1926 flight to the North Pole. Bernard Shaw addressed the intelligent woman on political theory.

1929

Fiction

1. All Quiet on the Western Front, by *Erich Maria Remarque.* Little, Brown
2. Dodsworth, by *Sinclair Lewis.* Harcourt, Brace
3. Dark Hester, by *Anne Douglas Sedgwick.* Houghton Mifflin
4. The Bishop Murder Case, by *S. S. Van Dine.* Scribner
5. Roper's Row, by *Warwick Deeping.* Knopf
6. Peder Victorious, by *O. E. Rölvaag.* Harper
7. Mamba's Daughters, by *DuBose Heyward.* Doubleday, Doran
8. The Galaxy, by *Susan Ertz.* Appleton
9. Scarlet Sister Mary, by *Julia Peterkin.* Bobbs-Merrill
10. Joseph and his Brethren, by *H. W. Freeman.* Holt

Nonfiction

1. The Art of Thinking, by *Ernest Dimnet.* Simon & Schuster
2. Henry the Eighth, by *Francis Hackett.* Liveright
3. The Cradle of the Deep, by *Joan Lowell.* Simon & Schuster
4. Elizabeth and Essex, by *Lytton Strachey.* Harcourt, Brace
5. The Specialist, by *Chic Sale.* Specialist Publishing Co.
6. A Preface to Morals, by *Walter Lippmann.* Macmillan
7. Believe It or Not, by *Robert L. Ripley.* Simon & Schuster
8. John Brown's Body, by *Stephen Vincent Benét.* Doubleday, Doran
9. The Tragic Era, by *Claude G. Bowers.* Houghton Mifflin
10. The Mansions of Philosophy, by *Will Durant.* Simon & Schuster

THE Coolidge boom turned into Hoover prosperity, only to totter in September with the first warning crash of this country's greatest financial depression. Black Tuesday, October 29, brought this country to the brink of financial disaster, but book sales were still booming. The great anti-war novel of World War I, *All Quiet on the Western Front,* written by the German-born Erich Maria Remarque, appeared eleven years after the war's close, to sell 300,000 in its first year. It was issued here in a first printing of 100,000; 700,000 copies were printed in Germany, many of them later to be burned by the Nazis. Famous all over the world, it was made into a Hollywood super-feature. Sinclair Lewis did another portrait of the American businessman in *Dodsworth,* a book that became a highly successful play, later a movie. S. S. Van Dine's *Bishop Murder Case* was as high on the list as his *Greene Murder Case* had been. Ole Rölvaag's *Peder Victorious* was a sequel to his first novel of the Dakota prairies, *Giants in the Earth* (1927). American regional literature was awakening more and more interest. The South provided two new novelists of distinction, DuBose Heyward of *Porgy* fame, and Julia Peterkin, who won the Pulitzer Prize with her first book. Perfecting its technique for selecting and developing best sellers, the young firm of Simon and Schuster, which had started only five years previously with *The Cross Word Puzzle Book,* was responsible for four books on the nonfiction list. *The Art of Thinking,* by a French writer, caught on with a public interested in self-improvement and sold 125,000 in 1929. The sensational spit-in-the-wind *Cradle of the Deep* followed in Trader Horn's footsteps. *Believe It or Not,* first of Robert Ripley's collections of his popular newspaper features, went over 50,000. *The Mansions of Philosophy* did not become quite the great success that Will Durant's *Story of Philosophy* had been. *Henry the Eighth* and *Elizabeth and Essex* were added to the many notable biographies of the period. Word-of-mouth publicity made Chic Sale's tiny little book of decidedly homely humor a runaway best seller. Since 1929 its sales have exceeded 1,500,000 copies. Walter Lippmann, outstanding political commentator, made his first appearance among best sellers in 1929. *John Brown's Body,* one of the early selections of the Book-of-the-Month Club, attained unusual sales for a book of poetry, in this case one long narrative sequence. Its first printing was 70,000 copies. At that time Book-of-the-Month Club's membership was about 50,000.

1930

Fiction

1. Cimarron, by *Edna Ferber*. Doubleday, Doran
2. Exile, by *Warwick Deeping*. Knopf
3. The Woman of Andros, by *Thornton Wilder*. A. & C. Boni
4. Years of Grace, by *Margaret Ayer Barnes*. Houghton Mifflin
5. Angel Pavement, by *J. B. Priestley*. Harper
6. The Door, by *Mary Roberts Rinehart*. Farrar & Rinehart
7. Rogue Herries, by *Hugh Walpole*. Doubleday, Doran
8. Chances, by *A. Hamilton Gibbs*. Little, Brown
9. Young Man of Manhattan, by *Katharine Brush*. Farrar & Rinehart
10. Twenty-Four Hours, by *Louis Bromfield*. Stokes

Nonfiction

1. The Story of San Michele, by *Axel Munthe*. Dutton
2. The Strange Death of President Harding, by *Gaston B. Means* and *May Dixon Thacker*. Guild Publishing Corp.
3. Byron, by *André Maurois*. Appleton
4. The Adams Family, by *James Truslow Adams*. Little, Brown
5. Lone Cowboy, by *Will James*. Scribner
6. Lincoln, by *Emil Ludwig*. Little, Brown
7. The Story of Philosophy, by *Will Durant*. Garden City Publishing Co.
8. The Outline of History, by *H. G. Wells*. Garden City Publishing Co.
9. The Art of Thinking, by *Ernest Dimnet*. Simon & Schuster
10. The Rise of American Civilization, by *Charles* and *Mary Beard*. Macmillan

1930 was a year of financial depression, bank crashes, and brokers' suicides, with the unemployed selling apples on the streets of New York, and with people turning to the inexpensive diversion of miniature golf to take their minds off money troubles. France started to build the Maginot Line that was designed to protect her forever from military aggression. Edna

Ferber led fiction sales for the second time in six years. Her *Cimarron* was a story of pioneer Oklahoma. The fame of his first novel carried Thornton Wilder's story of ancient Greece high on the list, though interest in it quickly flagged. *Years of Grace* was the first novel by a new writer from Chicago; it won the Pulitzer Prize and made its author one of the established favorites in the fiction scene. *The Good Companions,* published in 1929, had made a great audience for the English novelist, playwright, and essayist, J. B. Priestley, an audience that eagerly bought his new book, *Angel Pavement.* Mrs. Rinehart scored with another mystery novel twenty-one years after her *Man in Lower Ten* had become one of the first best sellers in American detective fiction. Hers was the first best seller on these lists to be published by the new firm of Farrar & Rinehart—established by John Farrar, formerly editor of *The Bookman,* and by two of Mrs. Rinehart's sons. The first book of the *Herries Chronicle* by Hugh Walpole was an immediate favorite and founded a fictional dynasty that rivaled Galsworthy's Forsytes in popularity. A young American writer scored a big success with *Young Man of Manhattan* (also a Farrar & Rinehart publication), combining realism and romance in a story of the uproarious 1920's. In nonfiction, leader of the year was Dr. Axel Munthe's *Story of San Michele,* one of those rare best sellers that start out in a modest way, catch on through recommendation by one reader to another until sales begin to pile up and advertising takes over. This, the first of many best-selling "doctor" books of the period, sold 181,000 copies. The vogue for autobiographies by notables or unusual figures in the professions began, but neither lawyers nor preachers proved as magnetic in the literary field at that time as doctors. The sensational *Strange Death of President Harding* (300,000 sold) had been preceded in 1927 by another book of the same caliber, *The President's Daughter,* revealing unsavory Washington scandal in an era of corruption. *Byron* was Maurois' third consecutive success, and Ludwig again offered a biography to an assured public. James Truslow Adams and the Beards made their first appearances as best-selling historians. Will James rose to popularity with his cowboy reminiscences and drawings. The Durant and Wells books both returned to the lists in new dollar hardbound editions. (The era of paperback reprints of such lengthy and meaty books was far in the future.)

Fiction

1. The Good Earth, by *Pearl S. Buck*. John Day
2. Shadows on the Rock, by *Willa Cather*. Knopf
3. A White Bird Flying, by *Bess Streeter Aldrich*. Appleton
4. Grand Hotel, by *Vicki Baum*. Doubleday, Doran
5. Years of Grace, by *Margaret Ayer Barnes*. Houghton Mifflin
6. The Road Back, by *Erich Maria Remarque*. Little, Brown
7. The Bridge of Desire, by *Warwick Deeping*. McBride
8. Back Street, by *Fannie Hurst*. Cosmopolitan Book Co.
9. Finch's Fortune, by *Mazo de la Roche*. Little, Brown
10. Maid in Waiting, by *John Galsworthy*. Scribner

Nonfiction

1. Education of a Princess, by *Grand Duchess Marie*. Viking Press
2. The Story of San Michele, by *Axel Munthe*. Dutton
3. Washington Merry-Go-Round, Anonymous (*Drew Pearson* and *Robert S. Allen*). Liveright
4. Boners. Viking Press
5. Culbertson's Summary, by *Ely Culbertson*. Bridge World
6. Contract Bridge Blue Book, by *Ely Culbertson*. Bridge World
7. Fatal Interview, by *Edna St. Vincent Millay*. Harper
8. The Epic of America, by *James Truslow Adams*. Little, Brown
9. Mexico, by *Stuart Chase*. Macmillan
10. New Russia's Primer, by *M. Ilin*. Houghton Mifflin

CONTRACT BRIDGE hit the nation with full force in this year of continued depression. Katharine Cornell was appearing on Broadway in *The Barretts of Wimpole Street* (one of the most popular plays presented for American soldiers overseas in World War II) and "De Lawd" made his appearance in *The Green Pastures. Of Thee I Sing,* with George Gershwin's music, was the first musical play ever to win the Pulitzer Prize. *The Good Earth,* by Pearl S. Buck, topped all novels of the year, making a permanent place in our literature for itself and her other novels of China. Mrs. Buck was awarded the Nobel Prize for Literature in 1938. Her book marked the first appearance on these lists of a publication of the John Day Company. There were five novelists new among best sellers in 1931, all of them women, all American but one. Willa Cather's books had been highly esteemed and widely read for years, but not until publication of *Shadows on the Rock* did one of them become a leading best seller. Bess Streeter Aldrich's preceding book, *A Lantern in Her Hand,* had won many readers by word-of-mouth publicity, gaining an audience for her next, *A White Bird Flying. Grand Hotel,* by the only one of the five not an American, is the most famous of them all. Fannie Hurst, fifth new name on the list, already had a great following among magazine and book readers, but it was *Back Street* that put her among the top-ranking best sellers. A new woman writer topped nonfiction as well. She was a member of the Russian royal family; the sale of her autobiography reflected the widespread interest in Russia. Through all these years many memoirs of imperial and revolutionary times in that country were published. The first best seller to illustrate public interest in the Soviet régime was M. Ilin's *New Russia's Primer. Washington Merry-Go-Round* was a natural successor to *Mirrors of Washington* of nearly a decade before, but it packed more dynamite. Published anonymously, it proved to have been written by columnists Drew Pearson and Robert Allen. *Boners* was another fad book in the *Cross Word Puzzle, Ask Me Another* and *Believe It or Not* line. With several succeeding volumes it sold into the hundreds of thousands. As the new contract bridge replaced auction, there was demand for new guides to the game; Ely Culbertson was the one who cashed in on the opportunity in a big way, taking the place held by Milton Work five years before, later to be succeeded himself by Charles Goren with his "point count" system. Edna St. Vincent Millay reached the list for the first time with *Fatal Interview,* and thus became the first new best-selling writer of serious poetry besides Stephen Vincent Benét since World War I days.

Fiction

1. The Good Earth, by *Pearl S. Buck*. John Day
2. The Fountain, by *Charles Morgan*. Knopf
3. Sons, by *Pearl S. Buck*. John Day
4. Magnolia Street, by *Louis Golding*. Farrar & Rinehart
5. The Sheltered Life, by *Ellen Glasgow*. Doubleday, Doran
6. Old Wine and New, by *Warwick Deeping*. Knopf
7. Mary's Neck, by *Booth Tarkington*. Doubleday, Doran
8. Magnificent Obsession, by *Lloyd C. Douglas*. Willett, Clark
9. Inheritance, by *Phyllis Bentley*. Macmillan
10. Three Loves, by *A. J. Cronin*. Little, Brown

Nonfiction

1. The Epic of America, by *James Truslow Adams*. Little, Brown
2. Only Yesterday, by *Frederick Lewis Allen*. Harper
3. A Fortune to Share, by *Vash Young*. Bobbs-Merrill
4. Culbertson's Summary, by *Ely Culbertson*. Bridge World
5. Van Loon's Geography, by *Hendrik Willem Van Loon*. Simon & Schuster
6. What We Live By, by *Ernest Dimnet*. Simon & Schuster
7. The March of Democracy, by *James Truslow Adams*. Scribner
8. Washington Merry-Go-Round, Anonymous (*Drew Pearson and Robert S. Allen*). Liveright; Blue Ribbon Books
9. The Story of My Life, by *Clarence Darrow*. Scribner
10. More Merry-Go-Round, Anonymous (*Drew Pearson and Robert S. Allen*). Liveright

IN THE WORST YEAR of the depression came the bonus march on Washington and the ensuing battle of Anacostia Flats. James J. Walker resigned under a cloud as Mayor of New York City. Radio was in full swing, with Rudy Vallee its topnotch artist. Father Coughlin's radio talks were gaining listeners. Technocracy was the newest theory on how to cure the depression. Colonel and Mrs. Lindbergh's small son was kidnaped from his crib in Hopewell, N. J. Japan seized Shanghai in her undeclared war on China. *The Good Earth* headed fiction for a second year. Pearl Buck's second novel, continuing the story of the same Chinese family, took third place. *The Fountain,* in second place, received unusual critical attention. Also from England came *Magnolia Street, Inheritance,* with which Macmillan vigorously reentered the field of best-selling fiction, and *Three Loves,* A. J. Cronin's first best seller, Ellen Glasgow and Booth Tarkington both continued their many years' popularity. Lloyd Douglas came rather quietly into the list in eighth place. He was a retired minister, over fifty, when his first novel was published. It was a book that caught on throughout the country, chiefly in the Midwest, by word-of-mouth personal recommendation, the first of many novels on religious themes that were to put him in the highest ranks of best-selling novelists. James Truslow Adams, who had been developing a reputation as an American historian, found a popular audience with two books, one of which, first in nonfiction in 1932, had also appeared on the previous year's list. Frederick Lewis Allen of *Harper's Magazine,* as Mark Sullivan had done with his *Our Times* books, found a waiting audience of people who enjoyed reading about things they remembered, events of the not-too-far-distant past. Vash Young, businessman like Bruce Barton before him, combined inspirational writing with practical advice in a little volume timed for that period of financial depression when salesmen, particularly, needed a lift. Hendrik Van Loon, going under Simon and Schuster's sponsorship, added another volume to his illustrated surveys of human knowledge. Ernest Dimnet followed his *Art of Thinking* with a new book, as did Pearson and Allen with *More Merry-Go-Round.* Their first book was still selling merrily, switching during the course of the year into a reprint edition. The trade policy regarding reprints was changing and nonfiction titles were now released much more quickly in popular-priced editions. Clarence Darrow, who, seven years before, had shared the spotlight in the Scopes trial, wrote a best-selling autobiography.

Fiction

1. Anthony Adverse, by *Hervey Allen*. Farrar & Rinehart
2. As the Earth Turns, by *Gladys Hasty Carroll*. Macmillan
3. Ann Vickers, by *Sinclair Lewis*. Doubleday, Doran
4. Magnificent Obsession, by *Lloyd C. Douglas*. Willett, Clark
5. One More River, by *John Galsworthy*. Scribner
6. Forgive Us Our Trespasses, by *Lloyd C. Douglas*. Houghton Mifflin
7. The Master of Jalna, by *Mazo de la Roche*. Little, Brown
8. Miss Bishop, by *Bess Streeter Aldrich*. Appleton-Century
9. The Farm, by *Louis Bromfield*. Harper
10. Little Man, What Now? by *Hans Fallada*. Simon & Schuster

Nonfiction

1. Life Begins at Forty, by *Walter B. Pitkin*. Whittlesey House
2. Marie Antoinette, by *Stefan Zweig*. Viking Press
3. British Agent, by *R. H. Bruce Lockhart*. Putnam
4. 100,000,000 Guinea Pigs, by *Arthur Kallet* and *F. J. Schlink*. Vanguard Press
5. The House of Exile, by *Nora Waln*. Little, Brown
6. Van Loon's Geography, by *Hendrik Willem Van Loon*. Simon & Schuster
7. Looking Forward, by *Franklin D. Roosevelt*. John Day
8. Contract Bridge Blue Book of 1933, by *Ely Culbertson*. Bridge World
9. The Arches of the Years, by *Halliday Sutherland*. Morrow
10. The March of Democracy, Vol. II, by *James Truslow Adams*. Scribner

"WHO's Afraid of the Big Bad Wolf?" was the theme song of 1933 as Franklin D. Roosevelt, taking office as chief executive of the nation, quickly declared a bank holiday. The NRA and the AAA were created. The World's Fair opened in Chicago. *Tobacco Road,* which by 1939 was to break the record for successive Broadway performances, was produced.

The United States abandoned the gold standard, liquor made a legitimate reappearance with the repeal of the 18th Amendment, the speakeasy era passed out of existence. Jigsaw puzzles became a big popular fad. In Berlin the Reichstag was burned. *Anthony Adverse,* selling 300,000 copies in its first six months, captured readers of many levels of taste and turned public interest definitely toward the historical novel for the first time since the first decade of the century. *Anthony Adverse,* too, began a trend toward the novel of unusual length, a feature which appealed to the public again in *Gone with the Wind.* Continuing its big-time fiction drive begun with Phyllis Bentley's *Inheritance* in 1932, Macmillan found in Gladys Hasty Carroll from Maine a new best-selling author. Lewis, Aldrich, and Bromfield repeated best-seller performances, as did Galsworthy with his third book in the new saga and Mrs. Aldrich with a schoolteacher predecessor of *Mr. Chips* and *Miss Dove.* Lloyd Douglas' *Magnificent Obsession* climbed steadily. In tenth place appeared a new writer from Germany, Hans Fallada, author of the first fiction success for the firm of Simon and Schuster that had up till now been outstanding in nonfiction. A new self-help book hit the nonfiction top for a long run, selling 88,897 copies in 1933. *Life Begins at Forty* added a new axiom to our language. Biography, with characters from France, Russia, China, and a doctor's story, *The Arches of the Years,* took four of the places on the list. Kallet and Schlink issued their interpretation of the claims of modern advertising in *100,000,000 Guinea Pigs,* a volume that led the way for many other books of the "exposure" type and drew increased attention to consumer movements. Culbertson continued to sell year after year. As Woodrow Wilson had done twenty years before, Franklin Roosevelt began his administration with a best-selling book on his policies. For the first time the firms of Whittlesey House, Morrow, and the Vanguard Press made their appearance on these lists. 1933 also saw a best seller from Appleton-Century, a combination of two publishing houses which had been individually responsible for many best-selling titles since the beginning of these records.

1934

Fiction

1. Anthony Adverse, by *Hervey Allen*. Farrar & Rinehart
2. Lamb in His Bosom, by *Caroline Miller*. Harper
3. So Red the Rose, by *Stark Young*. Scribner
4. Good-Bye, Mr. Chips, by *James Hilton*. Little, Brown
5. Within This Present, by *Margaret Ayer Barnes*. Houghton Mifflin
6. Work of Art, by *Sinclair Lewis*. Doubleday, Doran
7. Private Worlds, by *Phyllis Bottome*. Houghton Mifflin
8. Mary Peters, by *Mary Ellen Chase*. Macmillan
9. Oil for the Lamps of China, by *Alice Tisdale Hobart*. Bobbs-Merrill
10. Seven Gothic Tales, by *Isak Dinesen*. Smith & Haas

Nonfiction

1. While Rome Burns, by *Alexander Woollcott*. Viking Press
2. Life Begins at Forty, by *Walter B. Pitkin*. Whittlesey House
3. Nijinsky, by *Romola Nijinsky*. Simon & Schuster
4. 100,000,000 Guinea Pigs, by *Arthur Kallet* and *F. J. Schlink*. Vanguard Press
5. The Native's Return, by *Louis Adamic*. Harper
6. Stars Fell on Alabama, by *Carl Carmer*. Farrar & Rinehart
7. Brazilian Adventure, by *Peter Fleming*. Scribner
8. Forty-two Years in the White House, by *Ike Hoover*. Houghton Mifflin
9. You Must Relax, by *Edmund Jacobson*. Whittlesey House
10. The Life of Our Lord, by *Charles Dickens*. Simon & Schuster

THE Townsend plan and Upton Sinclair's EPIC party followed on the heels of Technocracy as economic cure-alls. Dillinger, greatest American bandit of the era, was killed, and the Dionne quintuplets were born. Parisians rioted over evidence of government corruption, and F.D.R. signed the Philippine Independence Act. Dust storms devastated Kansas and Oklahoma. *Anthony Adverse* sold 176,100 more copies in 1934, bringing it to the top of the fiction list again, but this was only the beginning! The South contributed two new novelists, Caroline Miller with the Pulitzer Prize novel, *Lamb in His Bosom,* and Stark Young with *So Red the Rose,* both books laid in the old South. Another two-year period of best-sellerdom began with James Hilton's first success, *Good-bye, Mr. Chips,* the first book, too, to achieve country-wide fame through radio commendation—the book about which Alexander Woollcott went "quietly mad." There were seven new names on the list in all. The English writer, Phyllis Bottome, scored a hit with her story of insanity, marking a trend toward novels studying abnormal psychological situations. Mary Ellen Chase, who had taught English to two decades of Smith College girls, proved that she herself could write vigorously. *Mary Peters* was another Maine story and subject of another big Macmillan promotion campaign. Alice Tisdale Hobart wrote a striking story of China; and *Seven Gothic Tales* introduced an author from Denmark whose unique tales created a devoted audience for her work in this country. Alexander Woollcott had become radio's favorite voice and expert story-teller as well as book promoter. People bought his own book, *While Rome Burns,* as well as those he recommended. In 1934 *While Rome Burns* sold 83,545 copies. Eventually it reached a sale of over 500,000. *Life Begins at Forty* was second in 1934, and another self-help book, *You Must Relax,* was in ninth place. Louis Adamic's extremely interesting account of his native Yugoslavia found many readers, as did Carl Carmer's picturesque interpretation of the State of Alabama, a book that inspired a popular song and laid the foundations for the author's reputation in the field of American folklore. A century-old book by the prince of best sellers, Charles Dickens, was rescued for a time from obscurity.

Fiction

1. Green Light, by *Lloyd C. Douglas*. Houghton Mifflin
2. Vein of Iron, by *Ellen Glasgow*. Harcourt, Brace
3. Of Time and the River, by *Thomas Wolfe*. Scribner
4. Time Out of Mind, by *Rachel Field*. Macmillan
5. Good-Bye, Mr. Chips, by *James Hilton*. Little, Brown
6. The Forty Days of Musa Dagh, by *Franz Werfel*. Viking Press
7. Heaven's My Destination, by *Thornton Wilder*. Harper
8. Lost Horizon, by *James Hilton*. Morrow
9. Come and Get It, by *Edna Ferber*. Doubleday, Doran
10. Europa, by *Robert Briffault*. Scribner

Nonfiction

1. North to the Orient, by *Anne Morrow Lindbergh*. Harcourt, Brace
2. While Rome Burns, by *Alexander Woollcott*. Viking Press
3. Life with Father, by *Clarence Day*. Knopf
4. Personal History, by *Vincent Sheean*. Doubleday, Doran
5. Seven Pillars of Wisdom, by *T. E. Lawrence*. Doubleday, Doran
6. Francis the First, by *Francis Hackett*. Doubleday, Doran
7. Mary Queen of Scotland and the Isles, by *Stefan Zweig*. Viking Press
8. Rats, Lice and History, by *Hans Zinsser*. Little, Brown
9. R. E. Lee, by *Douglas Southall Freeman*. Scribner
10. Skin Deep, by *M. C. Phillips*. Vanguard Press

THE NAZIS, in full power in Germany, intensified their anti-Jewish campaign. Mussolini invaded Ethiopia. In the U.S.A. the social security laws were passed and the WPA was inaugurated. Will Rogers was killed in an airplane crash. Boondoggling, Huey Long, and café society were conversational topics. Swing music hit the country, with Benny Goodman its leading exponent. George Gershwin's *Porgy and Bess,* originating in DuBose Heyward's novel, *Porgy,* was the first musical produced by the

Theatre Guild. With his third book, which sold 103,286 copies in 1935, Lloyd Douglas became the most popular novelist in the country. Ellen Glasgow, a best-selling author since 1904, achieved a high place with *Vein of Iron*. Six years previously, Thomas Wolfe's *Look Homeward, Angel* had brought him into literary prominence. His second novel, *Of Time and the River,* continued his prominence. Rachel Field, widely known as a writer and illustrator of books for children, made a national reputation with an adult novel. James Hilton's *Mr. Chips* went into its second year. One of his earlier novels, now reissued and also praised by Mr. Woollcott, was close behind it on the list. Eventually *Lost Horizon* became perhaps more famous than *Mr. Chips* and added a new word to our language, Shanghri-La. Both books also became famous movies. Although no yearly records were kept of juvenile best sellers, it is interesting to note that a famous juvenile, *The Little Colonel,* brought out in reprint edition, sold 100,000 copies in 1935. The name of Lindbergh reappeared on the nonfiction list after eight years. This time it was Anne Morrow Lindbergh who wrote of air adventure. It was her literary skill as well as her name, with all its associations from the first Paris flight through the tragic events of kidnapping and trial, that made her book nonfiction top seller of the year, reaching 185,000 copies. *While Rome Burns,* first in 1934, was second in 1935. *Life with Father,* as a book, laid the groundwork for the famous play's record run on Broadway. Vincent Sheean's *Personal History* forecast the important part that newspapermen were to play in the book field during the coming war years. The foundations for the success of *Seven Pillars of Wisdom* had been laid eight years previously by Lawrence's *Revolt in the Desert*. The legend of the man had grown and this, with a notable publicity campaign, accounted for the fact that an expensive book, one that was not "written down" for the sake of appeal to a wide public, was a best seller of the year. *Revolt in the Desert* had been in fact a popularization of part of the original *Seven Pillars of Wisdom*. It was to be the source for many years of books, movies and plays based on the Lawrence legend. Notable biographies by Hackett, Zweig, and Freeman had many readers. Hans Zinsser popularized some interesting aspects of medical lore; and *Skin Deep* became still another best-selling "consumer" book, following *100,000,000 Guinea Pigs*.

1936

Fiction

1. Gone with the Wind, by *Margaret Mitchell*. Macmillan
2. The Last Puritan, by *George Santayana*. Scribner
3. Sparkenbroke, by *Charles Morgan*. Macmillan
4. Drums Along the Mohawk, by *Walter D. Edmonds*. Little, Brown
5. It Can't Happen Here, by *Sinclair Lewis*. Doubleday, Doran
6. White Banners, by *Lloyd C. Douglas*. Houghton Mifflin
7. The Hurricane, by *Charles Nordhoff* and *James Norman Hall*. Little, Brown
8. The Thinking Reed, by *Rebecca West*. Viking Press
9. The Doctor, by *Mary Roberts Rinehart*. Farrar & Rinehart
10. Eyeless in Gaza, by *Aldous Huxley*. Harper

Nonfiction

1. Man the Unknown, by *Alexis Carrel*. Harper
2. Wake Up and Live! by *Dorothea Brande*. Simon & Schuster
3. The Way of a Transgressor, by *Negley Farson*. Harcourt, Brace
4. Around the World in Eleven Years, by *Patience, Richard,* and *Johnny Abbe*. Stokes
5. North to the Orient, by *Anne Morrow Lindbergh*. Harcourt, Brace
6. An American Doctor's Odyssey, by *Victor Heiser*. Norton
7. Inside Europe, by *John Gunther*. Harper
8. Live Alone and Like It, by *Marjorie Hillis*. Bobbs-Merrill
9. Life with Father, by *Clarence Day*. Knopf
10. I Write As I Please, by *Walter Duranty*. Simon & Schuster

THE Rome-Berlin Axis was announced and Germany entered the Rhineland. Edward VIII of England renounced his throne to marry the woman he loved. Revolution against the Republican government in Spain broke out in bloody civil war. American inventiveness turned to air conditioning and streamlining. Destructive floods rolled through the East and Mid-

121

west. Published in June, *Gone with the Wind* was to dominate all fiction sales for two years, creating publishing history with sales never before reached by fiction in so short a time. One million copies were sold at a retail price of $3 between June and the end of the year. But this was only the beginning for Margaret Mitchell's first and only published novel, which became literary legend in the author's lifetime. Millions more of the book were sold. Then came the movie, premiered in Atlanta. Years later a paperback edition was published, and, 40 years later, plans were afoot for television production of the original movie. George Santayana, Spanish by birth and long a professor of philosophy at Harvard, wrote a best-selling novel, *The Last Puritan,* first of a number of novels by various authors on patrician and intellectual Boston. Walter Edmonds was a new name in historical fiction, adding to the period's growing trend toward long historical novels which was started by *Anthony Adverse* and pointed up again by *Gone with the Wind.* Nordhoff and Hall were a writing team from the South Seas who had first written after World War I of their experiences in France and who had previously made a big hit with *Mutiny on the Bounty,* a sea chronicle based on historical records. Rebecca West and Aldous Huxley, notable English writers, appeared for the first time on an American annual best seller list. The nonfiction list was typical of the variety of authorship and subject matter which often comes to the fore in public approval. A surgeon writing for the layman headed the list, followed by a self-improvement book and a newspaperman's story. Fourth came the travel experiences of three smart youngsters, delightedly read by adults. Travel of all kinds predominated the list in this year when the rumblings of coming war were growing louder. Mrs. Lindbergh's book was still a best seller, followed by the narrative of the experiences in out-of-the-way countries of a doctor with a notable career throughout the world in medical research, which also marked the first appearance of the W. W. Norton imprint on these lists. *Inside Europe* was the first book in his long and excellent series on political interpretation the world over by reporter John Gunther. *Live Alone and Like It,* which sold 100,000 copies in 1936, was another self-help book written in humorous and entertaining fashion. Tenth was one of the first and one of the most notable books on the new Russia that foreign correspondents were to write.

Fiction

1. Gone with the Wind, by *Margaret Mitchell*. Macmillan
2. Northwest Passage, by *Kenneth Roberts*. Doubleday, Doran
3. The Citadel, by *A. J. Cronin*. Little, Brown
4. And So—Victoria, by *Vaughan Wilkins*. Macmillan
5. Drums Along the Mohawk, by *Walter D. Edmonds*. Little, Brown
6. The Years, by *Virginia Woolf*. Harcourt, Brace
7. Theatre, by *W. Somerset Maugham*. Doubleday, Doran
8. Of Mice and Men, by *John Steinbeck*. Covici, Friede
9. The Rains Came, by *Louis Bromfield*. Harper
10. We Are Not Alone, by *James Hilton*. Little, Brown

Nonfiction

1. How to Win Friends and Influence People, by *Dale Carnegie*. Simon & Schuster
2. An American Doctor's Odyssey, by *Victor Heiser*. Norton
3. The Return to Religion, by *Henry C. Link*. Macmillan
4. The Arts, by *Hendrik Willem Van Loon*. Simon & Schuster
5. Orchids on Your Budget, by *Marjorie Hillis*. Bobbs-Merrill
6. Present Indicative, by *Noel Coward*. Doubleday, Doran
7. Mathematics for the Million, by *Lancelot Hogben*. Norton
8. Life with Mother, by *Clarence Day*. Knopf
9. The Nile, by *Emil Ludwig*. Viking Press
10. The Flowering of New England, by *Van Wyck Brooks*. Dutton

U.S. TRAVELERS flocked to Paris for the Exposition and to London for the coronation of King George VI. Japan began her long war against China. The dirigible *Hindenburg* burst into fire as it made its first landing at Lakehurst, N.J. Charlie McCarthy, candid cameras, and skiing were current crazes in America, which was also swept by a wave of the new "sit-down" strikes. *Pins and Needles,* produced by the Labor Stage, was to break musical show records by 1939. *Gone with the Wind* swung into an even more triumphant leadership of fiction sales, eventually selling high in the millions. Translation rights were being sought in a score of languages and GWTW became as well-known initials as NBC or WPA. Kenneth Roberts of Maine had published four other historical novels before he achieved national recognition with *Northwest Passage.* A. J. Cronin was more popular than ever, with one of his best-liked novels, *The Citadel,* which sold 161,108 copies in 1937. A new writer of historical fiction from England, Vaughan Wilkins, made his debut on the list, as did Virginia Woolf and W. Somerset Maugham, although their books had had large American audiences for many years. John Steinbeck's first selling success came with *Of Mice and Men.* His *Tortilla Flat,* in 1935, had made its mark with the critics. Louis Bromfield departed from his usual American scene with a novel of India. Half the fiction was contributed in 1937 by English writers, half by American. The best-known self-help book of them all, *How to Win Friends and Influence People,* topped all nonfiction with sales of 729,000 copies in 1937, in addition to its 12,000 from the previous year. With its reappearance in a 25-cent edition (the paperback price of its time), it was to sell well into the millions. *The Return to Religion,* one of the few titles in the nonfiction religious field to reach the annual lists in some time, in contrast to the predominance of religion in both earlier and later years, sold 83,000 copies. Continuing his series of books on various fields of human knowledge, Hendrik Van Loon produced a best seller whose illustrations and format added to its sales appeal. Marjorie Hillis followed her *Live Alone and Like It* with another entertaining book along self-help lines, and Noel Coward first appeared among best sellers with his autobiography. *Mathematics for the Million* was not written down for mass interest; on the contrary, the public had to rise to the scholarly but effective presentation of a difficult subject. Clarence Day continued his delightful family chronicle with *Life with Mother.* Emil Ludwig deserted, temporarily, the lives of great men for the biography of a river. With *The Flowering of New England,* a distinguished literary critic began a series of books on American cultural history, though this was not the first volume chronologically.

Fiction

1. The Yearling, by *Marjorie Kinnan Rawlings.* Scribner
2. The Citadel, by *A. J. Cronin.* Little, Brown
3. My Son, My Son! by *Howard Spring.* Viking Press
4. Rebecca, by *Daphne du Maurier.* Doubleday, Doran
5. Northwest Passage, by *Kenneth Roberts.* Doubleday, Doran
6. All This, and Heaven Too, by *Rachel Field.* Macmillan
7. The Rains Came, by *Louis Bromfield.* Harper
8. And Tell of Time, by *Laura Krey.* Houghton Mifflin
9. The Mortal Storm, by *Phyllis Bottome.* Little, Brown
10. Action at Aquila, by *Hervey Allen.* Farrar & Rinehart

Nonfiction

1. The Importance of Living, by *Lin Yutang.* John Day
2. With Malice Toward Some, by *Margaret Halsey.* Simon & Schuster
3. Madame Curie, by *Eve Curie.* Doubleday, Doran
4. Listen! the Wind, by *Anne Morrow Lindbergh.* Harcourt, Brace
5. The Horse and Buggy Doctor, by *Arthur E. Hertzler.* Harper
6. How to Win Friends and Influence People, by *Dale Carnegie.* Simon & Schuster
7. Benjamin Franklin, by *Carl Van Doren.* Viking Press
8. I'm a Stranger Here Myself, by *Ogden Nash.* Little, Brown
9. Alone, by *Richard E. Byrd.* Putnam
10. Fanny Kemble, by *Margaret Armstrong.* Macmillan

"PEACE in our time" was declared at Munich after the Czech crisis and after Hitler had annexed Austria. American jitters were induced by a Martian radio attack, with Orson Welles as entrepreneur. *God Bless America,* which Irving Berlin had written in 1917, was revived by Kate Smith to become what some chose to call our second national anthem. Bingo and the big apple were fads of the year, and "Wrong-Way" Corrigan amused two continents. "Information Please!" the quiz program that topped all radio quiz programs, presented many authors as well as its "regulars" and, emceed by Clifton Fadiman, then literary critic of *The New Yorker,* added to the interest in and knowledge of books on the part of its vast radio audience. *The Yearling,* novel of a Florida boy and his beloved fawn, outsold other fiction and took its place as an American classic read by both young and old. *The Citadel,* third in 1937, went up to second place in 1938. From England came two writers new to the list and quickly taken up by the public, Howard Spring and Daphne du Maurier. *Rebecca* has gone on selling in reprint editions and was natural material for an extremely popular movie. *Northwest Passage* and *The Rains Came,* perhaps Bromfield's greatest fiction seller, carried on into their second years. Rachel Field's best-known novel, which also became a feature movie, was based upon events in her own family history. *And Tell of Time* was a historical story of Texas by a second new American woman writer on this list. Hervey Allen turned to American Civil War history with his first novel since the great *Anthony.* With the Sino-Japanese war going into its second year, an interpretation of China by a Chinese man of letters outsold all other nonfiction, reaching 124,415 copies in 1938. This included book club sales. Book club first printings were about 75,000 at this time. Margaret Halsey scored the British in her clever and humorous *With Malice Toward Some.* The daughter of Madame Curie told the story of her mother's life, which was taken to the hearts of readers aware of the woman scientist's greatness. *Listen! the Wind,* Mrs. Lindbergh's second account of flying experiences with her famous husband, followed her *North to the Orient* as a best seller. The autobiography of a country doctor was halfway down the list. The response to Carl Van Doren's definitive life of Franklin was enthusiastic. Another new best-selling American biographer was Margaret Armstrong, with *Fanny Kemble.* Ogden Nash was a constantly quoted favorite from the pages of *The New Yorker* and other magazines, even before the publication of *I'm a Stranger Here Myself,* one of the rare books of poetry to reach best-seller lists. Admiral Byrd gave his record of months in the Antarctic, newspaper accounts of which had previously thrilled and mystified millions.

1939

Fiction

1. The Grapes of Wrath, by *John Steinbeck*. Viking Press
2. All This, and Heaven Too, by *Rachel Field*. Macmillan
3. Rebecca, by *Daphne du Maurier*. Doubleday, Doran
4. Wickford Point, by *John P. Marquand*. Little, Brown
5. Escape, by *Ethel Vance*. Little, Brown
6. Disputed Passage, by *Lloyd C. Douglas*. Houghton Mifflin
7. The Yearling, by *Marjorie Kinnan Rawlings*. Scribner
8. The Tree of Liberty, by *Elizabeth Page*. Farrar & Rinehart
9. The Nazarene, by *Sholem Asch*. Putnam
10. Kitty Foyle, by *Christopher Morley*. Lippincott

Nonfiction

1. Days of Our Years, by *Pierre van Paassen*. Hillman-Curl
2. Reaching for the Stars, by *Nora Waln*. Little, Brown
3. Inside Asia, by *John Gunther*. Harper
4. Autobiography with Letters, by *William Lyon Phelps*. Oxford University Press
5. Country Lawyer, by *Bellamy Partridge*. Whittlesey House
6. Wind, Sand and Stars, by *Antoine de St. Exupéry*. Reynal & Hitchcock
7. Mein Kampf, by *Adolf Hitler*. Reynal & Hitchcock
8. A Peculiar Treasure, by *Edna Ferber*. Doubleday, Doran
9. Not Peace But a Sword, by *Vincent Sheean*. Doubleday, Doran
10. Listen! the Wind, by *Anne Morrow Lindbergh*. Harcourt, Brace

THE New York World's Fair opened, with exhibits from nearly all the countries of the world except Germany, and was visited by the King and Queen of England George VI and Elizabeth. The Spanish Civil War ended with the surrender of the Loyalists. Late in the year Germany invaded Poland—the period of peace between two world wars had ended. A novel of the "Okies," those dispossessed by the dust storms of 1934, made John Steinbeck top best seller of the nation. Bookstores sold 300,000 copies during the year. *All This, and Heaven Too* and *Rebecca* both climbed higher on the best-seller ladder in their second year. John P. Marquand had written a penetrating novel of Boston, *The Late George Apley,* in 1937. Known popularly as the writer of the "Mr. Moto" spy stories, he attained critical and commercial success with his first serious novel, though it did not make the list of the year in which it was published. As often happens with a newly prominent writer, the second book after a first success achieved greater national sales in its first year of publication, though not necessarily total sales, than did the earlier book. *Escape,* written by Grace Zaring Stone under the pseudonym of Ethel Vance, was the first best-selling fiction based upon events in Hitler's Germany. Continuing the trend of the long historical novel was *The Tree of Liberty.* Another trend—toward fiction of Biblical times—was marked by the sales of *The Nazarene,* scholarly story by a writer new to this country, whose work was translated from the Yiddish. Christopher Morley, long-beloved poet, essayist, and novelist, found a best-selling audience with his portrayal of a modern working girl, *Kitty Foyle,* later played on the screen by Ginger Rogers. Contemporary history began to loom large in the world of books. Best seller of nonfiction was written by Pierre van Paassen, a Hollander who took a world view of political events in his reminiscences, as had Vincent Sheean in 1935. In *Reaching for the Stars,* Nora Waln described the tragedy of life in Germany under the Nazis as she had witnessed it. Gunther continued his political surveys with *Inside Asia.* Long an influential commentator on books, Professor Phelps of Yale had an assured audience for his autobiography and Oxford University Press (American branch) had its first big popular seller. *Country Lawyer,* amusing narrative of old-time upstate New York life, introduced the legal profession into best sellerdom, where medical lives were already well established. *Wind, Sand and Stars,* by a French writer and aviator, added to the literature of flight. *Mein Kampf,* Bible of Nazi Germany, was published with its full text for the first time over here. A best seller over many years in the fiction field, Edna Ferber wrote best-selling nonfiction as well with her autobiography, *A Peculiar Treasure.*

1940

Fiction

1. How Green Was My Valley, by *Richard Llewellyn*. Macmillan
2. Kitty Foyle, by *Christopher Morley*. Lippincott
3. Mrs. Miniver, by *Jan Struther*. Harcourt, Brace
4. For Whom the Bell Tolls, by *Ernest Hemingway*. Scribner
5. The Nazarene, by *Sholem Asch*. Putnam
6. Stars on the Sea, by *F. van Wyck Mason*. Lippincott
7. Oliver Wiswell, by *Kenneth Roberts*. Doubleday, Doran
8. The Grapes of Wrath, by *John Steinbeck*. Viking Press
9. Night in Bombay, by *Louis Bromfield*. Harper
10. The Family, by *Nina Fedorova*. Little, Brown

Nonfiction

1. I Married Adventure, by *Osa Johnson*. Lippincott
2. How to Read a Book, by *Mortimer Adler*. Simon & Schuster
3. A Smattering of Ignorance, by *Oscar Levant*. Doubleday, Doran
4. Country Squire in the White House, by *John T. Flynn*. Doubleday, Doran
5. Land Below the Wind, by *Agnes Newton Keith*. Little, Brown
6. American White Paper, by *Joseph W. Alsop, Jr.,* and *Robert Kintnor*. Simon & Schuster
7. New England: Indian Summer, by *Van Wyck Brooks*. Dutton
8. As I Remember Him, by *Hans Zinsser*. Little, Brown
9. Days of Our Years, by *Pierre van Paassen*. Dial Press
10. Bet It's a Boy, by *Betty B. Blunt*. Stephen Daye Press

AFTER MONTHS of the so-called "phony" war, the German blitz broke loose, engulfing Holland, Belgium, Luxembourg, France. Millions in America grabbed each new edition of the newspapers as the Nazis stormed nearer Paris. War gloom was at its deepest as Hitler attacked England from the air, and American sympathy went out to the besieged and bombarded Britishers. In the fall Wendell Willkie polled an enormous popular vote, but Franklin D. Roosevelt was elected President of the

United States for a third term. A novel of the Welsh coal miners, beauti-fully written and with emotional appeal, quickly made the best-seller grade, and brought a new name to the head of the fiction list. *How Green Was My Valley* sold 176,280 copies through the bookstores in 1940. Third, by a new English writer, was *Mrs. Miniver,* the central character of which charmed the American public in the book and the movie. Its author, Jan Struther, was possibly the most frequent guest on "Information, Please!" *For Whom the Bell Tolls,* Ernest Hemingway's first great best seller, told of an American in the Spanish Civil War. A new name in historical fiction was F. van Wyck Mason, though, like John P. Marquand, he had long been liked in another field of fiction—as a writer of inter-national adventure stories featuring an Army Intelligence hero. The first in his series of novels on the early maritime history of this country, *Three Harbours,* did not reach an annual list, but the second, *Stars on the Sea,* did. It was a novel of unusual length, as was *Oliver Wiswell,* another Kenneth Roberts historical novel. *I Married Adventure,* Osa Johnson's narrative of years in far, wild countries with her explorer husband, Martin Johnson, topped nonfiction with sales of 288,000, including book club copies. *How to Read a Book* was an interesting success. "Information, Please!" contributed another book success when one of its most popular stars, the whimsical and musical Oscar Levant, entertained with *A Smat-tering of Ignorance. Country Squire in the White House,* campaign litera-ture of 1940, sold over 100,000 copies. *Land Below the Wind* was an Atlantic-Little, Brown prize-winning book about Borneo. With the ex-ception of *American White Paper* and *Days of Our Years* (the first Dial Press book on these lists), it is amazing to note that by the end of the first year of the war no nonfiction best seller could in any way be con-sidered a "war book." *New England: Indian Summer* was the second volume of Van Wyck Brooks' best-selling literary history. *As I Remember Him* was the biography of his "romantic self" by Hans Zinsser, author of *Rats, Lice and History. Bet It's a Boy,* a little cartoon book of obstetrical humor, sold over 100,000 in the year, a forerunner of the many popular "non-books" of the sixties.

1941

Fiction

1. The Keys of the Kingdom, by *A. J. Cronin*. Little, Brown
2. Random Harvest, by *James Hilton*. Little, Brown
3. This Above All, by *Eric Knight*. Harper
4. The Sun Is My Undoing, by *Marguerite Steen*. Viking Press
5. For Whom the Bell Tolls, by *Ernest Hemingway*. Scribner
6. Oliver Wiswell, by *Kenneth Roberts*. Doubleday, Doran
7. H. M. Pulham, Esquire, by *John P. Marquand*. Little, Brown
8. Mr. and Mrs. Cugat, by *Isabel Scott Rorick*. Houghton Mifflin
9. Saratoga Trunk, by *Edna Ferber*. Doubleday, Doran
10. Windswept, by *Mary Ellen Chase*. Macmillan

Nonfiction

1. Berlin Diary, by *William L. Shirer*. Knopf
2. The White Cliffs, by *Alice Duer Miller*. Coward-McCann
3. Out of the Night, by *Jan Valtin*. Alliance Book Corp.
4. Inside Latin America, by *John Gunther*. Harper
5. Blood, Sweat and Tears, by *Winston S. Churchill*. Putnam
6. You Can't Do Business with Hitler, by *Douglas Miller*. Little, Brown
7. Reading I've Liked, ed. by *Clifton Fadiman*. Simon & Schuster
8. Reveille in Washington, by *Margaret Leech*. Harper
9. Exit Laughing, by *Irvin S. Cobb*. Bobbs-Merrill
10. My Sister and I, by *Dirk van der Heide*. Harcourt, Brace

"NEVER had so many owed so much to so few" as England's gallant airmen defended their island. The worst threat of invasion was over but Germany had attacked Russia and held nearly all the continent as her own *Festung Europa*. One Sunday afternoon toward the end of the year, when most American families had their radios tuned to the Philharmonic, came the stunning announcement that the Japanese had attacked Pearl Harbor. The United States immediately entered the war against Japan, Germany, and Italy. War books predominated the 1941 list of best sellers, although we were actually at war only during the last month of the year.

In fiction two best-selling war novels, both by English authors, were in second and third places. James Hilton had already written several best sellers (his *Random Harvest* was about World War I), but Eric Knight, later killed in a plane crash, was best known as the author of an outstanding dog story, *Lassie Come-Home*. First on the list was the latest Cronin novel, rival in popularity to *The Citadel*. *The Keys of the Kingdom* sold 236,496 copies through the trade, plus 234,328 through the Book-of-the-Month Club, whose membership had reached a figure far beyond that of its early years. Marguerite Steen, author of many novels, joined best sellers with a long historical novel. *For Whom the Bell Tolls* and *Oliver Wiswell* appeared for a second year, and John P. Marquand added another portrait of consequence to his gallery of Bostonians. *Mr. and Mrs. Cugat,* introduced another new author. Edna Ferber had a story of Saratoga's heyday, and Mary Ellen Chase a second best seller about Maine. The war led in earnest in nonfiction. Correspondent William Shirer's *Berlin Diary* made history by forming opinion and preparing American understanding of one of the enemies with whom we were to be at war by December. It sold 213,769 copies through the bookstores, 236,496 through the Book-of-the-Month Club in 1941. *The White Cliffs,* first Coward-McCann best seller on these lists, a narrative poem of wartime England, later basis of a movie and a popular song, made a record sale for a book of poetry, reaching 250,000 copies in its first three years. The underground life of Gestapo vs. Communist was the basis of Jan Valtin's *Out of the Night*. John Gunther followed his *Inside Europe* and *Inside Asia* with a third best seller. American interest in England's great crisis was reflected in the sales of Prime Minister Winston Churchill's speeches. *You Can't Do Business with Hitler* struck an important prewar note. The touching story of a Dutch refugee boy, *My Sister and I,* a title which also inspired a popular song of the day, made a total of seven books on the 1941 nonfiction list that were concerned with the war in one way or another. The other three places were filled by Clifton Fadiman's anthology, *Reading I've Liked,* arousing interest in a wide audience because of his great popularity on "Information, Please!" and as book critic of *The New Yorker*; by a historical portrait of Washington, D.C., *Reveille in Washington*; and by the autobiography of a long-time favorite author and humorist, Irvin S. Cobb.

Fiction

1. The Song of Bernadette, by *Franz Werfel*. Viking Press
2. The Moon Is Down, by *John Steinbeck*. Viking Press
3. Dragon Seed, by *Pearl S. Buck*. John Day
4. And Now Tomorrow, by *Rachel Field*. Macmillan
5. Drivin' Woman, by *Elizabeth Pickett*. Macmillan
6. Windswept, by *Mary Ellen Chase*. Macmillan
7. The Robe, by *Lloyd C. Douglas*. Houghton Mifflin
8. The Sun Is My Undoing, by *Marguerite Steen*. Viking Press
9. Kings Row, by *Henry Bellamann*. Simon & Schuster
10. The Keys of the Kingdom, by *A. J. Cronin*. Little, Brown

Nonfiction

1. See Here, Private Hargrove, by *Marion Hargrove*. Holt
2. Mission to Moscow, by *Joseph E. Davies*. Simon & Schuster
3. The Last Time I Saw Paris, by *Elliot Paul*. Random House
4. Cross Creek, by *Marjorie Kinnan Rawlings*. Scribner
5. Victory Through Air Power, by *Major Alexander P. de Seversky*. Simon & Schuster
6. Past Imperfect, by *Ilka Chase*. Doubleday, Doran
7. They Were Expendable, by *W. L. White*. Harcourt, Brace
8. Flight to Arras, by *Antoine de St. Exupéry*. Reynal & Hitchcock
9. Washington Is Like That, by *W. M. Kiplinger*. Harper
10. Inside Latin America, by *John Gunther*. Harper

THE EARLY MONTHS of 1942 marked the low point of the war as far as the United States was concerned. The Philippines were overrun after MacArthur's desperate stand on Corregidor, Australia and our lifelines to that continent were threatened, and Singapore fell. Then in April we struck our first offensive blow with the bombing of Tokyo. In August came the first attack on Guadalcanal. Americans were introduced to rationing, and pleasure-driving in automobiles was prohibited. The death of ex-Kaiser Wilhelm of Germany in exile caused little stir in comparison with tremendous daily developments in World War II. Again the appeal of religious fiction was evidenced by the great sale of *The Song of Bernadette,* which reached almost half a million copies in 1942. With its reprint edition, timed for the release of a notable movie, it sold over 900,000 in two years. John Steinbeck's *The Moon Is Down,* later a stage play, was a story of the German occupation of Norway; it, like *Bernadette,* approached the 500,000 mark in 1942. Pearl Buck's novel of war in China, *Dragon Seed,* sold around 400,000 copies in its original edition and was also made into a notable 1944 movie. *The Robe,* published in October, a novel of the time of Christ, started toward its record-breaking sales figure—it was still high on best seller lists the country over two years later. In that time it was never less than fifth on the monthly National Best Seller List of *Publishers' Weekly,* and it passed the 1,000,000 mark on its second birthday. In 1953 with the release of the movie based upon it, *The Robe* in a cheaper "movie edition" was the best selling novel of the year. The rookie of World War II, Private Hargrove, was the star of the hit book of 1942 nonfiction; sales in all editions went over 2,000,000, far outdistancing the comparable *Dere Mable* of World War I. Seven war books dominated the nonfiction list. Besides *Private Hargrove* there were Ambassador Davies' report on Russia (later a controversial movie); *The Last Time I Saw Paris* (first Random House best seller on these lists), nostalgic portrait of the Paris that had been, by Elliot Paul, whose *Life and Death of a Spanish Town* had previously portrayed the coming of fascism to Spain; *Victory Through Air Power,* a noted flyer, plane designer, and manufacturer's forecast of strategy; *They Were Expendable,* first American record of personal exploits in World War II to become a national best seller, by correspondent W. L. White, the first book to be named an "Imperative" by the newly formed Council on Books in Wartime; *Flight to Arras,* war experiences of the French aviator who had written *Wind, Sand and Stars*; and *Inside Latin America* in its second year. Marjorie Rawlings, of *The Yearling* fame in fiction, contributed charming sketches of her Florida countryside. A highly entertaining autobiography by a star of stage, movie, and radio, and a picture of Washington life completed the unwarlike part of the list.

1943

Fiction

1. The Robe, by *Lloyd C. Douglas*. Houghton Mifflin
2. The Valley of Decision, by *Marcia Davenport*. Scribner
3. So Little Time, by *John P. Marquand*. Little, Brown
4. A Tree Grows in Brooklyn, by *Betty Smith*. Harper
5. The Human Comedy, by *William Saroyan*. Harcourt, Brace
6. Mrs. Parkington, by *Louis Bromfield*. Harper
7. The Apostle, by *Sholem Asch*. Putnam
8. Hungry Hill, by *Daphne du Maurier*. Doubleday, Doran
9. The Forest and the Fort, by *Hervey Allen*. Farrar & Rinehart
10. The Song of Bernadette, by *Franz Werfel*. Viking Press

Nonfiction

1. Under Cover, by *John Roy Carlson*. Dutton
2. One World, by *Wendell L. Willkie*. Simon & Schuster
3. Journey Among Warriors, by *Eve Curie*. Doubleday, Doran
4. On Being a Real Person, by *Harry Emerson Fosdick*. Harper
5. Guadalcanal Diary, by *Richard Tregaskis*. Random House
6. Burma Surgeon, by *Lt. Col. Gordon Seagrave*. Norton
7. Our Hearts Were Young and Gay, by *Cornelia Otis Skinner* and *Emily Kimbrough*. Dodd, Mead
8. U. S. Foreign Policy, by *Walter Lippmann*. Little, Brown
9. Here Is Your War, by *Ernie Pyle*. Holt
10. See Here, Private Hargrove, by *Marion Hargrove*. Holt

WITH the landing of a great Allied armada in North Africa came the turning point of the war. Our troops moved on into Sicily and Italy. From Britain, Germany and the occupied countries of Europe were blasted from the air. In the Pacific our Navy began moving in on enemy-held islands. Again a religious novel topped fiction—*The Robe,* which had been published late the previous year. With paper supply cut to 90 per cent of the 1942 level, Houghton Miffin was hard put to meet the demand. As new printings of *The Robe* appeared, the book shrank in height and thickness, though the text was not cut. Marcia Davenport was a new best-selling author whose *Valley of Decision,* story of a Pennsylvania mine-owning family, met with great success. The daughter of Alma Gluck, she had already written two well-liked books with musical background, a biography of Mozart and a novel, *Of Lena Geyer.* By the end of 1943, *Valley of Decision* had been on 14 consecutive monthly lists and *Bernadette* on 13. Novels reflected the war only slightly; it was the background for only two best sellers of the year, *So Little Time,* in which John Marquand deserted his customary Boston scene, and William Saroyan's tender and moving story of a California family, which became a memorable movie as well. This was Saroyan's first appearance on an annual best seller list. A new author with a first novel whose title was to become as familiar as *Gone with the Wind* was Betty Smith, who put neglected Brooklyn on the fiction map. The four other authors were all familiar names among best sellers—Sholem Asch with his second religious novel, Daphne du Maurier with a successor to *Rebecca,* Hervey Allen with the first book of his projected series of American historical novels, and Franz Werfel with *The Song of Bernadette* in its second year. Three novels on the 1943 list were religious in theme. Only two titles on the nonfiction list were not "war books." These were Dr. Fosdick's *On Being a Real Person,* which sold over 200,000, and the lively reminiscences of a trip to pre-World War I Europe by Cornelia Otis Skinner and Emily Kimbrough. *Under Cover,* an opinion-making report of subversive activities in this country, sold 600,000 copies in its original edition. Wendell Willkie's wartime trip around the world created an eager market for his report, which then absorbed 1,500,000 copies. Since it was published simultaneously in a cloth and a paperbound edition, the latter greatly outselling the former and having a wide newsstand and drugstore sale, Willkie's book might well have stood at the head of this list. But these lists were based upon bookstore sales only, and therefore the reports on *Under Cover* outdistanced those on *One World. One World* was also an "Imperative" of the Council on Books in Wartime, was translated into sixteen languages, and sold well over 3,000,000 copies throughout the world. Eve Curie was again a best seller, this time with an account of her trip to the war fronts of the globe. *Guadalcanal Diary* was a correspondent's report of our hard-fought campaign. *Burma Surgeon* related the experiences of a doctor who became an Army medical officer when the Japanese took over the country in which he had labored long as a medical missionary. Walter Lippmann, influential newspaper columnist who had been a best seller in 1929 with *A Preface to Morals,* gave his views on what our foreign policy had been and should be, another Council "Imperative." In *Here Is Your War* newspaperman Ernie Pyle revealed the human qualities of the infantryman as he saw them in North Africa—a book that found country-wide response as had the newspaper articles upon which it was based. *See Here, Private Hargrove* was still going strong in its second year.

Fiction

1. Strange Fruit, by *Lillian Smith*. Reynal & Hitchcock
2. The Robe, by *Lloyd C. Douglas*. Houghton Mifflin
3. A Tree Grows in Brooklyn, by *Betty Smith*. Harper
4. Forever Amber, by *Kathleen Winsor*. Macmillan
5. The Razor's Edge, by *W. Somerset Maugham*. Doubleday, Doran
6. The Green Years, by *A. J. Cronin*. Little, Brown
7. Leave Her to Heaven, by *Ben Ames Williams*. Houghton Mifflin
8. Green Dolphin Street, by *Elizabeth Goudge*. Coward-McCann
9. A Bell for Adano, by *John Hersey*. Knopf
10. The Apostle, by *Sholem Asch*. Putnam

Nonfiction

1. I Never Left Home, by *Bob Hope*. Simon & Schuster; Home Guide
2. Brave Men, by *Ernie Pyle*. Holt
3. Good Night, Sweet Prince, by *Gene Fowler*. Viking Press
4. Under Cover, by *John Roy Carlson*. Dutton
5. Yankee from Olympus, by *Catherine Drinker Bowen*. Little, Brown
6. The Time for Decision, by *Sumner Welles*. Harper
7. Here Is Your War, by *Ernie Pyle*. Holt
8. Anna and the King of Siam, by *Margaret Landon*. John Day
9. The Curtain Rises, by *Quentin Reynolds*. Random House
10. Ten Years in Japan, by *Joseph C. Grew*. Simon & Schuster

THE NEWS of the invasion of northern Europe that the world had been waiting and hoping for so long was broadcast early on the morning of June 6. With the Allies closing in on Germany from all sides, confidence rose that the end of the war was in sight. In the fall, as Dewey and Roosevelt campaigned for the Presidency, two influential and greatly admired men on the national political scene died within a few days of each other, Al Smith and Wendell Willkie, the latter the author of one of the great best sellers, *One World. Strange Fruit,* poignant first novel of white and black in the South, published by the comparatively new firm of Reynal & Hitchcock, was first on the fiction list of the year. It was later banned in Boston as was another first novel, fourth among best sellers, *Forever Amber.* Kathleen Winsor was the much publicized and photogenic author of *Forever Amber,* a novel of Restoration England which emphasized the bawdiness of the period. There were two religious novels on the list—*The Robe* in its third year of best-sellerdom and *The Apostle* in its second. Another first novel, *A Tree Grows in Brooklyn,* was in third place. It had been fourth the year before. The war was the background in only two novels, in *The Razor's Edge* and in *A Bell for Adano,* which was John Hersey's first novel but third book about the war. It was the story of an American AMG officer in Italy and of the problems he faced in administering the affairs of a region recently swept of the Nazis. Ben Ames Williams, long a favorite fiction and magazine writer, appeared on a yearly list for the first time. *Green Dolphin Street* was a historical novel which won for its author, Elizabeth Goudge, the $125,000 prize offered by the film producers Metro-Goldwyn-Mayer. War books of 1944, seven out of the ten in nonfiction, were notable because of their timeliness, their coverage of the diverse phases of the war, and their excellence of presentation. One was written by a comedian who journeyed to the war fronts to entertain the troops (Bob Hope, many years later, was still making Christmas trips to entertain American soldiers on foreign soil); three by war correspondents; one by an investigator of subversive activities; and two by statesmen. Bob Hope's book, published in a paper as well as a cloth edition, far outstripped the rest in sales, going well over the million mark. Ernie Pyle was the newspaperman responsible for two books on the list. He was awarded a Pulitzer Prize for his reporting from the war fronts where he was later to be killed. Quentin Reynolds had written many excellent books, from the war correspondent's vantage point, since the start of the war, but not until *The Curtain Rises* was published did he make the annual list. The books by former Under Secretary of State Sumner Welles and former Ambassador Grew were outstanding examples of those which, like *Berlin Diary* and *One World,* influenced American thinking. First of the three non-war books of the year was *Good Night, Sweet Prince,* a biography of one of the most famous stars of stage and screen, John Barrymore of the glamorous theatrical family. The other two non-war books were also biographies. *Yankee from Olympus,* in fifth place, was primarily the story of Justice Holmes but included as well other members of a family that held a prominent place in American life and letters over many years.

138

Anna and the King of Siam was the interesting story of a woman who went to Siam in the 19th century as governess to the King's daughters. It became, many years later, basis of a movie and as "The King and I," the basis of a popular musical, and still another movie.

1945

Fiction

1. Forever Amber, by *Kathleen Winsor*. Macmillan
2. The Robe, by *Lloyd C. Douglas*. Houghton Mifflin
3. The Black Rose, by *Thomas B. Costain*. Doubleday
4. The White Tower, by *James Ramsey Ullman*. Lippincott
5. Cass Timberlane, by *Sinclair Lewis*. Random House
6. A Lion Is In the Streets, by *Adria Locke Langley*. Whittlesey House
7. So Well Remembered, by *James Hilton*. Little, Brown
8. Captain from Castile, by *Samuel Shellabarger*. Little, Brown
9. Earth and High Heaven, by *Gwethalyn Graham*. Lippincott
10. Immortal Wife, by *Irving Stone*. Doubleday

Nonfiction

1. Brave Men, by *Ernie Pyle*. Holt
2. Dear Sir, by *Juliet Lowell*. Duell, Sloan & Pearce
3. Up Front, by *Bill Mauldin*. Holt
4. Black Boy, by *Richard Wright*. Harper
5. Try and Stop Me, by *Bennett Cerf*. Simon & Schuster
6. Anything Can Happen, by *George and Helen Papashvily*. Harper
7. General Marshall's Report. Simon & Schuster
8. The Egg and I, by *Betty MacDonald*. Lippincott
9. The Thurber Carnival, by *James Thurber*. Harper
10. Pleasant Valley, by *Louis Bromfield*. Harper

THE WORLD was shocked by President Roosevelt's death at Warm Springs in April. Long-awaited VE day came in May and, in August, VJ day, after the atomic bomb had exploded over Hiroshima and Nagasaki. The UN charter was signed in San Francisco. War shortages still prevailed in the book industry; though "thin" books were necessary to conserve paper and other production materials a very "fat" book was 1945's best-selling novel, the already-famous *Forever Amber,* selling 868,630 copies in its second year. Two hundred and seventy thousand copies of the second novel on the 1945 list were sold during that year, also its second year, bringing the total of *The Robe* close to 2,000,000 at that time. These two novels at the top of the 1945 list were the only ones that year that were not book club selections or dividends or issued in the Armed Services Editions of which 90,000,000 books had been distributed to men in the service. The war years were the peak years for the book clubs: their paper quotas were high, under paper rationing, compared to the publishers'. This fact accounted for some of the big sales of fiction, particularly historical fiction. Nearly all the novels on the 1945 list sold over half a million copies, including such extra-bookstore distribution. Three new novelists achieved prominence—James Ramsey Ullman, Adria Locke Langley, and Gwethalyn Graham—most of the others were well-known and popular writers. There were no war novels on the 1945 fiction list; historical fiction predominated. War books, however, took first, second, third and seventh places in nonfiction. *Brave Men,* published late in 1944 and second for that year, sold 687,450 copies through the bookstores, and, with its book club sales, well over a million. *Dear Sir,* the little book of war humor, unexpectedly showed up with the total of 654,391. The leading autobiography of 1945, *Black Boy,* sold 195,000 copies, and, with book club, 546,000. *General Marshall's Report* sold 133,770 copies, of which 15,000 were clothbound, 118,770, paperbound—representing a trend toward two editions, in cloth and paper, of a single title which was further developed in succeeding years. In general nonfiction did not attain the high sales of fiction, though *Brave Men* (its author had been killed early in the year by a Japanese sniper's bullet) outdistanced every book in both classifications.

1946

Fiction

1. The King's General, by *Daphne du Maurier*. Doubleday
2. This Side of Innocence, by *Taylor Caldwell*. Scribner
3. The River Road, by *Frances Parkinson Keyes*. Messner
4. The Miracle of the Bells, by *Russell Janney*. Prentice-Hall
5. The Hucksters, by *Frederic Wakeman*. Rinehart
6. The Foxes of Harrow, by *Frank Yerby*. Dial Press
7. Arch of Triumph, by *Erich Maria Remarque*. Appleton-Century
8. The Black Rose, by *Thomas B. Costain*. Doubleday
9. B. F.'s Daughter, by *John P. Marquand*. Little, Brown
10. The Snake Pit, by *Mary Jane Ward*. Random House

Nonfiction

1. The Egg and I, by *Betty MacDonald*. Lippincott
2. Peace of Mind, by *Joshua L. Liebman*. Simon & Schuster
3. As He Saw It, by *Elliott Roosevelt*. Duell, Sloan & Pearce
4. The Roosevelt I Knew, by *Frances Perkins*. Viking Press
5. Last Chapter, by *Ernie Pyle*. Holt
6. Starling of the White House, by *Thomas Sugrue* and *Col. Edmund Starling*. Simon & Schuster
7. I Chose Freedom, by *Victor Kravchenko*. Scribner
8. The Anatomy of Peace, by *Emery Reves*. Harper
9. Top Secret, by *Ralph Ingersoll*. Harcourt, Brace
10. A Solo in Tom-Toms, by *Gene Fowler*. Viking Press

1946 WAS the year in which the American public first listened to an atomic explosion—at Bikini Atoll, via radio. The end of World War II was officially proclaimed by President Truman. Mother Cabrini was the first American citizen to be raised to sainthood. *Call Me Mister* and *Annie Get Your Gun* were popular stage productions and *The Best Years of Our Lives,* the movie of the year. Daphne du Maurier, whose *The King's General* headed the 1946 best seller list, was a novelist familiar to readers of best sellers. Her *Hungry Hill* was a best seller of 1943 and her famous *Rebecca* appeared on the lists of both 1938 and 1939. Through the bookstores, 228,235 copies of *The King's General* were sold in 1946; including sales through three book clubs, its total in 1946 was 1,095,571. Besides *The King's General,* there were four other historical novels on the 1946 list of best-selling fiction. *This Side of Innocence,* by Taylor Caldwell, took second place with a bookstore sale of about 221,000 copies. This novel had, in addition, the largest sale ever attained at that time by any Literary Guild selection, over 1,055,000. Another longtime popular novelist, Frances Parkinson Keyes, reached the annual list for the first time with her *River Road,* with sales of 225,000, plus a book club sale adding up to 950,000. Fourth of the historical novels was a first novel by Frank Yerby, later to become one of the biggest-selling novelists of the '40's and '50's. *The Foxes of Harrow* sold 172,000 through the bookstores, and, with sales from three book clubs, attained a total of 1,200,000 during the year. Eighth was *The Black Rose,* a Thomas B. Costain historical. A widely publicized first novel, *The Miracle of the Bells,* by Russell Janney, reached fourth place, the only title on the fiction list which was not the selection of any book club. Another writer new to the best seller lists, Frederic Wakeman, had a trade sale of over 180,000 for his realistic novel about the advertising business, *The Hucksters,* with a total of 712,434, including book club sales. *Arch of Triumph,* by Erich Maria Remarque, whose great novel of World War I, *All Quiet on the Western Front,* topped the 1929 best seller list, was in seventh place. *B. F.'s Daughter,* by John P. Marquand, a favorite novelist over many years, sold 129,000 copies through the trade plus 680,000 book club copies. *The Snake Pit,* by Mary Jane Ward, who made her first appearance on the list and started a trend for novels about psychiatric problems, sold about 125,000, which, with the book club sale, made a total of 600,000. All these figures for fiction in the first postwar year seemed staggering in the cold light of less prosperous earlier and later years. With production problems still keeping publishers busy trying to keep up with demand, hardbound books were sold in quantities never before reached, though the actual number of new titles was at its lowest in about 40 years. Said *Publishers' Weekly,* "Never before have so few titles gone to so many readers . . . the major book clubs . . . think nothing of printing a half-million copies of a current selection." Nonfiction figures were not quite so startling. Though Betty MacDonald's first book, *The Egg and I,* sold 496,000 copies through the bookstores and a total of 1,038,500 with its book club sale, Joshua L. Liebman's *Peace of Mind,* which was to be the nonfiction best seller of 1947 and still on the annual list in 1948, reached second place with a mere 242,000 copies. There were two biographies of the late President among 1946 best sellers, and a volume of White House reminiscences, two war books, a book on the peace, and two biographies, one a Russian political autobiography.

1947

Fiction

1. The Miracle of the Bells, by *Russell Janney*. Prentice-Hall
2. The Moneyman, by *Thomas B. Costain*. Doubleday
3. Gentleman's Agreement, by *Laura Z. Hobson*. Simon & Schuster
4. Lydia Bailey, by *Kenneth Roberts,* Doubleday
5. The Vixens, by *Frank Yerby*. Dial Press
6. The Wayward Bus, by *John Steinbeck*. Viking Press
7. House Divided, by *Ben Ames Williams*. Houghton Mifflin
8. Kingsblood Royal, by *Sinclair Lewis*. Random House
9. East Side, West Side, by *Marcia Davenport*. Scribner
10. Prince of Foxes, by *Samuel Shellabarger*. Little, Brown

Nonfiction

1. Peace of Mind, by *Joshua L. Liebman*. Simon & Schuster
2. Information Please Almanac, 1947, ed. by *John Kieran*. Garden City Publishing Co.
3. Inside U.S.A., by *John Gunther*. Harper
4. A Study of History, by *Arnold J. Toynbee*. Oxford University Press
5. Speaking Frankly, by *James F. Byrnes*. Harper
6. Human Destiny, by *Pierre Lecomte du Noüy*. Longmans, Green
7. The Egg and I, by *Betty MacDonald*. Lippincott
8. The American Past, by *Roger Butterfield*. Simon & Schuster
9. The Fireside Book of Folk Songs, ed. by *Margaret B. Boni*. Simon & Schuster
10. Together, by *Katharine T. Marshall*. Tupper & Love

THE Taft-Hartley Act was passed by Congress in 1947 and the Marshall Plan announced; the Freedom Train, exhibiting the great historical documents of the U.S.A., and the Friendship Train, bearing food for devastated Europe, were started on their ways. Street-cars disappeared from Manhattan Island and flying saucers were seen in the sky. New Yorkers went to the theatre to see *All My Sons, A Streetcar Named Desire* and the first operas by Gian-Carlo Menotti to be produced here. Henry Ford died at his home in Michigan, leaving an estate of over 500 million dollars. Titles which rang up most sales in the bookstores during 1947 were *The Miracle of the Bells,* a first novel by Russell Janney, in fiction, and *Peace of Mind,* by Rabbi Liebman, in nonfiction. The nonfiction title outsold the fiction title by about 30,000 copies. Both books had also appeared on the 1946 best seller list. *The Miracle of the Bells* had a larger sale, one of over 240,000 copies, in its second year. With book club sales it had reached an overall figure, by the end of 1947, of approximately 400,000. Only two novels and three books of nonfiction on the combined list had no book club or extra-bookstore sales whatever. Half the fiction list in 1947 was made up of historical novels. Thomas B. Costain's *The Moneyman,* in second place in fiction, selling 185,000 through the trade, started out with an advance sale double that of his 1946 best-selling historical romance, *The Black Rose.* The other historical novels on the 1947 list were *Lydia Bailey, The Vixens, House Divided,* and *Prince of Foxes,* all by well-known and popular authors. *The Vixens* sold 152,706 copies through bookstores, plus Fiction Book Club sales of over 125,000. *House Divided,* one of the two "bookstore only" novels on the list, sold just over 125,000. *Prince of Foxes* sold 107,000 copies—with its Literary Guild sales, over 1,125,000. The heightened postwar interest in problems of race relations was reflected in the sale of *Gentleman's Agreement,* by Laura Z. Hobson, dealing with Jewish-Gentile relations, and *Kingsblood Royal,* in which Sinclair Lewis presented what was then the dilemma of a white man who discovered that he had Negro blood. *Gentleman's Agreement* sold 172,615 copies through bookstores, over a million in 1947 through all media. The Lewis book had an overall sale of about 800,000, of which 115,000 were sold in the stores. *The Wayward Bus,* by John Steinbeck, sold 520,000, including trade, book club, and Armed Services Editions. *East Side, West Side,* by Marcia Davenport, the other of the two "bookstore only" novels, had a sale of approximately 111,000. *Peace of Mind,* one of the first of the big sellers in the "inspirational" market that boomed in the '40's and '50's, had a bigger sale in its second year in the bookstores, 270,669. Its overall sale by the end of 1947 was 577,693. Nearly 300,000 copies of the first *Information Please Almanac* were sold—the famous radio program was at the height of its popularity—and the *Almanac* was the second best seller of the year. John Gunther's 1947 "Inside" book, *Inside U.S.A.,* was in third place, with 187,000 copies printed. It was among the four nonfiction best sellers which may be classified as historical and political. The others were Arnold Toynbee's *A Study of History,* with 123,000 trade sale plus 60,000 book club; *Speaking Frankly,* Secretary of State Byrnes' memoirs of the war years, with 125,000 printed; and *The American Past,* picture history by Roger Butterfield, with a sale of about 68,000.

Besides *Peace of Mind,* another religious book was a big 1947 seller. *Human Destiny,* by Pierre Lecomte du Noüy, reached sixth place with a sale of 105,000 and a book club printing of 320,000. *The Egg and I,* which had been the 1946 leader in nonfiction, appeared again in 1947 with sales of 101,138 copies in its second year. Its two-year total was in the neighborhood of a million and a quarter. Besides the MacDonald book, the only other 1947 best seller which could be classified as biography, a category that formerly dominated nonfiction lists, was *Together,* the life of General Marshall written by his wife. It sold 59,156 copies through the stores, 300,000 with its book club sales. *The Fireside Book of Folk Songs,* like *The American Past,* a fast seller as a Christmas gift book, reached a sale of about 68,000. Those two were the only books among nonfiction best sellers which were not distributed in part through sales agencies other than bookstores.

1948

Fiction

1. The Big Fisherman, by *Lloyd C. Douglas*. Houghton Mifflin
2. The Naked and the Dead, by *Norman Mailer*. Rinehart
3. Dinner at Antoine's, by *Frances Parkinson Keyes*. Messner
4. The Bishop's Mantle, by *Agnes Sligh Turnbull*. Macmillan
5. Tomorrow Will Be Better, by *Betty Smith*. Harper
6. The Golden Hawk, by *Frank Yerby*. Dial Press
7. Raintree County, by *Ross Lockridge, Jr*. Houghton Mifflin
8. Shannon's Way, by *A. J. Cronin*. Little, Brown
9. Pilgrim's Inn, by *Elizabeth Goudge*. Coward-McCann
10. The Young Lions, by *Irwin Shaw*. Random House

Nonfiction

1. Crusade in Europe, by *Dwight D. Eisenhower*. Doubleday
2. How to Stop Worrying and Start Living, by *Dale Carnegie*. Simon & Schuster
3. Peace of Mind, by *Joshua L. Liebman*. Simon & Schuster
4. Sexual Behavior in the Human Male, by *A. C. Kinsey* and others. Saunders
5. Wine, Women and Words, by *Billy Rose*. Simon & Schuster
6. The Life and Times of the Shmoo, by *Al Capp*. Simon & Schuster
7. The Gathering Storm, by *Winston Churchill*. Houghton Mifflin
8. Roosevelt and Hopkins, by *Robert E. Sherwood*. Harper
9. A Guide to Confident Living, by *Norman Vincent Peale*. Prentice-Hall
10. The Plague and I, by *Betty MacDonald*. Lippincott

AMERICANS were talking about the "pumpkin papers" in the Chambers-Hiss case in 1948. They were watching and listening to the first symphony and opera telecasts, and seeing *Mister Roberts* and *Kiss Me Kate* on the stage. *Slow Boat to China, Nature Boy* and Citation became familiar words. Published in mid-November of 1948, Lloyd C. Douglas's second Biblical novel *The Big Fisherman* outdistanced all the other fiction titles

147

of that year. It had an advance of 245,000 copies and, by the end of the year, had sold 366,692. Comparable figures for *The Robe,* issued in 1942, were an advance of 42,000 and a sale of about 100,000 by the end of the year. *The Robe* was a best seller for 32 months, a record at that time. The first outstanding postwar novel about World War II was in second place. This was *The Naked and the Dead,* by Norman Mailer, a new writer who, with his first book, attained an important place in American literature. His novel sold 137,185 copies in the stores plus about 60,000 through the Book Find Club. Another World War II novel and also a first novel, though its author, Irwin Shaw, was well known as a playwright and short story writer, reached tenth place on the list. His *The Young Lions* had a sale of 78,050 in 1948. There was another first novelist on 1948's list, also highly regarded by the critics, Ross Lockridge, Jr., who committed suicide not long after his *Raintree County* had achieved great success. All the rest of the best-selling novels of 1948 were by authors of longtime popularity. Frances Parkinson Keyes' *Dinner at Antoine's* was in third place with a sale of 114,249 copies. It was followed by Agnes Sligh Turnbull's novel with a religious theme, *The Bishop's Mantle,* which sold over 100,000 copies through the trade, its Dollar Book Club and other sales bringing it close to the million mark. Betty Smith's successor to *A Tree Grows in Brooklyn, Tomorrow Will Be Better,* was fifth. With its bookstore sale of 102,163 and its Dollar Book Club sales, Frank Yerby's *The Golden Hawk* passed the million mark, making it probably the best-selling novel of the year in sales to the public through all media. Memoirs of war years were prominent among the nonfiction best sellers. General Eisenhower's *Crusade in Europe* topped them with sales in a little over a month, of 239,265 copies plus a large book club sale. Prime Minister Churchill's first volume in his great history of World War II, *The Gathering Storm,* was seventh on the list, and Robert E. Sherwood's *Roosevelt and Hopkins,* eighth. The trend toward big sales for books on our psychological, spiritual, and physical problems accelerated. Four books on the list could be placed in such categories: *How to Stop Worrying and Start Living, Peace of Mind, Sexual Behavior in the Human Male,* and *A Guide to Confident Living.* Dale Carnegie's book followed his great success, *How to Win Friends and Influence People,* with a sale of 235,636 in its first year. Joshua Liebman's *Peace of Mind,* in its third year as a leading seller was close behind it with 227,705. Book phenomenon of the year, the Kinsey Report, issued by a publisher of medical books, sold about 225,000 copies. Dr. Peale's first best seller, *A Guide to Confident Living,* had sales of 78,000 copies in 1948. Three books in lighter moods completed the list: entrepreneur Billy Rose's *Wine, Women and Words,* with sales of 155,655; cartoonist Al Capp's *The Life and Times of the Shmoo,* selling 141,977; and egg fancier Betty MacDonald's *The Plague and I.*

148

Fiction

1. The Egyptian, by *Mika Waltari*. Putnam
2. The Big Fisherman, by *Lloyd C. Douglas*. Houghton Mifflin
3. Mary, by *Sholem Asch*. Putnam
4. A Rage to Live, by *John O'Hara*. Random House
5. Point of No Return, by *John P. Marquand*. Little, Brown
6. Dinner at Antoine's, by *Frances Parkinson Keyes*. Messner
7. High Towers, by *Thomas B. Costain*. Doubleday
8. Cutlass Empire, by *Van Wyck Mason*. Doubleday
9. Pride's Castle, by *Frank Yerby*. Dial Press
10. Father of the Bride, by *Edward Streeter*. Simon & Schuster

Nonfiction

1. White Collar Zoo, by *Clare Barnes, Jr.* Doubleday
2. How to Win at Canasta, by *Oswald Jacoby*. Doubleday
3. The Seven Storey Mountain, by *Thomas Merton*. Harcourt, Brace
4. Home Sweet Zoo, by *Clare Barnes, Jr.* Doubleday
5. Cheaper by the Dozen, by *Frank B. Gilbreth, Jr.* and *Ernestine Gilbreth Carey*. Crowell
6. The Greatest Story Ever Told, by *Fulton Oursler*. Doubleday
7. Canasta, the Argentine Rummy Game, by *Ottilie H. Reilly*. Ives Washburn
8. Canasta, by *Josephine Artayeta de Viel* and *Ralph Michael*. Pellegrini & Cudahy
9. Peace of Soul, by *Fulton J. Sheen*. Whittlesey House
10. A Guide to Confident Living, by *Norman Vincent Peale*. Prentice-Hall

As President Truman began a second term, people were disturbed by high coffee prices and returned to coffee hoarding. New Yorkers were asked to conserve water because of shortage—until the disastrous floods came to the northeastern states in the latter part of 1949. Tickets for *South Pacific,* the biggest musical hit in years, were only obtainable at what were then considered impossible prices. Historical novels came back into their own in 1949, comprising more than half the fiction list, two of the six built on Biblical characters. Best-selling novel was *The Egyptian,* by Mika Waltari. It was a story of ancient Egypt and the Near East, a translation from the Finnish of a writer not previously published in this country. Though sales of *The Big Fisherman* were much smaller in 1949 than in 1948, when it topped the annual list, it was, nevertheless, second for the year, selling 162,615 in comparison with 1948's 366,692. Another Biblical novel, *Mary,* by Sholem Asch, was third. Historical romances by the perennially best-selling authors, Costain, Mason, and Yerby were in seventh, eighth and ninth places. *High Towers* had a trade sale of 84,710 plus a Dollar Book Club sale of 824,434. *Cutlass Empire* also had a large book club sale in addition to its 80,668 through bookstores. *Pride's Castle* sold 73,503 plus a Dollar Book Club sale that brought it up over the million mark. On a theme far from Biblical was modern novelist John O'Hara's *A Rage to Live.* Its sales were 135,000 copies. *Point of No Return,* by John P. Marquand, later to be the basis of a very successful stage play, as was his *Late George Apley,* was fifth with 128,164 copies sold through the trade and a total sale, including book club, of 528,164. *Dinner at Antoine's,* which had been third on the 1948 list, sold 95,000 more copies in 1949. With its Dollar Book Club sale it reached over a million. Thirty-one years after publication of his big seller of World War I *Dere Mable,* Edward Streeter reappeared as the author of an entertaining novel, *Father of the Bride* (later a movie), which sold 73,281 copies plus Book-of-the-Month Club distribution. Feature of 1949 nonfiction was the predominance of what could be called non-reading books—picture books and game books. The hilarious "Zoo" books by Clare Barnes, Jr., photographs of animals caricaturing human behavior, were the big hits of the year. *White Collar Zoo* took first place with its sale of 395,000 copies. *Home Sweet Zoo,* published on December 2, wound up in fourth place, selling 262,000 copies in the last month of the year. The Canasta craze that hit the U.S. was reflected in the high sales of three Canasta books. Oswald Jacoby's *How to Win at Canasta* was second on the list with a sale of 385,333. *Canasta, the Argentine Rummy Game,* by Ottilie H. Reilly, sold 206,000 copies. *Canasta,* by Josephine Artayeta de Viel and Ralph Michael, sold over 200,000 in the bookstores and, in a cheaper edition, about 400,000 more through other outlets. Thomas Merton's *The Seven Storey Mountain* led the religious titles which made up most of the remainder of the non-fiction list. It sold 307,400 copies in 1949. Fulton Oursler's *The Greatest Story Ever Told* was sixth with 205,426 sold through the trade, 286,906 through book clubs. *Peace of Soul,* the then Monsignor Fulton J. Sheen's rejoinder to Dr. Liebman's *Peace of Mind,* was ninth with a total of 182,652. *A Guide to Confident Living,* which had been ninth on the

150

1948 list, was tenth in 1949, selling 158,000 copies, 15,000 of them in the month of December. The remaining "reading" book on the list, in fact the only one not religious, not a picture or game book, was the humorous family biography, *Cheaper by the Dozen,* by Frank B. Gilbreth, Jr. and Ernestine Gilbreth Carey. It sold 241,093 copies in the stores and 257,000 through the Book-of-the-Month Club.

Fiction

1. The Cardinal, by *Henry Morton Robinson*. Simon & Schuster
2. Joy Street, by *Frances Parkinson Keyes*. Messner
3. Across the River and Into the Trees, by *Ernest Hemingway*. Scribner
4. The Wall, by *John Hersey*. Knopf
5. Star Money, by *Kathleen Winsor*. Appleton-Century-Crofts
6. The Parasites, by *Daphne du Maurier*. Doubleday
7. Floodtide, by *Frank Yerby*. Dial Press
8. Jubilee Trail, by *Gwen Bristow*. Crowell
9. The Adventurer, by *Mika Waltari*. Putnam
10. The Disenchanted, by *Budd Schulberg*. Random House

Nonfiction

1. Betty Crocker's Picture Cook Book. McGraw-Hill
2. The Baby. Simon & Schuster
3. Look Younger, Live Longer, by *Gayelord Hauser*. Farrar, Straus & Young
4. How I Raised Myself from Failure to Success in Selling, by *Frank Bettger*. Prentice-Hall
5. Kon-Tiki, by *Thor Heyerdahl*. Rand McNally
6. Mr. Jones, Meet the Master, by *Peter Marshall*. Revell
7. Your Dream Home, by *Hubbard Cobb*. Wise
8. The Mature Mind, by *H. A. Overstreet*. Norton
9. Campus Zoo, by *Clare Barnes, Jr.* Doubleday
10. Belles on Their Toes, by *Frank Gilbreth, Jr.* and *Ernestine Gilbreth Carey*. Crowell

TELEVISION came into its own in 1950 with the tremendous interest shown in the Kefauver committee's crime investigation hearings. The President recalled General MacArthur after the start of the Korean War and authorized continued work on the H bomb. The theatre-in-the-round was arousing interest, and people were humming *Goodnight, Irene*. Heavyweight champion Joe Louis met defeat before the gloves of Ezzard Charles.

George Bernard Shaw died at the age of 94. The majority of the 1950 fiction best sellers were modern stories in contrast to the predominance of historical novels in 1949. *The Cardinal,* top seller of the year, was by an author new to the best seller lists, as also were *Jubilee Trail* and *The Disenchanted.* All the others were by authors who had appeared on annual best seller lists at least once. Trade interest in *The Cardinal* was heightened by its publication in both cloth and paperbound editions, the first major trial of this merchandising method for a best-selling novel. It sold 435,516 copies in paper, 152,879 in cloth, a total of 588,395. Frances Parkinson Keyes' *Joy Street,* second in fiction sales, reached its place with only one month in the bookstores. It was published on December 1 with an advance of 110,000. Re-orders made its total, by the end of the year, 140,285. Third and fourth were two novels by well-known writers in which World War II was the background—a much less important background in Ernest Hemingway's *Across the River and Into the Trees* than in John Hersey's fine novel of the Jewish quarter in Nazi-occupied Warsaw. *Across the River and Into the Trees* sold 104,000 copies. *The Wall* sold 97,860 plus a Book-of-the-Month Club distribution of 230,000. Kathleen Winsor followed up the success of *Forever Amber* with the story of a modern girl, *Star Money.* The total sale of *The Parasites* by Daphne du Maurier, including that of the Book League, was 401,891. Its trade sale was 82,347 copies. From seventh to ninth places came the only best-selling historical novels of the year. Frank Yerby's *Floodtide,* 81,000, outsold his *Pride's Castle* of 1949. In addition, it had a large Dollar Book Club sale. *Jubilee Trail,* by Gwen Bristow, was over half a million with its Literary Guild copies. Ninth was *The Adventurer,* by Mika Waltari, whose *The Egyptian* had topped the 1949 list. Budd Schulberg's novel, presumably based on the life of F. Scott Fitzgerald, *The Disenchanted,* wound up the fiction. It sold 70,000 through the trade, 255,000 including book club copies. Again in 1950 "reading" books were scarce among the top ten sellers in non-fiction. Eight out of the ten fell into "how to," picture book, or "self-help" categories, if the Marshall and Overstreet books may be included in the last-named group. The two remaining titles, *Kon-Tiki,* by Thor Heyerdahl and *Belles on Their Toes,* by the Gilbreth writing team, sold respectively 128,848 copies and over 300,000 with book club copies. Leading the bookstore list of 1950 nonfiction best sellers was *Betty Crocker's Picture Cook Book,* with a trade sale of 300,000. General Mills sold about 200,000 more. *The Baby,* humorous picture book, sold about 250,000 copies in the bookstores, with a sale, including newsstands, of 322,236. *Look Younger, Live Longer,* by Gayelord Hauser, sold about 200,000 copies in bookstores, with its health food store sale, 275,135. Frank Bettger's *How I Raised Myself from Failure to Success in Selling,* in fourth position, sold 195,000 copies. Sixth was *Mr. Jones, Meet the*

Master, by Peter Marshall, Chaplain of the U.S. Senate, reaching a sale of 125,000. *Your Dream Home,* by Hubbard Cobb, sold over 100,000 copies through bookstores, close to one million by mail, making it actually the top best seller of the year through all channels. *The Mature Mind,* by H. A. Overstreet, was the only title among the first ten that appeared on every monthly list through 1950. It sold 91,341 copies plus a Book-of-the-Month Club sale of 247,500. *Campus Zoo,* another humorous picture book, compiled by Clare Barnes, Jr., two of whose "Zoo" books were on the 1949 list, sold 81,724.

1951

Fiction

1. From Here to Eternity, by *James Jones.* Scribner
2. The Caine Mutiny, by *Herman Wouk.* Doubleday
3. Moses, by *Sholem Asch.* Putnam
4. The Cardinal, by *Henry Morton Robinson.* Simon & Schuster
5. A Woman Called Fancy, by *Frank Yerby.* Dial Press
6. The Cruel Sea, by *Nicholas Monsarrat.* Knopf
7. Melville Goodwin, U.S.A., by *John P. Marquand.* Little, Brown
8. Return to Paradise, by *James A. Michener.* Random House
9. The Foundling, by *Cardinal Spellman.* Scribner
10. The Wanderer, by *Mika Waltari.* Putnam

Nonfiction

1. Look Younger, Live Longer, by *Gayelord Hauser.* Farrar, Straus & Young
2. Betty Crocker's Picture Cook Book. McGraw-Hill
3. Washington Confidential, by *Jack Lait and Lee Mortimer.* Crown
4. Better Homes and Gardens Garden Book. Meredith
5. Better Homes and Gardens Handyman's Book. Meredith
6. The Sea Around Us, by *Rachel L. Carson.* Oxford University Press
7. Thorndike-Barnhart Comprehensive Desk Dictionary, ed. by *Clarence L. Barnhart.* Doubleday
8. Pogo, by *Walt Kelly.* Simon & Schuster
9. Kon-Tiki, by *Thor Heyerdahl.* Rand McNally
10. The New Yorker Twenty-Fifth Anniversary Album. Harper

NEARLY seven years after the end of World War II an Army novel with a Pearl Harbor finale topped the fiction sales of the year, and three other novels with war backgrounds were high on the list. In England Winston Churchill resumed his post as Prime Minister, two British diplomats disappeared behind the Iron Curtain, and King George opened the Festival of Britain. Sinclair Lewis and Henri-Philippe Pétain died, the former aged 65; the latter, 95. In the United States, people were stirred by General MacArthur's address to Congress after his recall from the Far East command. Joe DiMaggio retired from baseball, and Ben Hogan won the Open Golf Championship. "The King and I," staring Gertrude Lawrence and Yul Brunner, based upon the 1944 best seller *Anna and the King of Siam,* was one of the great musicals of the New York season. Television was developing into a threat to the motion picture theatres. War novels were a feature of the 1951 fiction best seller list. *From Here to Eternity,* James Jones' first novel, outsold every other fiction title in the bookstores, reaching a total of 240,000. *The Caine Mutiny,* by Herman Wouk, story of the wartime Navy, was not far behind it with a sale of 236,000 copies. In sixth place was another war novel of the sea, *The Cruel Sea,* by Nicholas Monsarrat, which sold approximately 70,000 copies. Seventh, was John P. Marquand's latest best seller, with a war background, *Melville Goodwin, USA.* Religious novels took third, fourth and ninth places: *Moses,* by Sholem Asch; *The Cardinal,* by Henry Morton Robinson, which was the top 1950 seller and which sold 88,709 copies in 1951; and *The Foundling,* by Cardinal Spellman, with sales of 61,000. There were only two historical novels on the list: *A Woman Called Fancy,* by Frank Yerby (75,666), and *The Wanderer,* by Mika Waltari. James A. Michener's postwar *Return to Paradise* sold 65,000 copies. This was Michener's first novel to make the annual list. His *Tales of the South Pacific,* on which the famous musical "South Pacific" was based, was published in 1947. On the nonfiction list the title which was third in 1950 took top place in 1951, Gayelord Hauser's *Look Younger, Live Longer.* Including the sales of the new edition which came out in 1951, but not including sales through health food stores, its total for the year was 286,735. *Betty Crocker's Picture Cook Book,* which was first in 1950, was second in 1951 with sales of 233,500 copies. Third was one of only three books on the nonfiction list that can be called "reading" books to distinguish them from the "subject" and picture books that comprise seven out of the ten. That was *Washington Confidential,* the first of the "Confidential" books by Jack Lait and Lee Mortimer to make an annual list. It sold 227,131 copies. The two other "reading" titles were Rachel L. Carson's *The Sea Around Us,* forerunner of the many ecological volumes that were to occupy serious reader attention for years to come, with a sale of 167,181, and *Kon-Tiki,* by Thor Heyerdahl (fifth in 1950), which sold 140,461 copies in 1951. Continuing the "subject" books, two *Better Homes and Gardens* titles, the *Garden Book* and the *Handyman's Book,* were fourth and fifth, with sales through bookstores of 221,213 and 206,989 copies. The *Thorndike-Barnhart Comprehensive Desk Dictionary* sold 162,623 copies, not including book club or school distribution. Eighth and tenth were the two "picture" books, Walt Kelly's comic strip book for adults, *Pogo,* selling 145,731 copies, and the cartoon collection, *The New Yorker Twenty-Fifth Anniversary Album.* As a rule standard works like dictionaries and cook books were not included on these *Publishers' Weekly* annual best seller lists except in the years when they were originally published as brand new titles. That is why the Thorndike-Barnhart dictionary was included on the 1951 list but other standard works like the *World Almanac,* Lasser's *Your Income Tax,* other leading cook books, dictionaries, reference works, and Bibles were not.

Fiction

1. The Silver Chalice, by *Thomas B. Costain*. Doubleday
2. The Caine Mutiny, by *Herman Wouk,* Doubleday
3. East of Eden, by *John Steinbeck*. Viking Press
4. My Cousin Rachel, by *Daphne du Maurier*. Doubleday
5. Steamboat Gothic, by *Frances Parkinson Keyes*. Messner
6. Giant, by *Edna Ferber*. Doubleday
7. The Old Man and the Sea, by *Ernest Hemingway*. Scribner
8. The Gown of Glory, by *Agnes Sligh Turnbull*. Houghton Mifflin
9. The Saracen Blade, by *Frank Yerby*. Dial Press
10. The Houses in Between, by *Howard Spring*. Harper

Nonfiction

1. The Holy Bible: Revised Standard Version. Nelson
2. A Man Called Peter, by *Catherine Marshall*. McGraw-Hill
3. U.S.A. Confidential, by *Jack Lait and Lee Mortimer*. Crown
4. The Sea Around Us, by *Rachel L. Carson*. Oxford University Press
5. Tallulah, by *Tallulah Bankhead*. Harper
6. The Power of Positive Thinking, by *Norman Vincent Peale*. Prentice-Hall
7. This I Believe, ed. by *Edward P. Morgan;* foreword by *Edward R. Murrow*. Simon & Schuster
8. This Is Ike, ed. by *Wilson Hicks*. Holt
9. Witness, by *Whittaker Chambers*. Random House
10. Mr. President, by *William Hillman*. Farrar, Straus & Young

IN CONTRAST to the best sellers of a few preceding years, those of 1952 showed few new trends, and, in general, their sales totals were lower. The year was notable, however, for the appearance of Ernest Hemingway's short novel *The Old Man and the Sea* which became a classic in the author's lifetime. All the novels on the list were by well-established authors, most of whom had appeared on annual best seller lists many times. In 1951 there were four war novels among the best sellers; in 1952 the only one was a repeat, *The Caine Mutiny*. There were two historical novels as there were the previous year; two with religious themes as compared with 1951's three. Because of a very large December sale *The Silver Chalice* won top place in fiction to the surprise even of its publisher because the second place title, *The Caine Mutiny,* also a Doubleday book and a best seller for 21 months, had been running ahead throughout the year. When their sales were totaled, however, *The Silver Chalice* turned up with a sale of 221,000 copies, *The Caine Mutiny* with 189,000. *East of Eden* sold 140,000; *My Cousin Rachel* 130,000; *Steamboat Gothic* over 120,000; *Giant* 119,000; *The Gown of Glory* 62,500 and *The Saracen Blade* over 55,000. Outstanding on the 1952 nonfiction list was the Bible, Revised Standard Version, with its close to two-million-copy sale. Three other titles of religious interest among the 1952 best sellers again pointed up the continuing popular appeal of religious books. *A Man Called Peter,* the biography of the late Chaplain of the U.S. Senate, written by his wife, which had been on the list for 15 months, was second with sales of 205,000 copies. *The Power of Positive Thinking* was in sixth place with a total of 102,340 sold and *This I Believe* seventh with 98,500. *U.S.A. Confidential,* third, sold 163,961 copies. *The Sea Around Us,* on the list for 17 months and seventh in 1951 with a sale of 167,181, was fourth for 1952, selling 105,795. Four biographies, two of them of political figures, as befitted the election year, made up the rest of the nonfiction list: *Tallulah; This Is Ike,* which sold about 90,000 copies, including both cloth and paperbound editions; *Witness,* selling 80,000 copies; and *Mr. President* totalling 77,246. Sales of nonfiction titles on the best seller list were larger than those of fiction but still they did not equal by any means the sales of the titles on the similar list in 1951. One reason is that "how-to" books, with their very large sales, made up most of 1951's list. For 1952, the cook books which had been out for several years and the cartoon books, which were current popular novelty items, were omitted in order to give a better picture from the literary point of view of what general topics interested the public most. Outside the book field, TV played its part, for the first time in an election campaign, the campaign in which General Eisenhower defeated Adlai Stevenson. The McCarthy campaign continued as did the FBI raids on Communists. Juvenile delinquency was an urgent problem. Pizzas, scrabble, nylon and dacron, and chlorophyll products were all taken up in a big way by the American consumer.

Fiction

1. The Robe, by *Lloyd C. Douglas*. Houghton Mifflin
2. The Silver Chalice, by *Thomas B. Costain*. Doubleday
3. Désirée, by *Annemarie Selinko*. Morrow
4. Battle Cry, by *Leon M. Uris*. Putnam
5. From Here to Eternity, by *James Jones*. Scribner
6. The High and the Mighty, by *Ernest K. Gann*. Sloane
7. Beyond This Place, by *A. J. Cronin*. Little, Brown
8. Time and Time Again, by *James Hilton*. Little, Brown
9. Lord Vanity, by *Samuel Shellabarger*. Little, Brown
10. The Unconquered, by *Ben Ames Williams*. Houghton Mifflin

Nonfiction

1. The Holy Bible: Revised Standard Version. Nelson
2. The Power of Positive Thinking, by *Norman Vincent Peale*. Prentice-Hall
3. Sexual Behavior in the Human Female, by *Alfred C. Kinsey* and others. Saunders
4. Angel Unaware, by *Dale Evans Rogers*. Revell
5. Life Is Worth Living, by *Fulton J. Sheen*. McGraw-Hill
6. A Man Called Peter, by *Catherine Marshall*. McGraw-Hill
7. This I Believe, ed. by *Edward P. Morgan;* foreword by *Edward R. Murrow*. Simon & Schuster
8. The Greatest Faith Ever Known, by *Fulton Oursler* and *G. A. O. Armstrong*. Doubleday
9. How to Play Your Best Golf, by *Tommy Armour*. Simon & Schuster
10. A House Is Not a Home, by *Polly Adler*. Rinehart

THERE WERE record-breaking floods in the low-lying countries of Europe in 1953. Josef Stalin died in Moscow early in the year. King George VI of England had died in 1952; Elizabeth II was crowned in June 1953. General George C. Marshall was awarded the Nobel Peace Prize and Winston Churchill the Nobel Prize in literature. Eugene O'Neill died in

Boston on November 27. An armistice in the Korean War was signed on July 27. Edmund Hillary and Tenzing Norkey conquered the world's highest peak, Mount Everest. The unusual aspect of 1953's fiction best seller list was that the leading novel and two others were popularly-priced editions of older novels, which had been best sellers several years previously in their original editions. Two were re-priced and re-publicized to coincide with new movies based upon them. The biggest fiction sales of 1953 were chalked up by the $1.98 movie edition of *The Robe,* which had been originally published in 1942. It was the top seller of 1943, second in 1944 and in 1945. It is remarkable that, eleven years after its first publication, it topped all fiction with its sale of 180,000. In addition, 8,000 copies of the $3.75 edition were sold. The movie of the same title was the first film to be shown in the then new CinemaScope process. In second place on the fiction list was 1952's best seller, *The Silver Chalice.* After a sale of 221,000 copies in 1952, it sold 135,000 in 1953 including about 89,000 in the $1.98 edition, which was on sale only in the last three months of the year. *Désirée,* leader of sales among novels that were published in 1953, was third with 115,773 copies. It was one of five historical novels, half the list, in comparison with two each in 1952 and in 1951. The author was one of three new to the annual best seller lists. The other two were Leon M. Uris, author of *Battle Cry,* and Ernest K. Gann, author of *The High and the Mighty,* which sold 63,857 copies in the bookstores. *Battle Cry* was the only war novel on the list unless one can so consider the army novel, *From Here to Eternity,* which was fifth with 68,500 copies sold in its $2.69 movie edition. It had been 1951's top-selling novel in its original edition. If outlets other than bookstores had been considered for these annual lists, *From Here to Eternity* would have outdistanced by far any other novel, for 2,000,000 copies of its paperbound 75-cent edition, brought out to coincide with the appearance of the movie, were sold. It was at just about this time that paperback reprints of popular novels became the impressive big sellers. These best seller lists, have, however continued to be confined to hardbound originals. The theme of religion dominated nonfiction best sellers in 1953 as it had in many preceding years, and nonfiction continued, title for title, to outsell fiction in the bookstores. For the second year the *Revised Standard Version* of the Bible outsold all other current titles. It had been averaging 49,700 copies a month in buckram and 41,790 in leather throughout the year. With its big December sale, it went over 1,100,000 for the year. Of the other six books of religious appeal Norman Vincent Peale's *The Power of Positive Thinking* was second with a sale of 340,000 (it had been sixth on the 1952 list); *Angel Unaware* fourth with sales of 257,176; *Life Is Worth Living,* with sales of 142,000, fifth; in sixth place, *A Man Called Peter,* sales in 1953, 130,000; *This I Believe* seventh, as it had been in 1952, its 1953 sales 115,000; and eighth, *The Greatest Faith Ever Known,* selling 96,000. The three remaining non-religious, nonfiction best sellers of the year were *Sexual Behavior in the Human Female,* second of the Kinsey Reports, in third place with sales of 275,000 copies; *How to Play Your Best Golf,* by golf pro Tommy Armour, sales 90,000; and *A House Is Not a Home,* by Polly Adler, a pro of a different kind, in tenth place with 86,000 sold.

1954

Fiction

1. Not As a Stranger, by *Morton Thompson*. Scribner
2. Mary Anne, by *Daphne du Maurier*. Doubleday
3. Love Is Eternal, by *Irving Stone*. Doubleday
4. The Royal Box, by *Frances Parkinson Keyes*. Messner
5. The Egyptian, by *Mika Waltari*. Putnam
6. No Time for Sergeants, by *Mac Hyman*. Random House
7. Sweet Thursday, by *John Steinbeck*. Viking Press
8. The View from Pompey's Head, by *Hamilton Basso*. Doubleday
9. Never Victorious, Never Defeated, by *Taylor Caldwell*. McGraw-Hill
10. Benton's Row, by *Frank Yerby*. Dial Press

Nonfiction

1. The Holy Bible: Revised Standard Version. Nelson
2. The Power of Positive Thinking, by *Norman Vincent Peale*. Prentice-Hall
3. Better Homes and Gardens New Cook Book. Meredith
4. Betty Crocker's Good and Easy Cook Book. Simon & Schuster
5. The Tumult and the Shouting, by *Grantland Rice*. A. S. Barnes
6. I'll Cry Tomorrow, by *Lillian Roth, Gerold Frank* and *Mike Connolly*. Frederick Fell
7. The Prayers of Peter Marshall, ed. by *Catherine Marshall*. McGraw-Hill
8. This I Believe, 2, ed. by *Raymond Swing*. Simon & Schuster
9. But We Were Born Free, by *Elmer Davis*. Bobbs-Merrill
10. The Saturday Evening Post Treasury, ed. by *Roger Butterfield*. Simon & Schuster

As AMERICANS watched the McCarthy hearings on TV, were hopeful about the Salk polio tests, lived through hurricanes Carol to Hazel, and learned to pronounce Dien Bien Phu, they also bought more copies of the Bible in the *Revised Standard Version* than of any other book. In

1954 R.S.V.B. held its top position among best sellers for the third consecutive year. Its sales were smaller than they had been in preceding years, but large enough to outsell any other title, fiction or nonfiction, by almost 200,000. It sold 710,359 copies in 1954, making a three-year total of 3,141,670. The majority of novels among the ten best sellers of the year were by authors whose names have appeared on these lists many times before, authors of well-established popularity. The exceptions were: the top title of the year, *Not As a Stranger,* by Morton Thompson, which pointed up the perennial interest in "medical" stories; *No Time for Sergeants,* the only first novel on the list, its author, Mac Hyman, bringing out delightfully some of the more humorous aspects of life in the U.S. armed forces; and *The View from Pompey's Head.* The author of the last-named title, Hamilton Basso, although a well-known writer, had not previously placed among the top ten. *No Time for Sergeants* sold 66,216 copies plus a 100,000 book club sale; *The View from Pompey's Head* sold 58,000 plus book club copies. Fifth on the fiction list was *The Egyptian.* It had been the top-selling fiction title of 1949, brought back in a $1.98 edition to coincide with the release of the movie based upon it. More than half the fiction list was made up of period novels. Along with *The Egyptian* there were *Mary Anne* with a sale of 127,000; *Love Is Eternal* with an 88,000-copy sale; *The Royal Box,* which sold 83,234; *Never Victorious, Never Defeated,* sales 57,442; and *Benton's Row,* which, in one month, sold 54,724. The one remaining novel, neither historical nor by an author making his first appearance on an annual list, was *Sweet Thursday,* which sold 65,000 copies and which later became a Broadway play. Sales of the nonfiction titles in the top ten places of the year were greater by over 1,600,000 than the sales of the top ten novels, and nonfiction also outsold fiction title by title right down the list. Besides the number one book, the Bible, there were three other best sellers of religious interest in comparison with 1953's six. *The Power of Positive Thinking,* which was second also in 1953 and sixth in 1952, sold 531,336 copies in 1954, making a total of 971,336 for the three years. In seventh place *The Prayers of Peter Marshall* sold 91,000, followed by the second series of *This I Believe* selling 89,867—19,887 in the clothbound edition, 69,980 in the paperbound. Two cook books took third and fourth places among nonfiction, The *Better Homes and Gardens New Cook Book* with a sale of 359,468 copies and *Betty Crocker's Good and Easy Cook Book,* which sold 290,000 copies, both these sales only through the trade, exclusive of sales through magazines and manufacturers. Two autobiographies—that of Grantland Rice, late sports columnist, and of Lillian Roth of the entertainment world, were in fifth and sixth places, both somewhat surprise sellers. *The Tumult and the Shouting* sold 133,498 copies;

I'll Cry Tomorrow, 115,000. *But We Were Born Free,* by Elmer Davis, was the only book on current affairs on the list. *The Saturday Evening Post Treasury,* handsome, illustrated gift book, did especially well at Christmas time, selling 73,159 copies in two months.

Fiction

1. Marjorie Morningstar, by *Herman Wouk*. Doubleday
2. Auntie Mame, by *Patrick Dennis*. Vanguard Press
3. Andersonville, by *MacKinlay Kantor*. World Publishing Co.
4. Bonjour Tristesse, by *Françoise Sagan*. Dutton
5. The Man in the Gray Flannel Suit, by *Sloan Wilson*. Simon & Schuster
6. Something of Value, by *Robert Ruark*. Doubleday
7. Not As a Stranger, by *Morton Thompson*. Scribner
8. No Time for Sergeants, by *Mac Hyman*. Random House
9. The Tontine, by *Thomas B. Costain*. Doubleday
10. Ten North Frederick, by *John O'Hara*. Random House

Nonfiction

1. Gift from the Sea, by *Anne Morrow Lindbergh*. Pantheon Books
2. The Power of Positive Thinking, by *Norman Vincent Peale*. Prentice-Hall
3. The Family of Man, by *Edward Steichen*. Simon & Schuster and Maco Magazine Corp.
4. A Man Called Peter, by *Catherine Marshall*. McGraw-Hill
5. How to Live 365 Days a Year, by *John A. Schindler*. Prentice-Hall
6. Better Homes and Gardens Diet Book. Meredith
7. The Secret of Happiness, by *Billy Graham*. Doubleday
8. Why Johnny Can't Read, by *Rudolf Flesch*. Harper
9. Inside Africa, by *John Gunther*. Harper
10. Year of Decisions, by *Harry S. Truman*. Doubleday

THE PUBLIC's choice of novels during 1955 ranged from some concerned with young love to others about the complex problems of modern life, from one laid in the South during the Civil War, to scenes of strife in Kenya. No trends were particularly discernible, except that there were fewer historical novels than usual on the list, only two. Four of the year's best-selling novels were by new or little-known writers—Patrick Dennis, Françoise Sagan, Sloan Wilson and Mac Hyman. Top novel in sales was *Marjorie Morningstar,* by Herman Wouk, whose *The Caine Mutiny* was second in 1952. *Marjorie Morningstar* sold 191,349 copies during the year. *Auntie Mame* was second with 150,000 copies sold. *Andersonville* was published late in the year but had a total of 121,000 exclusive of book club sales. *Bonjour Tristesse* was by a young French writer, Françoise Sagan, the only author on both fiction and nonfiction lists not an American, and the only woman author on the fiction list. It sold 120,000 copies. *The Man in the Gray Flannel Suit* sold just under 100,000. Total for *Something of Value* was 93,757. *Not As a Stranger* was the top fiction seller of 1954. Sales of the original edition and of the $2.69 edition, timed with the movie based upon it, brought it in its second year to seventh place. *No Time for Sergeants,* also in its second year, and the basis of a Broadway hit, sold 92,000 copies in 1955. Its two-year total plus a book club sale was over a quarter of a million. *The Tontine* was by a writer long familiar to readers of best sellers. It sold 75,298 copies. *Ten North Frederick,* published on Thanksgiving Day, sold 65,900 in just over a month. In reporting the nonfiction best sellers of each year, it had become *Publishers' Weekly's* policy not to include standard works such as dictionaries and cook books, and, in the case of the 1955 list, the Bible, after such volumes had appeared on the lists for one, two, or more years. *The Bible, Revised Standard Version,* had headed the annual list for three years. Its sales of 800,000 copies, more than in 1954, would have made it top for 1955 as well. It seemed to be an established fact up through the mid-twentieth century, that the Bible, in whatever version, was always the best seller. Therefore, in order to mirror more transient contemporary reading taste, it was omitted from this list and *Gift from the Sea* took first place with its sale of 430,000. There were three books of religious interest on the 1955 best-seller list: *The Power of Positive Thinking,* appearing for the fourth consecutive year, sold 378,000; *A Man Called Peter,* with 275,000 sold in its $1.98 movie edition; and *The Secret of Happiness,* by the popular evangelist, which sold 115,697. Third for 1955 was the beautiful book of photographs plus text, by Edward Steichen, *The Family of Man,* which had its big sale, of 364,000 copies, in the paperbound edition. In addition there was a hardbound edition sale of about 15,000. The self-help book, *How to Live 365 Days a Year,* was fifth with a sale of 235,000. The *Better Homes and Gardens Diet Book* sold 130,021 copies in 1955. Winding up the list, in eighth, ninth, and tenth places, were three books of topical importance: *Why Johnny Can't Read, Inside Africa,* and *Year of Decisions* by former President Harry S. Truman. This first volume in President Truman's autobiography sold 74,820 copies. Following the recent trend, the ten top nonfiction titles outsold the ten top fiction by almost two to one. The total sale of the nonfiction through the bookstores amounted to 2,168,701 volumes; that of the fiction, 1,102,761. As 1955 ended the country was still in alarm over President Eisenhower's illness, wondering whether he could again be a candidate for the presidency. The stock market was high, unemployment at a low figure. A new generation had learned all about Davy Crockett. Winston Churchill had retired as British Prime Minister and had been knighted by Queen Elizabeth. Most imminent cloud in the political sky was the threat of a clash in the Near East. On the interplanetary scene came the government's announcement of its project for the launching of manmade satellites.

Fiction

1. Don't Go Near the Water, by *William Brinkley*. Random House
2. The Last Hurrah, by *Edwin O'Connor*. Little, Brown
3. Peyton Place, by *Grace Metalious*. Messner
4. Auntie Mame, by *Patrick Dennis*. Vanguard Press
5. Eloise, by *Kay Thompson*. Simon & Schuster
6. Andersonville, by *MacKinlay Kantor*. World Publishing Co.
7. A Certain Smile, by *Françoise Sagan*. Dutton
8. The Tribe That Lost Its Head, by *Nicholas Monsarrat*. Sloane
9. The Mandarins, by *Simone de Beauvoir*. World Publishing Co.
10. Boon Island, by *Kenneth Roberts*. Doubleday

Nonfiction

1. Arthritis and Common Sense. Revised Edition, by *Dan Dale Alexander*. Witkower Press
2. Webster's New World Dictionary of the American Language. Concise Edition, edited by *David B. Guralnik*. World Publishing Co.
3. Betty Crocker's Picture Cook Book. Revised and Enlarged Second Edition. McGraw-Hill
4. Etiquette, by *Frances Benton*. Random House
5. Better Homes and Gardens Barbecue Book. Meredith
6. The Search for Bridey Murphy, by *Morey Bernstein*. Doubleday
7. Love or Perish, by *Smiley Blanton, M.D.* Simon & Schuster
8. Better Homes and Gardens Decorating Book. Meredith
9. How To Live 365 Days a Year, by *John A. Schindler*. Prentice-Hall
10. The Nun's Story, by *Kathryn Hulme*. Little, Brown

THE SECOND NOVELS by two prominent writers topped fiction: reference, "how-to" and cook books dominated the nonfiction list in this year which saw the re-election of Eisenhower and Nixon. It was the year in which

Grace Kelly married Prince Rainier, in which the Egyptian government seized the Suez Canal, and in which the last veteran of the Civil War Union Army died and the G.A.R. officially went out of existence. There were terrorist activities in Cyprus, disputes between Israel and Jordan, Russia crushed the Hungarian uprising, and the F.B.I. reported more major crimes committed in the U.S. than in any previous year. Elvis Presley was singing "Love Me Tender" and people had given up trying to get seats for "My Fair Lady," Broadway's biggest hit. William Brinkley's *Don't Go Near the Water,* most popular novel of the year, a humorous tale of Navy life on a Pacific isle during World War II, sold 165,000 copies in the bookstores, plus a book club sale, and was bought for movie production for $350,000. Also making a six-figure movie sale was a first novel, *Peyton Place,* which, in the long run, proved to be one of the top-selling American novels of all time, and a perennial television serial, though it reached only third place in fiction in its first year of publication. *Auntie Mame* was in its second year, racking up some 124,000 copies in 1956. It, too, was destined for bigger triumphs—as a starring vehicle for Rosalind Russell, as a movie, as a great paperback seller, and, over ten years later, as a Broadway musical hit. *Eloise,* terror of the Plaza, took her first bow in the book by Kay Thompson, with illustrations by Hilary Knight. It sold 100,000 copies in 1956 as did MacKinlay Kantor's great Civil War novel and Pulitzer Prize winner, *Andersonville*. There were two best sellers by French women novelists on the 1956 list. Françoise Sagan followed her *Bonjour Tristesse* with *A Certain Smile*. Simone de Beauvoir made her first appearance among best sellers with *The Mandarins*.

Leading all nonfiction with a sale of over 255,000 in the year was a book offering help to arthritis sufferers. Issued by a small Connecticut publisher, *Arthritis and Common Sense* leapt into prominence when it was recommended on the Arthur Godfrey program. A new dictionary was second on this list with a sale of 250,000 copies. *Etiquette* by Frances Benton, co-edited by the General Federation of Women's Clubs, sold over 156,000. Cookbooks, home guides, helps to business and personal problems filled up almost all the rest of the list, each with sales of well over 100,000. There were two exceptions. One was *The Search for Bridey Murphy,* a curious book that captured the imagination of the public. It told about a Colorado housewife, who, in many hypnotic trances, convinced a good number of people that she was the reincarnation of an eighteenth century Irishwoman. The other was *The Nun's Story,* a book of literary merit which reached tenth place. Kathryn Hulme's biography of a Belgian nun was later brought magnificently to the screen by Audrey Hepburn.

1957

Fiction

1. By Love Possessed, by *James Gould Cozzens*. Harcourt, Brace
2. Peyton Place, by *Grace Metalious*. Messner
3. Compulsion, by *Meyer Levin*. Simon & Schuster
4. Rally Round the Flag, Boys! by *Max Shulman*. Doubleday
5. Blue Camellia, by *Frances Parkinson Keyes*. Messner
6. Eloise in Paris, by *Kay Thompson*. Simon & Schuster
7. The Scapegoat, by *Daphne du Maurier*. Doubleday
8. On the Beach, by *Nevil Shute*. Morrow
9. Below the Salt, by *Thomas B. Costain,* Doubleday
10. Atlas Shrugged, by *Ayn Rand*. Random House

Nonfiction

1. Kids Say the Darndest Things! by *Art Linkletter*. Prentice-Hall
2. The FBI Story, by *Don Whitehead*. Random House
3. Stay Alive All Your Life, by *Norman Vincent Peale*. Prentice-Hall
4. To Live Again, by *Catherine Marshall*. McGraw-Hill
5. Better Homes and Gardens Flower Arranging. Meredith
6. Where Did You Go? Out. What Did You Do? Nothing, by *Robert Paul Smith*. Norton
7. Baruch: My Own Story, by *Bernard M. Baruch*. Holt
8. Please Don't Eat the Daisies, by *Jean Kerr*. Doubleday
9. The American Heritage Book of Great Historic Places. American Heritage Publishing Co. and Simon & Schuster
10. The Day Christ Died, by *Jim Bishop*. Harper

THE INTERNATIONAL GEOPHYSICAL YEAR of 1957-58 was inaugurated on July 1 with scientists from many nations cooperating in studies of the earth and its environment. In the first half of the year both the USSR and the USA had been setting off series of greater and greater nuclear tests. In June the American Cancer Society and the Public Health Service had issued warnings on the association between cigarette smoking and lung cancer. Through the summer and fall the Little Rock school integration disturbances continued. French and Algerian warfare went on. Russia launched Sputnik I and Sputnik II, which carried a dog. Albert Camus won the Nobel Prize for Literature. Eugene O'Neill's "Long Day's Journey into Night" won both the Pulitzer Prize and that of the Drama Critics' Circle. "West Side Story," with score by Leonard Bernstein was an outstanding Broadway musical. Rock 'n' roll vied with the hit song "Around the World in 80 Days." In books, a serious novel by James Gould Cozzens sold about 100,000 more copies in the stores than did *Peyton Place,* in second place in its second year. *By Love Possessed,* which sold 217,000 copies, analyzed closely the professional and emotional problems of a New England lawyer. James Gould Cozzens' *Guard of Honor* had won the Pulitzer Prize in 1948 but it was not until publication of *By Love Possessed* that the author made the annual best seller list. In fourth and fifth places were authors new to these lists, with two novels which could scarcely be of greater contrast. *Compulsion,* by Meyer Levin, was generally considered to be based upon the theme of the Leopold-Loeb murder case in Chicago many years before. A play based upon the novel was produced in 1957, later a movie. Max Shulman's *Rally Round the Flag, Boys!* which also became a movie, gave a humorous picture of what happened to a Connecticut exurban town when it became the site of a missile base. *Eloise* popped up again, this time in Paris, with another 100,000-copy sale. Nevil Shute, long-established writer, made his first appearance on an annual best seller list with his widely-publicized story of a world devastated by fallout, man's last stand in Australia. *On the Beach* was later produced as a movie.

Books of information and entertainment filled the nonfiction list, though the usually ubiquitous "how-to" books were strangely absent. *Better Homes and Gardens Flower Arranging* was the only housewife's aid on the list, in fifth place, with a sale of 116,000. *Please Don't Eat the Daisies,* by Jean Kerr, eighth, with nearly 107,000 sold, was not a garden book, as its title suggested, but a volume of witty and delightful essays which became the basis of a popular Broadway play. Top of nonfiction for the year was *Kids Say the Darndest Things!,* made of material from Art Linkletter's TV and radio shows, with illustrations by the popular "Peanuts" cartoonist, Charles M. Schulz. *The FBI Story* was second with a sale of 173,000. Dr. Norman Vincent Peale, who had had many books on the best seller lists over the past decade, returned with *Stay Alive All Your Life.* Following on the list was Catherine Marshall's account of personal adjustment after the death of her husband, Peter Marshall, former Chaplain of the Senate, *To Live Again.* In sixth place was a unique book of childhood reminiscences by Robert Paul Smith, the title of which alone could have made it a best seller, *Where Did You Go? Out. What Did You Do? Nothing.*

172

The autobiography of the elder statesman, Bernard M. Baruch, sold over 110,000 copies. Jim Bishop followed his successful *The Day Lincoln Was Shot* with a book on a similar plan, *The Day Christ Died,* a reconstruction of Christ's last twenty-four hours on earth.

Fiction

1. Doctor Zhivago, by *Boris Pasternak*. Pantheon Books
2. Anatomy of a Murder, by *Robert Traver*. St. Martin's Press
3. Lolita, by *Vladimir Nabokov*. Putnam
4. Around the World with Auntie Mame, by *Patrick Dennis*. Harcourt, Brace
5. From the Terrace, by *John O'Hara*. Random House
6. Eloise at Christmastime, by *Kay Thompson*. Random House
7. Ice Palace, by *Edna Ferber*. Doubleday
8. The Winthrop Woman, by *Anya Seton*. Houghton, Mifflin
9. The Enemy Camp, by *Jerome Weidman*. Random House
10. Victorine, by *Frances Parkinson Keyes*. Messner

Nonfiction

1. Kids Say the Darndest Things! by *Art Linkletter*. Prentice-Hall
2. 'Twixt Twelve and Twenty, by *Pat Boone*. Prentice-Hall
3. Only in America, by *Harry Golden*. World Publishing Co.
4. Masters of Deceit, by *Edgar Hoover*. Holt
5. Please Don't Eat the Daisies, by *Jean Kerr*. Doubleday
6. Better Homes and Gardens Salad Book. Meredith Publishing Co.
7. The New Testament in Modern English, translated by *J. P. Phillips*. Macmillan
8. Aku-Aku, by *Thor Heyerdahl*. Rand McNally
9. Dear Abby, by *Abigail Van Buren*. Prentice-Hall
10. Inside Russia Today, by *John Gunther*. Harper

THINGS WERE a bit quieter in the world at large as the USSR halted its nuclear testing and tentative plans for a summit conference were made. But there was trouble nearer home: violent demonstrations against Vice President Nixon marked his visit to Caracas; Castro started his drive against the Batista government; and Governor Faubus closed all the Little Rock high schools as a counter-move to desegregation. In Europe, the Pope died and a new Pope was elected; General deGaulle became

President of the New Fifth Republic of France; and Van Cliburn of Texas won first prize in Moscow in the international Tschaikovsky piano competition. Two leading novels of the year in U.S. bookstores were by authors of Russian origin. Leading the best seller list was *Doctor Zhivago,* which came successfully to the screen some seven years later. In its two months on sale in 1958, the book sold nearly half a million copies, exclusive of book club sale. A story of a Russian doctor-poet's experiences in the harrowing years after the Russian Revolution, it was not published in the USSR, and, because of Soviet pressure, the author refused the Nobel Prize awarded him. The title, *Lolita,* became widely known as a descriptive word in this country, mainly because of the movie, which actually had little resemblance to the novel of more serious intent. *Lolita* reached third place in fiction with a sale of 153,000 copies. In second place in fiction, with a bookstore sale of 166,000 copies was that rarity among annual best sellers, a mystery story. *Anatomy of a Murder* was the story of a murder and a trial in northern Michigan, with authentic court atmosphere provided by its author, Court Justice John D. Voelker, writing under the pen-name of Robert Traver. The following year *Anatomy of a Murder* sold close to three million in its Dell paperback edition. *Lolita* sold more than three million as a Crest paperback. Aside from the top three, the best-selling novels of 1958 were by long-established authors. *From the Terrace,* modern novel by the perennial best-selling author, John O'Hara, sold 96,000 copies in one month of 1958; its later Bantam paperback sale placed it close to two million. Patrick Dennis continued Auntie Mame's fame with a sale of 117,000 copies for *Around the World with Auntie Mame.* Edna Ferber's *Ice Palace* was timed with the approaching statehood of Alaska. Though they had previously published popular books, Anya Seton and Jerome Weidman made their first appearances on an annual list. *The Winthrop Woman* was a historical novel of the Massachusetts Bay Colony. *The Enemy Camp* portrayed the tensions of a Gentile-Jewish marriage.

As usual, during these years of the '50's, few "literary" books became nonfiction best sellers. There was, of course, the fine new modern English translation of the *New Testament* by the English clergyman, J. B. Phillips, which sold 154,000. Harry Golden, editor of the *Carolina Israelite* and television personality, made his first appearance on the list with his book of wise and witty comments on a wide range of subjects, both topical and nostalgic. His *Only in America* sold 165,000 copies. A Pocket Book paperback sale brought it over one and one-quarter million in 1960. *Masters of Deceit* by the head of the FBI described communist activities in this country for a 160,000-copy sale. *Please Don't Eat the Daisies* appeared for a second year with almost a 265,000-copy two-year sale. With its Crest paperback sale, it eventually reached more than two million. *Aku-Aku* was an account of another Thor Heyerdahl expedition, this time exploring the archaeological secrets of Easter Island. *Inside Russia Today* was a new report by John Gunther, whose many "Inside" books were all best sellers. Art Linkletter's *Kids Say the Darndest Things!* was nonfiction leader for the second year, with a 1958 total of 241,000 copies. With its later Pocket Book paperback edition, it went well over three million. In the five weeks of 1958 during which the book by the movie actor, Pat Boone, who had had a phenomenal rise to popularity, was on sale, it reached a total of 187,000. *'Twixt Twelve and Twenty* contained his conservative advice to teen-agers. *Dear Abby* in ninth place, was a collection of lovelorn letters and the answers to them by Abby Van Buren, syndicated column conductor. The cook book of the year was *Better Homes and Gardens Salad Book,* which sold 156,000 copies in bookstores.

Fiction

1. Exodus, by *Leon Uris*. Doubleday
2. Doctor Zhivago, by *Boris Pasternak*. Pantheon Books
3. Hawaii, by *James Michener*. Random House
4. Advise and Consent, by *Allen Drury*. Doubleday
5. Lady Chatterley's Lover, by *D. H. Lawrence*. Grove Press
6. The Ugly American, by *William J. Lederer* and *Eugene L. Burdick*. Norton
7. Dear and Glorious Physician, by *Taylor Caldwell*. Doubleday
8. Lolita, by *Vladimir Nabokov*. Putnam
9. Mrs. 'Arris Goes to Paris, by *Paul Gallico*. Doubleday
10. Poor No More, by *Robert Ruark*. Holt

Nonfiction

1. 'Twixt Twelve and Twenty, by *Pat Boone*. Prentice-Hall
2. Folk Medicine, by *D. C. Jarvis*. Holt
3. For 2¢ Plain, by *Harry Golden*. World Publishing Co.
4. The Status Seekers, by *Vance Packard*. McKay
5. Act One, by *Moss Hart*. Random House
6. Charley Weaver's Letters from Mamma, by *Cliff Arquette*. Winston
7. Elements of Style, by *William Strunk, Jr.* and *E. B. White*. Macmillan
8. The General Foods Kitchens Cookbook. Random House
9. Only in America, by *Harry Golden*. World Publishing Co.
10. Mine Enemy Grows Older, by *Alexander King*. Simon & Schuster

FALLOUT WARNINGS because of atmosphere nuclear testing and advice on building fallout shelters were perhaps of less immediate concern to U.S. citizens than the reports of contamination of their Thanksgiving cranberries. Tension heightened over Berlin. There were anti-white riots in the Congo. Castro consolidated his position in Cuba and took office as premier early in the year. Congress began inquiries about "rigged" TV quiz shows and radio-TV "payola" in the same year that the long-established "Hit Parade" expired. The movie industry, however, showed signs of resuscitation. "The Nun's Story" was one of the year's big movies and "Gigi," with Maurice Chevalier, won the Oscar. On its international tour, Leonard Bernstein's New York Philharmonic gave 18 concerts in the USSR. The USSR Supreme Court announced that foreign writers were not entitled to royalties on their works published in Russia. Pasternak's *Doctor Zhivago* rolled up its sales in the U.S. to well over half a million copies for two years. Another holdover from the 1958 list was Nabokov's *Lolita.* The best-selling novel of 1959 was *Exodus,* story of the making of modern Israel, by Leon Uris, its hardbound total around the 400,000 mark. Later in the year the Bantam paperback edition ran its sales into the millions. *Hawaii,* James Michener's long novel based on the history of the Islands from the time they first emerged from the sea, was published in November. In only two months it made third place on the list with sales close to 200,000 copies. This was the year in which Hawaii became the fiftieth State of the Union. Novels of political implications reached fourth and sixth places. These were Allen Drury's first novel, *Advise and Consent,* laid in Washington, later a Broadway play, and *The Ugly American,* by William J. Lederer and Eugene L. Burdick, which title quickly added a new slogan to our language. Its controversial matter concerned American diplomatic behavior in a small southeastern Asian country. Between these two, in fifth place, appeared the unexpurgated edition of the 1932 novel, *Lady Chatterley's Lover,* long a best seller in previous editions. There were court battles over the right to send D. H. Lawrence's celebrated book through the mails as well as various suits between hardbound and paperback publishers. Sales of the Grove Press edition in 1959 were about 160,000. Books by popular novelists completed the list of the ten best: *Dear and Glorious Physician,* Taylor Caldwell's Biblical novel about Luke; *Mrs. 'Arris Goes to Paris,* in which Paul Gallico's popular heroine made her first appearance; and *Poor No More,* story of a ruthless businessman by Robert Ruark, whose *Something of Value* had been a big seller four years before.

"How-to" books loomed large in 1959's nonfiction, the list headed by actor-singer Pat Boone's advice to teen-agers, *'Twixt Twelve and Twenty,* which had been second on the list the previous year. Its two-year total was 457,388 copies. *Folk Medicine: A Vermont Doctor's Guide to Good Health* was in second place with a 1958-59 sale of 265,816 copies. A distinguished and unique best seller, a compact little book on correct style in English, was *Elements of Style* by the late Cornell professor William Strunk, Jr., in a revised edition by E. B. White. It was seventh on the list with combined trade clothbound and paperback college edition sales of more than 150,000. It was also distributed as a dividend by the

Book-of-the-Month Club. Direct mail sales by General Foods (which were not included in this compilation) made the fourth "how-to" best seller, *The General Foods Kitchens Cookbook,* probably the year's best seller. Sales by the book trade brought it to eighth place. Television, specifically their authors' appearances on the Jack Paar Tonight Show, aided the sales of four nonfiction titles, Harry Golden's two books, *For 2¢ Plain* and *Only in America, Charley Weaver's Letters from Mamma,* and Alexander King's first essay in autobiography, *Mine Enemy Grows Older.* The more interesting "reading" books among best-selling nonfiction of the year appeared in fourth and fifth positions. These were *The Status Seekers,* commentary, both biting and entertaining, on American class symbols, by Vance Packard, and *Act One* by Moss Hart, chronicle of the famous playwright's early experiences in the theatre.

1960

Fiction

1. Advise and Consent, by *Allen Drury*. Doubleday
2. Hawaii, by *James A. Michener*. Random House
3. The Leopard, by *Giuseppe di Lampedusa*. Pantheon Books
4. The Chapman Report, by *Irving Wallace*. Simon & Schuster
5. Ourselves To Know, by *John O'Hara*. Random House
6. The Constant Image, by *Marcia Davenport*. Scribner
7. The Lovely Ambition, by *Mary Ellen Chase*. Norton
8. The Listener, by *Taylor Caldwell*. Doubleday
9. Trustee from the Toolroom, by *Nevil Shute*. Morrow
10. Sermons and Soda-Water, by *John O'Hara*. Random House

Nonfiction

1. Folk Medicine, by *D. C. Jarvis*. Holt, Rinehart & Winston
2. Better Homes and Gardens First Aid for Your Family. Meredith Publishing Co.
3. The General Foods Kitchens Cookbook. Random House
4. May This House Be Safe from Tigers, by *Alexander King*. Simon & Schuster
5. Better Homes and Gardens Dessert Book. Meredith Publishing Co.
6. Better Homes and Gardens Decorating Ideas. Meredith Publishing Co.
7. The Rise and Fall of the Third Reich, by *William L. Shirer*. Simon & Schuster
8. The Conscience of a Conservative, by *Barry Goldwater*. Victor Publishing Co.
9. I Kid You Not, by *Jack Paar*. Little, Brown
10. Between You, Me and the Gatepost, by *Pat Boone*. Prentice-Hall

THIS WAS a troubled year, politically, with unrest around the world—in Algeria, Laos, Venezuela, Japan, the Congo, Cuba, and the Dominican Republic—much of it anti-American in tone. No Nobel Peace Prize was

180

awarded in 1960. On May 1 the U.S. U-2 reconnaissance plane piloted by Francis Gary Powers was brought down in Russia. Khrushchev broke off the summit conference in Paris because of the incident. Israeli agents captured Nazi Adolf Eichmann. In September, with the opening of the General Assembly of the UN and the arrival of both Khrushchev and Castro, New York City turned into what looked like an armed state. Heavy police guards were on 24-hour duty at all the Iron Curtain consulates and armed cavalcades dashed back and forth between the UN and the delegates' domiciles at all hours. The U.S. continued to be entertained by foreign movies: the French "Hiroshima Mon Amour," the British "Our Man in Havana," the Greek "Never on Sunday," and the Cannes Grand Prix winner, the Italian "La Dolce Vita." The juke boxes ground out "Teenie Weenie Bikini." In November John Fitzgerald Kennedy and Lyndon Baines Johnson were elected President and Vice President of the United States. In the publishing world, which found in these events of 1960 an abundance of material for future books, there were many mergers of old-line firms. There was a tremendous increase in original paperback publishing both for the mass market and in the so-called "quality" lines. There were 20 new paperback firms established and many long-established hardbound publishers entered the paperback field. Prices of paperbacks went up. The original 25-cent price for reprints of novels was long past. Sixty cents and 95 cents became more usual prices as longer and better novels and nonfiction became important paperback merchandise, with paperback publishers offering high prices for reprint rights. The two leading novels in bookstore sales in 1960 were holdovers from the 1959 list, both published late in 1959. In third and fourth places were novels by the only authors among the ten who were new to annual best seller lists, Giuseppe di Lampedusa and Irving Wallace. *The Leopard,* story of a noble Sicilian family, was the first and only book by the late Italian nobleman. *The Chapman Report,* which became a popular movie, drew its plot from a statistical survey similar to that upon which the Kinsey Report was based. John O'Hara was the first novelist in 25 years, not since James Hilton in 1935, to place two books on an annual list. In 1959, Harry Golden was the first author to have two books on the nonfiction list in 10 years.

During the 1950's, reversing the order of many years before, the ten nonfiction best sellers outsold the ten fiction best sellers in overall total. In 1959, nonfiction had an edge of about 110,000 copies over fiction, but in 1960 the ten nonfiction titles sold almost twice as many copies as the corresponding fiction. Again "how-to" books predominated, comprising more than half the list. *Folk Medicine* moved up from second place the previous year to first, with an additional sale of 262,000 copies for a two-year total of 486,018. The publisher's imprint on this title was no longer

Henry Holt & Co. Pointing up the many mergers in the book business, was the three-publisher combine of Holt, Rinehart & Winston. Three *Better Homes and Gardens* books for the homemaker were in second, fifth and sixth places, with trade sales respectively of 213,013, 148,183, and 145,-471 copies. Third place was occupied by a repeater from 1959. *The General Foods Kitchens Cookbook* added another 180,000 copies through the trade. Pat Boone's 1960 best seller, *Between You, Me and the Gatepost,* following his 1959 leader, *'Twixt Twelve and Twenty,* reached tenth place. Most impressive of the 1960 nonfiction was *The Rise and Fall of the Third Reich,* by William L. Shirer, whose *Berlin Diary* had helped to make history in 1941. In only two months of publication this weighty historical volume, priced at $10, sold 111,871 copies. In addition, the Book-of-the-Month Club printed 270,000 copies. Senator Barry Goldwater's statement of his political faith, *The Conscience of a Conservative,* reached eighth place with a sale of 97,000. The paperback sale brought it close to the half-million mark. Jack Paar, at the height of his television popularity, gave added publicity to the remaining two books of the first ten—his own autobiography, in ninth place, and more Alexander King autobiography mingled with witty comment, *May This House Be Safe from Tigers,* which sold 148,714 copies for fourth position on the list.

1961

Fiction

1. The Agony and the Ecstasy, by *Irving Stone*. Doubleday
2. Franny and Zooey, by *J. D. Salinger*. Little, Brown
3. To Kill a Mockingbird, by *Harper Lee*. Lippincott
4. Mila 18, by *Leon Uris*. Doubleday
5. The Carpetbaggers, by *Harold Robbins*. Simon & Schuster
6. Tropic of Cancer, by *Henry Miller*. Grove Press
7. Winnie Ille Pu, translated by *Alexander Lenard*. Dutton
8. Daughter of Silence, by *Morris West*. Morrow
9. The Edge of Sadness, by *Edwin O'Connor*. Little, Brown
10. The Winter of Our Discontent, by *John Steinbeck*. Viking Press

Nonfiction

1. The New English Bible: The New Testament. Cambridge University Press and Oxford University Press
2. The Rise and Fall of the Third Reich, by *William Shirer*. Simon & Schuster
3. Better Homes and Gardens Sewing Book. Meredith Publishing Co.
4. Casserole Cook Book. Meredith Publishing Co.
5. A Nation of Sheep, by *William Lederer*. Norton
6. Better Homes and Gardens Nutrition for Your Family. Meredith Publishing Co.
7. The Making of the President, 1960, by *Theodore H. White*. Atheneum Press
8. Calories Don't Count, by *Dr. Herman Taller*. Simon & Schuster
9. Betty Crocker's New Picture Cook Book: New Edition. McGraw-Hill
10. Ring of Bright Water, by *Gavin Maxwell*. Dutton

THE YEAR of the "twist" craze, the beginning of the Civil War Centennial celebration, and of major advances in space exploration—Major Yuri Gagarin of Russia was the first man to orbit the earth and Alan B. Shepard, Jr. was the first U.S. astronaut to rocket off in a space capsule—was also the year of such disasters as the Bay of Pigs invasion, the closing of the border between East and West Germany, and the death of UN Secretary General Dag Hammarskjöld in a plane crash in Northern Rhodesia. The 1961 Nobel Prize was awarded to him posthumously. The Peace Corps for service in underdeveloped foreign countries was established. There was continued international exchange of orchestras. The Metropolitan Museum bought a Rembrandt painting for the highest auction price ever paid. Cellist Pablo Casals played a return engagement at the White House; the last time he had played there had been for President Theodore Roosevelt in 1904. The state of the American theatre was called distressing. Although Broadway productions bogged down, many local repertory companies were springing up throughout the rest of the country. The best-selling novels of the year were definitely high in interest and excellence. The leaders of the year, Irving Stone's great novel of the life of Michelangelo, *The Agony and the Ecstasy,* and J. D. Salinger's second novel, *Franny and Zooey* (his *Catcher in the Rye,* which originally made him famous, did not make an annual list), at the head of 1961's fiction, were challenged by a newcomer, first novelist Harper Lee. Her *To Kill a Mockingbird,* a sensitive and compelling story of a small southern town in the 1930's, published in 1960, won the Pulitzer Prize. Its two-year total was close to 200,000 plus sales by three book clubs. Following his *Exodus* of two years before, Leon Uris wrote a story of the Warsaw ghetto in World War II, *Mila 18,* which was fourth on the list with 134,397 sold. Popular novelist Harold Robbins made his first appearance on an annual list with a novel of modern American life considered a *roman à clef, The Carpetbaggers,* with over 108,000 sold. In sixth and seventh places appeared two dissimilar titles, both, however, originally published over 25 years before. Henry Miller's *Tropic of Cancer,* long an under-the-counter item, and considered the most-banned book of its time, was openly published in the less-strictured 1960's. It sold 100,000 copies in hardcover plus a later paperback sale of two and one-half million. *Winnie Ille Pu,* forerunner of a vogue for publishing well-loved English language books in other languages, was a Latin translation by Alexander Lenard of A. A. Milne's *Winnie the Pooh,* which was first published as a children's book in 1926, but, as often happens to such classics, taken over for adult reading. *Winnie Ille Pu* was the first book in a language other than English to appear on any of these yearly lists. Books by Morris West with his first best seller on an annual list and by the perennially popular John Steinbeck wound up the fiction, along with *The Edge of Sadness,* novel with a priest as protagonist, by Edwin O'Connor. It was the winner of the Pulitzer Prize.

A new translation of the Bible always reaffirms the aphorism that the

Bible is the best seller of all time. *The New Testament* issued jointly by Cambridge University Press and Oxford University Press as part of *The New English Bible* easily led nonfiction in 1961, selling 756,575 copies. In second place, in its second year was *The Rise and Fall of the Third Reich,* selling an additional 203,346 in 1961. Its book club sale brought it close to one million. The $265,000 which Dell Publishing Co. had paid for paperback reprint rights to *Return to Peyton Place* in 1959 was a record purchase. But only two years later Fawcett paid $400,000 for the paperback rights to William Shirer's big book, a lengthy one for paperback. Another paperback sale climax was to come in 1976 with Avon's $1,550,000 purchase of Woodward and Bernstein's *The Final Days.* Among other nonfiction titles for the general reader on the 1961 list were, in fifth place, selling 135,644 copies, *A Nation of Sheep,* by William Lederer, coauthor of *The Ugly American* of two years before. This new book was a critical discussion of U.S. foreign policy and of how news about foreign affairs reaches the public. Another book of political content was Theodore H. White's *The Making of the President, 1960,* the first of his "Making of the President" series, which won a Pulitzer Prize. A refreshing book wound up the list, Gavin Maxwell's *Ring of Bright Water,* an account of the author's home on the Scottish coast and of his nature adventures shared with two pet otters. The sales of the five other best sellers, books on sewing, cooking, and nutrition, added greatly to the big overall nonfiction count of the year.

1962

Fiction

1. Ship of Fools, by *Katherine Anne Porter*. Little, Brown
2. Dearly Beloved, by *Anne Morrow Lindbergh*. Harcourt, Brace & World
3. A Shade of Difference, by *Allen Drury*. Doubleday
4. Youngblood Hawke, by *Herman Wouk*. Doubleday
5. Franny and Zooey, by *J. D. Salinger*. Little, Brown
6. Fail-Safe, by *Eugene Burdick* and *Harvey Wheeler*. McGraw-Hill
7. Seven Days in May, by *Fletcher Knebel* and *Charles W. Bailey II*. Harper & Row
8. The Prize, by *Irving Wallace*. Simon & Schuster
9. The Agony and the Ecstasy, by *Irving Stone*. Doubleday
10. The Reivers, by *William Faulkner*. Random House

Nonfiction

1. Calories Don't Count, by *Dr. Herman Taller*. Simon & Schuster
2. The New English Bible: The New Testament. Cambridge University Press and Oxford University Press
3. Better Homes and Gardens Cook Book: New Edition. Meredith Publishing Co.
4. O Ye Jigs & Juleps! by *Virginia Cary Hudson*. Macmillan
5. Happiness Is a Warm Puppy, by *Charles M. Schulz*. Determined Productions
6. The Joy of Cooking: New Edition by *Irma S. Rombauer* and *Marion Rombauer Becker*. Bobbs-Merrill
7. My Life in Court, by *Louis Nizer*. Doubleday
8. The Rothschilds, by *Frederic Morton*. Atheneum Publishers
9. Sex and the Single Girl, by *Helen Gurley Brown*. Bernard Geis
10. Travels with Charley, by *John Steinbeck*. Viking Press

THERE WERE world-shaking events in the year 1962: the Cuban missile crisis; increased tension over the Berlin air corridor; the continuation of the Algerian violence by the OAS after official proclamation of the country's independence; resumption of atmospheric nuclear tests by both the USSR and the U.S.; and widening of the ideological breach between Russia and China. At home there was conflict over the admission of James H. Meredith to the University of Mississippi. American advances in space included our first manned earth orbit, by Lieutenant-Colonel John H. Glenn, Jr. and our first operation of a communications satellite, Telstar. Among notable plays were "Who's Afraid of Virginia Woolf?" Aside from teenagers' rock 'n' roll, the most popular song of the year was Anthony Newley's "What Kind of Fool Am I?" from his musical show, "Stop the World—I Want to Get Off." The New York Philharmonic, under Leonard Bernstein, opened Philharmonic Hall (later Avery Fisher Hall) in New York's Lincoln Center for the Performing Arts. In Rome, the Vatican Council was opened. In 1962 the number of books published in the United States reached an all-time high, with paperbacks accounting for 31 per cent of the total. The quality of the fiction best sellers of the year was high, with the names of notable writers appearing on the list. Leading was the novel, *Ship of Fools,* upon which Katherine Anne Porter had been working for 20 years. It sold almost 200,000 copies in the bookstores. Old-line publishers with new imprints issued the best sellers in second and seventh places. These were Harcourt, Brace & World and Harper & Row. Second was *Dearly Beloved,* the first novel ever written by Anne Morrow Lindbergh, whose accounts of pioneer air flights with her famous husband had been great best sellers over 20 years before. Just over the 100,000 mark was the record of books in third and fourth positions, *A Shade of Difference,* another political novel by the author of *Advise and Consent,* and *Youngblood Hawke* by Herman Wouk, author of many best sellers. His latest had a book publishing background, its central character resembling Thomas Wolfe. J. D. Salinger's *Franny and Zooey,* second in 1961, was fifth in 1962. Sixth and seventh were two exciting suspense stories, which, because of topical interest, attracted many readers. They were *Fail-Safe* by Eugene Burdick, co-author of *The Ugly American* with Harvey Wheeler, and *Seven Days in May,* about a presidential crisis. This was a novel by authors new to these lists, Washington newsmen Fletcher Knebel and Charles W. Bailey II. Both these novels sold more than a million copies each in their later paperback editions. Irving Wallace's *The Prize,* quite different in subject from his 1960 best seller, *The Chapman Report,* was a story about a Nobel Prize winner. *The Agony and the Ecstasy,* leader of 1961 fiction, was next with a two-year trade sale of 287,525 copies. The last book on the list, *The Reivers,* was a serio-comic novel by William Faulkner, who had been awarded the Nobel Prize for Literature for 1949. William Faulkner died just a month after publication of *The Reivers.* This, his last novel, won the Pulitzer Prize for the year.

There were a few more books of creative writing as distinguished from instructional guides and books of fleeting entertainment than there had been in the past few years in best-selling nonfiction. These were, in general, biographical and autobiographical. Surprise seller of the year was *O Ye Jigs & Juleps!* a diary recording observations, both naïve and perceptive, of life in a minister's household in the early 1900's. It was written by Virginia Cary Hudson when she was a child. Lawyer Louis Nizer's *My Life in Court,* which just missed making the first ten in 1961, came up in seventh place in 1962 with a sale of 143,695 copies and a two-year total of 218,410. Eighth was the biography of the famous international banking family *The Rothschilds* by Frederic Morton. John Steinbeck, novelist, 1962 winner of the Nobel Prize for Literature, was one of the authors who had appeared most frequently on these best seller lists during the previous 25 years. In 1962 he appeared for the first time as the author of a best-selling nonfiction title. *Travels with Charley* was John Steinbeck's delightful account of his camper journey with his dog from coast to coast. The book sold 110,000, exclusive of book club copies. *The New Testament (N.E.B.),* top seller in 1961, was second in 1962, with a 629,466 sale in cloth, paper, and leather bindings. Its two-year sale was 1,386,041. Topping nonfiction sales for the year was the controversial *Calories Don't Count* by Dr. Herman Taller, with a 1961-62 sale of 1,100,000. The first of the books by the popular cartoonist, Charles M. Schulz, to be published by the new firm, Determined Productions, was *Happiness Is a Warm Puppy,* which made a hit with 175,000 Christmas buyers. Few volumes of poetry had appeared on all these best seller lists. It was noteworthy that Robert Frost's *In the Clearing,* with a sale of 92,619, a total that might easily have placed it on the list in other years, just missed the first ten.

1963

Fiction

1. The Shoes of the Fisherman, by *Morris L. West.* Morrow
2. The Group, by *Mary McCarthy.* Harcourt, Brace & World
3. Raise High the Roof Beam, Carpenters, and Seymour—An Introduction, by *J. D. Salinger.* Little, Brown
4. Caravans, by *James A. Michener.* Random House
5. Elizabeth Appleton, by *John O'Hara.* Random House
6. Grandmother and the Priests, by *Taylor Caldwell.* Doubleday
7. City of Night, by *John Rechy.* Grove Press
8. The Glass-Blowers, by *Daphne du Maurier.* Doubleday
9. The Sand Pebbles, by *Richard McKenna.* Harper & Row
10. The Battle of the Villa Fiorita, by *Rumer Godden.* Viking Press

Nonfiction

1. Happiness Is a Warm Puppy, by *Charles M. Schulz.* Determined Productions
2. Security Is a Thumb and a Blanket, by *Charles M. Schulz.* Determined Productions
3. J.F.K.: The Man and the Myth, by *Victor Lasky.* Macmillan
4. Profiles in Courage: Inaugural Edition, by *John F. Kennedy.* Harper & Row
5. O Ye Jigs & Juleps! by *Virginia Cary Hudson.* Macmillan
6. Better Homes and Gardens Bread Cook Book. Meredith Publishing Co.
7. The Pillsbury Family Cookbook. Harper & Row
8. I Owe Russia $1200, by *Bob Hope.* Doubleday
9. Heloise's Housekeeping Hints. Prentice-Hall
10. Better Homes and Gardens Baby Book. Meredith Publishing Co.

POPE JOHN XXIII DIED—his *Pacem in Terris* was his last papal encyclical —and a new Pope elected. Pope Paul VI re-opened Vatican II in September. Sir Winston Churchill was proclaimed an honorary United States citizen. The Profumo case shocked the English-speaking world. Later there occurred the Great Mail Train Robbery near London. The USSR accepted the U.S. proposal for a direct communications link between Washington and Moscow to lessen the risk of accidental war—a catastrophe suggested by the 1962 best seller, *Fail-Safe*. Later in the year the U.K., USSR and U.S. signed a treaty banning nuclear testing in the atmosphere, in space, and under water. Anti-segregation demonstrations were augmented throughout many southern states during the summer, with a massive rally for civil rights in Washington late in August. November 22 was one of the most tragic days in American history, the day upon which President John F. Kennedy was assassinated in Dallas.

A novel based upon a religious theme, the story of a newly-elected Pope, topped all 1963's fiction with its 170,000-copy sale. *The Shoes of the Fisherman,* by Morris West, was the fastest-selling title Morrow had until then on the market. Mary McCarthy, though a writer of note, had never had a really big best seller until *The Group* sold some 130,000 copies and reached second place on the list. This story of the lives of some Vassar girls, revealed ten years after their graduation from college, became the basis of a much-publicized feature movie. J. D. Salinger followed his two-year best seller, *Franny and Zooey,* with more episodes in the life of the Glass family. *Raise High the Roof Beam, Carpenters, and Seymour—An Introduction* sold about 100,000 copies. In fourth, fifth, and sixth places were books by novelists who had built great audiences over the years, James Michener, John O'Hara, and Taylor Caldwell. *Caravans,* Michener's novel of Afghanistan adventure, sold over 90,000 plus its book club sale. O'Hara's *Elizabeth Appleton* was set in his favorite fictional Pennsylvania town. Taylor Caldwell's *Grandmother and the Priests* related episodes of Irish family and religious life. There were two first novelists who achieved best sellerdom in 1963. John Rechy's *City of Night* was a picture of the homosexual world in some of the large American cities. With *The Sand Pebbles,* story of a U.S. Navy gunboat in China in the 1920's, Richard McKenna won the 1963 Harper Prize Novel award. Two of the most popular novelists in this country had new books with sales of some 50,000 copies, just missing the first ten. They were Ian Fleming with *On Her Majesty's Secret Service* and Helen MacInnes with *The Venetian Affair*. Sales of both these books zoomed in their later paperback editions. These years of the '60's marked the height of the Ian Fleming craze, with movie after movie appearing to increase the popularity of James Bond—007. "Dr. No" was one of the most popular pictures of the year, along with such other movies made from books as *The Birds, Lord of the Flies, The Leopard,* which won the top award at the Cannes Film Festival, and *Tom Jones,* Oscar winner of the year.

Outstanding on the nonfiction list was John F. Kennedy's Pulitzer Prize-winning *Profiles in Courage* in the Inaugural Edition, issued early in 1961.

190

In paperback form (not the Inaugural Edition) *Profiles in Courage,* of which Pocket Books had already sold about two million copies since 1957, rose in sales, selling about two and one-quarter million in 1963 alone. The clothbound Inaugural Edition was in fourth place on the list. Just preceding it was a political biography sharply critical of Kennedy, *J.F.K.: The Man and the Myth* by Victor Lasky. *O Ye Jigs & Juleps!* continued its 1962 success. The only other nonfiction title among the first ten not a book of specific instruction or seasonal entertainment was Bob Hope's hilarious travel saga, *I Owe Russia $1200.* It sold 111,585 copies plus book club distribution. The two Charles M. Schulz books of pictures with captions which topped all nonfiction were *Happiness Is a Warm Puppy* and *Security Is a Thumb and a Blanket.* The first was fifth in the previous year. In 1963 it sold 825,054 copies for a million-copy total. The newer title racked up 356,000 copies. The other four books on 1963's list were books of information for homemakers, each selling more than 100,000.

Fiction

1. The Spy Who Came in From the Cold, by *John Le Carré*. Coward-McCann
2. Candy, by *Terry Southern and Mason Hoffenberg*. Putnam
3. Herzog, by *Saul Bellow*. Viking Press
4. Armageddon, by *Leon Uris*. Doubleday
5. The Man, by *Irving Wallace*. Simon & Schuster
6. The Rector of Justin, by *Louis Auchincloss*. Houghton Mifflin
7. The Martyred, by *Richard E. Kim*. Braziller
8. You Only Live Twice, by *Ian Fleming*. New American Library
9. This Rough Magic, by *Mary Stewart*. Morrow
10. Convention, by *Fletcher Knebel* and *Charles W. Bailey, II*. Harper & Row

Nonfiction

1. Four Days, by *American Heritage* and *United Press International*. Simon & Schuster
2. I Need All the Friends I Can Get, by *Charles M. Schulz*. Determined Productions
3. Profiles in Courage: Memorial Edition, by *John F. Kennedy*. Harper & Row
4. In His Own Write, by *John Lennon*. Simon & Schuster
5. Christmas Is Together-Time, by *Charles M. Schulz*. Determined Productions
6. A Day in the Life of President Kennedy, by *Jim Bishop*. Random House
7. The Kennedy Wit, compiled by *Bill Adler*. Citadel Press
8. A Moveable Feast, by *Ernest Hemingway*. Scribner
9. Reminiscences, by *General Douglas MacArthur*. McGraw-Hill
10. The John F. Kennedys, by *Mark Shaw*. Farrar, Straus & Giroux

THE WORLD'S FAIR opened in New York; the official celebration of the 400th anniversary of Shakespeare's birth began at Stratford-on-Avon. For the first time since their establishment in 1917, no Pulitzer Prizes were awarded in fiction, drama, or music. Jean-Paul Sartre, French exponent of existentialism, refused the Nobel Prize for Literature. The Nobel Peace Prize went to the Reverend Martin Luther King, Jr., Negro civil rights leader. In January Pope Paul made a three-day flying visit to the Holy Land. He was the first Pope to travel by air and the first Pope to leave Italy in 150 years. Deaths of notables in 1964 included those of Herbert Clark Hoover at the age of 90, Prime Minister Nehru of India, and General Douglas MacArthur. Nikita S. Khrushchev was removed from all his governmental and Communist Party offices. The war in Vietnam was escalated, there was mounting trouble in Cyprus, Panama, and the Congo, and race riots in eight northern cities of the U.S. In November Lyndon B. Johnson and Hubert S. Humphrey were elected President and Vice President. The movies had their most successful year since television had become their chief competitor. Sean Connery portrayed Agent 007 in a number of films based on the Fleming books. Mary Poppins, popular character of children's books for many years, was a big hit in a Walt Disney film. For the first time movies were shown to passengers on air flights. Discothèques became the most popular nighttime resorts, where people danced the frug, the swim, and the watusi. The Beatles were the top performers in England and in America. There were smash musicals on Broadway—"Hello Dolly!," "Funny Girl," "Fiddler on the Roof," and "Golden Boy." In publishing there were acquisitions, consolidations, mergers galore by publishers with eyes on the tremendous expansion of the school market. Many old-line houses "went public" on the stock exchange.

Never before had a "thriller" headed all fiction titles of a year. *The Spy Who Came in from the Cold,* aided by unusual word-of-mouth praise, sold a whopping 230,000 copies through bookstores. In 1965 *The Spy* sold more than two million in paperback. Not only the leader, but two other suspense stories were best sellers, illustrating the great appeal of espionage and romantic mystery in the 1960's. In eighth and ninth places, Ian Fleming and Mary Stewart made their first appearances on an annual list, that of Ian Fleming unfortunately just after his death. *This Rough Magic,* like other Mary Stewart novels, represented the best type of romantic mystery, with colorful background. There were four other best-selling novels of 1964 by authors making their first appearances on a yearly list, but only one of them by a first novelist. He was Richard E. Kim, a young Korean, whose *The Martyred* sold 70,000 copies. This novel also marked the first appearance of the publishing firm of George Braziller, Inc. on an annual list. New American Library as a hardcover publisher and Citadel Press also made their débuts on the lists. In second place was *Candy* by Terry Southern and Mason Hoffenberg, who wrote the story as a spoof on the rising tide of "dirty" books. It sold 140,000 copies in

1964, almost one and one-half million in paperback in 1965. Third was the novel that had highest critical praise of the year, *Herzog.* Its author, Saul Bellow, was a long-established writer just reaching a very large audience. In similar situation was Louis Auchincloss, author of *The Rector of Justin.* The other three fiction leaders of the year were by authors who had appeared a number of times on these lists. *Armageddon,* by Leon Uris was one of the two war novels—the other, *The Martyred. The Man* by Irving Wallace and *Convention,* by Fletcher Knebel and Charles W. Bailey II, were both concerned with timely political topics.

In contrast to many previous years, the nonfiction list was free of "how-to" books. This was due, in part, to the great number of best sellers related to the late President Kennedy. They comprised half the list of ten, including his own *Profiles in Courage* issued in February in a Memorial Edition. Top of nonfiction, which, overall, outsold the ten fiction titles two to one, was *Four Days,* documentary and pictorial account of the tragic November days of 1963, with a preface by historian Bruce Catton. It was compiled by *American Heritage* magazine and United Press International. Simon and Schuster distributed a half million copies of the deluxe edition through the trade. U.P.I. sold two and one-half million copies. In sixth place, with sales of 139,000 was Jim Bishop's *A Day in the Life of President Kennedy,* a book which the author had completed just a week before the President's death. It was a chronicle of one day in the President's working and home life, from 7 A.M. to midnight. Following was *The Kennedy Wit,* with sales of 103,000, compiled by Bill Adler from comments made by JFK through his entire political life, both in formal speeches and in off-the-cuff repartee. Winding up the list was *The John F. Kennedys,* subtitled "A Family Album," and containing about 150 photographs of the Kennedy family in Georgetown, Cape Cod, Washington, and other places. Of the remaining five nonfiction best sellers, two were Charles M. Schulz picture books. *I Need All the Friends I Can Get* was second, selling 175,000 copies. *Christmas Is Together-Time,* fifth, sold 150,000. In fourth place was the book of poems and stories by Beatle John Lennon. Its 150,000-copy sale was pushed along by the Beatles' visit to the U.S. Two books, very different in background and personality, both autobiographical and both posthumously published, were eighth and ninth on the list. They were *A Moveable Feast* by Ernest Hemingway and *Reminiscences* by General Douglas MacArthur.

1965

Fiction

1. The Source, by *James A. Michener*. Random House
2. Up the Down Staircase, by *Bel Kaufman*. Prentice-Hall
3. Herzog, by *Saul Bellow*. Viking Press
4. The Looking Glass War, by *John Le Carré*. Coward-McCann
5. The Green Berets, by *Robin Moore*. Crown
6. Those Who Love, by *Irving Stone*. Doubleday
7. The Man with the Golden Gun, by *Ian Fleming*. New American Library
8. Hotel, by *Arthur Hailey*. Doubleday
9. The Ambassador, by *Morris West*. Morrow
10. Don't Stop the Carnival, by *Herman Wouk*. Doubleday

Nonfiction

1. How To Be a Jewish Mother, by *Dan Greenburg*. Price/Stern/Sloan
2. A Gift of Prophecy, by *Ruth Montgomery*. Morrow
3. Games People Play, by *Eric Berne, M.D.* Grove Press
4. World Aflame, by *Billy Graham*. Doubleday
5. Happiness Is a Dry Martini, by *Johnny Carson*. Doubleday
6. Markings, by *Dag Hammarskjöld*. Knopf
7. A Thousand Days, by *Arthur Schlesinger, Jr.* Houghton Mifflin
8. My Shadow Ran Fast, by *Bill Sands*. Prentice-Hall
9. Kennedy, by *Theodore C. Sorensen*. Harper & Row
10. The Making of the President, 1964, by *Theodore H. White*. Atheneum

EARLY in 1965, Sir Winston Churchill, dominating world figure for many years, died at the age of 90. President Johnson's first State of the Union message announced his "Great Society" program, continuing the Kennedy "New Frontier" program. President Lyndon Johnson also ordered sustained air bombardment of North Vietnam. Congress passed the Medicare bill and a bill authorizing federal aid to elementary and secondary education. The latter bill was to have a highly stimulating effect upon the book industry. A Soviet astronaut and a U.S. astronaut became the first men to walk in space. Events arousing great public interest were Pope Paul's one-day visit to the UN in New York, with his celebration of mass at the Yankee Stadium, and the power failure that blacked out most of the Northeast States and part of Canada. In entertainment go-go dancers and the discothèque were the vogue. Such older night spots as the Stork Club in New York, the Trocadero in London, and the Peppermint Lounge, home of the twist, passed out of existence. The average price of books, which had been $5.29 in 1957-59, rose to $7.65 in 1965, still less than the price of a Broadway musical ticket. Best-selling novel on the year's list, mostly comprised of books by well-known authors, was James Michener's *The Source.* This long novel about Israel past and present sold well over a quarter of a million. The other established authors among the first ten were Saul Bellow, repeating the success of *Herzog* for the second year (it sold more than a million in paperback in 1965, 145,000 in hardcover); John Le Carré, with his second espionage best seller, *The Looking Glass War*; Irving Stone, long a best-selling writer of historical and biographical novels, whose *Those Who Love* was based upon the lives of Abigail and John Adams; Ian Fleming, making his second appearance on the yearly hardcover list with his last full-length James Bond adventure, *The Man with the Golden Gun*; Morris West, whose *The Ambassador* was a story of a U.S. diplomat in South Vietnam; and Herman Wouk with *Don't Stop the Carnival,* entertaining story of a man who retired from the public relations business to run a hotel on a Caribbean island. There were three novelists who appeared for the first time among a year's best sellers. Surprise hardcover seller of the year, second in sales only to *The Source,* was *Up the Down Staircase,* clever and touching story of a New York schoolteacher's lot. This was Bel Kaufman's first novel, selling 222,519 copies. *The Green Berets,* another best seller with a Vietnamese setting, sold close to 100,000 copies in hardcover. The book came out in paperback in November and became the phenomenon of the year, with 1,200,000 printed in only two months. A second novel about a big hotel was by Arthur Hailey, also new to the list. His *Hotel* was in tenth place, selling 93,000 copies.

Emphasis in the nonfiction best ten was on little books of humor, books of information, and on special subjects, though there was not the preponderance of "non-books" that there had often been. Leader was *How To Be a Jewish Mother,* an entertaining little book on the complex art of momism by Dan Greenburg, issued by the new firm of Price/Stern/Sloan, with pictures by Gerry Gersten. It sold 270,000 copies. Another bestselling "entertainment" was the Tonight Show MC Johnny Carson's *Happiness Is a Dry Martini.* Typical Carson one-liners were illustrated by

Whitney Darrow, Jr., and sold 172,000, reaching fifth place on the list. Books on unusual topics were in second and third places in nonfiction. Ruth Montgomery's *A Gift of Prophecy,* an account of "the phenomenal Jeane Dixon" and her predictions of future events sold 210,000. In *Games People Play: The Psychology of Human Relationships,* Eric Berne, M.D. explained his theories about the roles people assume, usually to conceal the real facts about themselves from others. His book sold 205,000 copies. One of the few religious best sellers of the past few years reached fourth place with a sale of 198,000. This was evangelist Billy Graham's *World Aflame. Markings* by the late Secretary General of the UN, Dag Hammarskjöld, could be called his spiritual autobiography, containing his poems, thoughts, and short essays arranged chronologically. Published late in 1964, this volume had an impressive two-year total of 270,647. Adding to the five best sellers of 1964 about President Kennedy were two more in 1965. *A Thousand Days* by Arthur Schlesinger, Jr. sold 140,000 copies through bookstores and won the Pulitzer Prize for biography. *Kennedy* by Theodore C. Sorensen was a record of the late President's public life by a close associate, his Special Counsel. Tenth was *The Making of the President, 1964,* second best seller in Theodore H. White's narratives of presidential elections. *My Shadow Ran Fast* was an autobiographical account, by Bill Sands, of his prison experiences as a young man in San Quentin and of his later work organizing rehabilitation programs for convicts and ex-convicts.

Fiction

1. Valley of the Dolls, by *Jacqueline Susann*. Bernard Geis
2. The Adventurers, by *Harold Robbins*. Trident Press
3. The Secret of Santa Vittoria, by *Robert Crichton*. Simon & Schuster
4. Capable of Honor, by *Allen Drury*. Doubleday
5. The Double Image, by *Helen MacInnes*. Harcourt, Brace & World
6. The Fixer, by *Bernard Malamud*. Farrar, Straus & Giroux
7. Tell No Man, by *Adela Rogers St. Johns*. Doubleday
8. Tai-Pan, by *James Clavell*. Atheneum Publishers
9. The Embezzler, by *Louis Auchincloss*. Houghton Mifflin
10. All in the Family, by *Edwin O'Connor*. Atlantic-Little, Brown

Nonfiction

1. How to Avoid Probate, by *Norman F. Dacey*. Crown
2. Human Sexual Response, by *William Howard Masters* and *Virginia E. Johnston*. Little, Brown
3. In Cold Blood, by *Truman Capote*. Random House
4. Games People Play, by *Eric Berne, M.D.* Grove Press
5. A Thousand Days, by *Arthur M. Schlesinger, Jr.* Houghton Mifflin
6. Everything But Money, by *Sam Levenson*. Simon & Schuster
7. The Random House Dictionary of the English Language. Random House
8. Rush to Judgment, by *Mark Lane*. Holt, Rinehart & Winston
9. The Last Battle, by *Cornelius Ryan*. Simon & Schuster
10. Phyllis Diller's Housekeeping Hints, by *Phyllis Diller*. Doubleday

BEST-SELLING books of 1966 were chiefly concerned with history, with sex and psychology, and with entertainment. Some of the outstanding world events of the year were to be reflected in the lists of later years: France's withdrawal from NATO; the activation of Medicare in the U. S.;

the escalation of the war in Vietnam; the first television pictures from the moon by Surveyor I; U. S. astronauts' first docking operation and walk in space. The former German Chancellor Konrad Adenauer visited Israel. Some U. S. H-bombs were accidentally dropped on and recovered from Spanish soil and sea. The New Metropolitan Opera House offered a new American opera for its gala opening at Lincoln Center. Most popular records of the year were "Winchester Cathedral" and the album of Jeanette MacDonald and Nelson Eddy favorites. "Man of La Mancha," based upon *Don Quixote,* offered strong rivalry to the Broadway musical hits "Mame" and "Hello Dolly." Publication of the Catholic edition of the Bible in the *Revised Standard Version* was considered a milestone in the mid-century ecumenical movement. A new dictionary, *The Random House Dictionary of the English Language,* sold out its first printing of 150,000 copies in the two months before Christmas.

Leading all sales of the year was an unusual volume, offering advice on making wills and avoiding estate litigation, *How To Avoid Probate* by Norman F. Dacey. It sold 575,000 copies. Like the *Kinsey Reports* of nearly twenty years before, a book planned as a scholarly medical work became a leading best seller. This was *Human Sexual Response* by William Howard Masters and Virginia E. Johnston. Third in nonfiction was the "nonfiction novel" by Truman Capote, *In Cold Blood,* report of a particularly brutal and senseless murder of the members of a Kansas farm family. Fourth and fifth were repeaters from 1965, *Games People Play,* with a two-year total of 465,000 copies, and *A Thousand Days,* which won the Pulitzer Prize in 1966. A second book relating to the late President Kennedy was eighth on the list. Mark Lane's *Rush to Judgment* was the best seller among a number of 1966 books questioning the validity of the *Report of the Warren Commission.*

As usual, the ten leading nonfiction titles of the year outsold the ten leading novels two to one. The first ten in nonfiction sold over 100,000 copies each; only the three top novels sold in that quantity in the bookstores. Two of these were first novels. Heading the list was *Valley of the Dolls* with a sale of 275,808 copies. Jacqueline Susann's novel described the aspirations of three girls in the entertainment world, telling what the use of barbiturates, pep pills, and alcohol did to those aspirations. In third place was Robert Crichton's *The Secret of Santa Vittoria.* This entertaining story of a little Italian village in 1943 sold 116,704 copies in four months. Between the two first novels, in second place, came Harold Robbins' sexiest novel to date, *The Adventurers.* It sold 187,000 copies during the year, was scheduled for movie production and the largest printing before paperback publication that Pocket Books had ever undertaken, 1,625,000 copies. Two novels of the American political scene, *Capable of Honor* and *All in the Family,* a spy story *The Double*

Image, a novel with a religious theme *Tell No Man,* and *The Embezzler* a contemporary novel of manners, all by established authors, appeared on the 1966 list. An author new to best sellers was James Clavell. His *Tai-Pan* was a long historical novel about Hong Kong. Best reviewed best seller of the year was *The Fixer* by Bernard Malamud. This story of a "fixer" or handyman in Czarist Russia, who was victim of a wave of anti-Semitism, became the winner of both the National Book Award and the Pulitzer Prize.

1967

Fiction

1. The Arrangement, by *Elia Kazan*. Stein & Day
2-3. The Confessions of Nat Turner, by *William Styron*. Random House
2-3. The Chosen, by *Chaim Potok*. Simon & Schuster
4. Topaz, by *Leon Uris*. McGraw-Hill
5. Christy, by *Catherine Marshall*. McGraw-Hill
6. The Eighth Day, by *Thornton Wilder*. Harper & Row
7. Rosemary's Baby, by *Ira Levin*. Random House
8. The Plot, by *Irving Wallace*. Simon & Schuster
9. The Gabriel Hounds, by *Mary Stewart*. Morrow
10. The Exhibitionist, by *Henry Sutton*. Bernard Geis

Nonfiction

1. Death of a President, by *William Manchester*. Harper & Row
2. Misery Is a Blind Date, by *Johnny Carson*. Doubleday
3. Games People Play, by *Eric Berne, M.D.* Grove Press
4. Stanyan Street & Other Sorrows, by *Rod McKuen*. Random House
5. A Modern Priest Looks at His Outdated Church, by *Father James Kavanaugh*. Trident Press
6. Everything but Money, by *Sam Levenson*. Simon & Schuster
7. Our Crowd, by *Stephen Birmingham*. Harper & Row
8-9-10. Edgar Cayce—The Sleeping Prophet, by *Jess Stearn*. Doubleday
8-9-10. Better Homes and Gardens Favorite Ways with Chicken. Meredith Press
8-9-10. Phyllis Diller's Marriage Manual, by *Phyllis Diller*. Doubleday

THOUGH THE United States was pouring more men and materiel into Vietnam and student revolt was building up on college campuses throughout the nation, from Columbia to Berkeley, these tones of the country were not reflected in the best sellers of the year. Instead, the top best seller of all harkened back to the death of John F. Kennedy in 1963. With much advance publicity and controversy *Death of a President* by William Manchester exceeded all other new nonfiction and fiction sold in American bookstores, by more than 500,000. It was followed by a second opus by Johnny Carson, emcee of the "Tonight Show," *Misery Is a Blind Date.* Its sales were 179,000. Another "Tonight Show" frequent performer, Phyllis Diller, tied for 8-9-10 on the list with a sale of 125,000 for her *Marriage Manual.* Popular poetry made the list for the first time in many years. Rod McKuen's books were to appear frequently during following years, but his *Stanyan Street & Other Sorrows,* described by the author as "love words . . . for music," marked his first appearance on an annual list, its sales in 1967, 137,542 copies.

Nonfiction was notable for the absence of "how-to" books; there was only one, tied for 8-9-10th place. There were some interesting newcomers: *A Modern Priest Looks at His Outdated Church* by Father James Kavanaugh; *Our Crowd* by Stephen Birmingham, novelist turning to nonfiction with an account of the Jewish wealthy aristocracy, particularly in New York City; and *Edgar Cayce—The Sleeping Prophet* by Jess Stearn.

In fiction, the leader was a first novel, *The Arrangement.* This story of a Beverly Hills personality was by a writer and director well known in the film and theater worlds. Elia Kazan's book sold about 212,500 copies in the stores and an additional large number through the Literary Guild and the Dollar Book Club. Still another first novel tied for second place, its sales 110,000 copies: Chaim Potok was critically acclaimed for *The Chosen.* The story, set in Brooklyn's Williamsburg section, tells about a boy rebelling against the Orthodox ways of life of his Hasidic rabbi father. Tying with *The Chosen,* in second place, was the story of a leader of a slave insurrection in Virginia in 1831. *The Confessions of Nat Turner* by William Styron had additional sales through Book-of-the-Month Club distribution. The rest of the fiction best sellers were by well-known authors. *The Eighth Day,* set in the early years of this century, was Thornton Wilder's first published novel in almost 20 years. There was an unusual number of best-selling suspense and/or politico-suspense novels on 1967's list: *Topaz* by Leon Uris; *Rosemary's Baby* by Ira Levin, much talked about both as a book and film in succeeding years; *The Plot* by Irving Wallace; and *The Gabriel Hounds* by Mary Stewart.

1968

Fiction

1. Airport, by *Arthur Hailey*. Doubleday
2. Couples, by *John Updike*. Knopf
3. The Salzburg Connection, by *Helen MacInnes*. Harcourt, Brace & World
4. A Small Town in Germany, by *John Le Carré*. Coward-McCann
5. Testimony of Two Men, by *Taylor Caldwell*. Doubleday
6. Preserve and Protect, by *Allen Drury*. Doubleday
7. Myra Breckinridge, by *Gore Vidal*. Little, Brown
8. Vanished, by *Fletcher Knebel*. Doubleday
9. Christy, by *Catherine Marshall*. McGraw-Hill
10. The Tower of Babel, by *Morris L. West*. Morrow

Nonfiction

1. Better Homes and Gardens New Cook Book. Meredith Press
2. The Random House Dictionary of the English Language: College Edition. Editor-in-chief *Laurence Urdang*. Random House
3. Listen to the Warm, by *Rod McKuen*. Random House
4. Between Parent and Child, by *Haim G. Ginott*. Macmillan
5. Lonesome Cities, by *Rod McKuen*. Random House
6. The Doctor's Quick Weight Loss Diet, by *Erwin M. Stillman* and *Samm Sinclair Baker*. Prentice-Hall
7. The Money Game, by *Adam Smith*. Random House
8. Stanyan Street & Other Sorrows, by *Rod McKuen*. Random House
9. The Weight Watcher's Cook Book, by *Jean Nidetch*. Hearthside Press
10. Better Homes and Gardens Eat and Stay Slim. Meredith Press

NIXON WON a Republican victory by a slight majority in the presidential race over a nonrunning Lyndon Johnson and a running Hubert Humphrey. Few national or international events were mirrored in 1968's best sellers—more were to come in the '70's. There were two exceptions. *The Tower of Babel* was a novel of Middle East tensions just before Israel's Six-Day War. *The Money Game* was an entertaining commentary on the stock market and its traders, still good reading in the bullish-bearish fluctuating economies of the '70's. George Goodman used the pseudonym Adam Smith as author of *The Money Game,* which attained a sale of 239,187 in 1968.

The suspense trend of 1967 continued through 1968. It was suspense in various forms from the excitement of a floundering plane in *Airport* to the espionage of *The Salzburg Connection* and *A Small Town in Germany* and the political tensions of *Preserve and Protect, Vanished,* and *The Tower of Babel. Airport* by Arthur Hailey was easily the fiction leader with a sale of 250,000. Second, with a sale of 180,858 plus a big book club distribution was *Couples,* the most critically approved novel on the list. John Updike its author, was one of two novelists who had not made previous appearances on annual lists; the other was Gore Vidal, author of *Myra Breckinridge.* Both Updike and Vidal also happened to write the "sexy" novels of the year.

Four of the best-selling novels of 1968 were published by Doubleday. In addition, five of the ten best sellers in nonfiction were published by Random House. Four of the Random House titles were the only four for "reading" as distinguished from books of reference, advice, and "how-to" books. Three out of these four books were by Rod McKuen, breaking other records—for poetry, and for the first time one author has had three titles on one annual list. McKuen's *Listen to the Warm* sold 310,157; *Lonesome Cities,* 267,063; and *Stanyan Street & Other Sorrows,* holdover from 1967, sold an additional 229,985 in 1968.

Nonfiction leader was the new edition of *Better Homes and Gardens New Cook Book,* which, according to its publisher, sold regularly a million copies a year through all outlets. The new edition sold 433,000 in bookstores during the last four months of 1968. Second was the new College Edition of the *Random House Dictionary* with its four months' sale of 395,471. Dr. Ginott's *Between Parent and Child,* which just missed the 1967 list added 300,000 more copies to its total in 1968, bringing it to fourth place. The other titles in nonfiction are all "slimness": *The Doctor's Quick Weight Loss Diet* by Erwin M. Stillman and Samm Sinclair Baker, 263,247 copies; *The Weight Watcher's Cook Book* by Jean Nidetch, 216,-567 copies; and *Better Homes and Gardens Eat and Stay Slim,* 190,000 copies.

1969

Fiction

1. Portnoy's Complaint, by *Philip Roth.* Random House
2. The Godfather, by *Mario Puzo.* Putnam
3. The Love Machine, by *Jacqueline Susann.* Simon & Schuster
4. The Inheritors, by *Harold Robbins.* Trident Press
5. The Andromeda Strain, by *Michael Crichton.* Knopf
6. The Seven Minutes, by *Irving Wallace.* Simon & Schuster
7. Naked Came the Stranger, by *Penelope Ashe.* Lyle Stuart
8. The Promise, by *Chaim Potok.* Knopf
9. The Pretenders, by *Gwen Davis.* World Publishing Co.
10. The House on the Strand, by *Daphne du Maurier.* Doubleday

Nonfiction

1. American Heritage Dictionary of the English Language. Editor-in-chief *William Morris.* Houghton Mifflin
2. In Someone's Shadow, by *Rod McKuen.* Random House
3. The Peter Principle, by *Laurence J. Peter* and *Raymond Hull.* Morrow
4. Between Parent and Teenager, by *Dr. Haim G. Ginott.* Macmillan
5. The Graham Kerr Cookbook, by the *Galloping Gourmet.* Doubleday
6. The Selling of the President 1968, by *Joe McGinniss.* Trident Press
7. Miss Craig's 21-Day Shape-Up Program for Men and Women, by *Marjorie Craig.* Random House
8. My Life and Prophecies, by *Jeane Dixon* with *René Noorbergen.* Morrow
9. Linda Goodman's Sun Signs, by *Linda Goodman.* Taplinger
10. Twelve Years of Christmas, by *Rod McKuen.* Random House

BEFORE NIXON'S INAUGURATION in January of 1969, there were half a million Americans serving in Vietnam, their peak strength. Richard Nixon had promised to bring them back and so began the period of his greatest popularity, heightened by the Kissinger-Nixon foreign-policy maneuvers, and the trips to Peking and Moscow. Joe McGinniss' *The Selling of the President 1968*, mildly critical of the campaign, was a nonfiction best seller, only reaching sixth place with 146,000 buyers. Almost entirely reversing its 20-year trend, the ten best-selling nonfiction outsold the fiction by less than 100,000, by a little more than two percent instead of the 100%. Half the nonfiction best sellers, nevertheless, were in the categories of "how-to" and reference. The overall best seller of 1969 was a book of reference, but it received perhaps more concerned critical attention than any other book of the year. This was the *American Heritage Dictionary of the English Language* which sold 440,000 copies during its 3½ months' selling period in 1969.

Again came Rod McKuen with two new books of poems. In second place was *In Someone's Shadow,* published in October, selling 235,000 and *Twelve Years of Christmas,* published at the end of November and selling 108,000 in just about one month. Interest in big business, in astrology, and in the occult was marked by the witty *The Peter Principle* by Laurence J. Peter and Raymond Hull; by *Linda Goodman's Sun Signs;* and by *My Life and Prophecies* by Jeane Dixon. *The Peter Principle,* third among nonfiction, sold 220,000. Dr. Ginott followed up his best-selling *Between Parent and Child* with *Between Parent and Teenager.* A cookbook by a television personality and a "shape-up" for physical fitness filled out the nonfiction.

Though fiction sales figures were high in 1969, the list was not notable for literary quality, but rather for eroticism; five of the novels, most of them deplored by the critics, were *The Love Machine* by Jacqueline Susann with its 293,000-copy sale; *The Inheritors* by Harold Robbins; *The Seven Minutes* by Irving Wallace; *Naked Came the Stranger* by Penelope Ashe, collective pseudonym of some journalists who set out to write a parody of the sex-in-suburbia story, but who were taken seriously by 98,000 book buyers; and *The Pretenders* by Gwen Davis. The biggest sales of the year in fiction, however, were rolled up by the much-disputed *Portnoy's Complaint,* in which Philip Roth described the plights of a Jewish mama-dominated boy. The novel's sale in 1969 was 418,000; its sales since 1969, in paperback, have surpassed those of many later best-selling paperbacks. The famous *The Godfather* by Mario Puzo, was second with 350,000 copies sold in hardcover at that time. Surprise best seller was Michael Crichton's *The Andromeda Strain,* based on the topic of retrieval of material from outer space. The astronaut moon shots, coinciding with the sales span of this title, undoubtedly focused public attention to aid in its 100,000 copy sale.

1970

Fiction

1. Love Story, by *Erich Segal.* Harper & Row
2. The French Lieutenant's Woman, by *John Fowles.* Little, Brown
3. Islands in the Stream, by *Ernest Hemingway.* Scribner
4. The Crystal Cave, by *Mary Stewart.* Morrow
5. Great Lion of God, by *Taylor Caldwell.* Doubleday
6. QB VII, by *Leon Uris.* Doubleday
7. The Gang that Couldn't Shoot Straight, by *Jimmy Breslin.* Viking Press
8. The Secret Woman, by *Victoria Holt.* Doubleday
9. Travels with My Aunt, by *Graham Greene.* Viking Press
10. Rich Man, Poor Man, by *Irwin Shaw.* Delacorte Press

Nonfiction

1. Everything You Wanted to Know about Sex but Were Afraid to Ask, by *David Reuben, M.D.* McKay
2. The New English Bible. *Oxford University Press* and *Cambridge University Press*
3. The Sensuous Woman, by *"J."* Lyle Stuart
4. Better Homes and Gardens Fondue and Tabletop Cooking. Meredith
5. Up the Organization, by *Robert Townsend.* Knopf
6. Ball Four, by *Jim Bouton.* World Publishing Co.
7. American Heritage Dictionary of the English Language. Editor-in-chief *William Morris.* Houghton Mifflin
8. Body Language, by *Julius Fast.* M. Evans
9. In Someone's Shadow, by *Rod McKuen.* Random House
10. Caught in the Quiet, by *Rod McKuen.* Random House

TEARS ROLLED DOWN the cheeks of more than 400,000 devoted readers from coast to coast as Erich Segal's *Love Story* filled bookstore windows early in 1970. Before the year was out the movie based on the novel appeared and a banner with the slogan "All New York Loves Love Story" stretched right across Times Square opposite the theater where it was playing. Nevertheless the book had its critics. When in an NBC year-end roundup the popularity of the book was remarked upon as an example of public reaction against pornography, one of the commentators called it "warm treacle." In general, it was true that 1970's fiction best sellers seemed a return to the traditional type of romance represented by big-name authors. Following *Love Story* on the list was John Fowles' first big hit, *The French Lieutenant's Woman,* a great romance of Victorian England. There were three more of 1970's leaders with historical settings: *The Crystal Cave* in which Mary Stewart told a fascinating story of Arthurian England based on the life of Merlin; Taylor Caldwell's historical-religious novel about St. Luke, *Great Lion of God;* and *The Secret Woman* marking Victoria Holt's first appearance on an annual list, though she had long been popular as a writer of Gothics.

Third in fiction was Ernest Hemingway's posthumous novel *Islands in the Stream* set in Bimini, Cuba, and "at sea," and selling 120,000. Jimmy Breslin's first novel *The Gang that Couldn't Shoot Straight,* about the comic misadventures of a Brooklyn Mafia family, piled up 97,000 copies in only about the last month of 1970. The long family saga by Irwin Shaw, *Rich Man, Poor Man* lived up to its slogan "something for everyone" with its tremendous popularity as a television four-part feature serial in 1976.

Sex-related books moved into the nonfiction best seller field in contra-distinction to their domination of fiction in the previous year. *Everything You Wanted to Know about Sex but Were Afraid to Ask* by David Reuben, M.D., swamped all other titles with a hardcover sale of 906,484, passing the million mark with book club and mail order sales. *The Sensuous Woman* by "J." sold 610,000 copies. *Body Language* by Julius Fast reached eighth place with a sale of 217,000.

Second in nonfiction, following Dr. Reuben, was *The New English Bible,* the new translation published jointly by Oxford University Press and Cambridge University Press. It sold 730,520 copies. The recurring themes of business and sports throughout the '70's were represented by *Up the Organization,* in which Robert Townsend entertainingly made some unorthodox suggestions about big business, and by an equally un-orthodox presentation of baseball by Jim Bouton in *Ball Four.* The *American Heritage Dictionary* sold 225,000 more copies in 1970. A cookbook and two more books of poetry by the ubiquitous Rod McKuen filled out the 1970 list.

1971

Fiction

1. Wheels, by *Arthur Hailey.* Doubleday
2. The Exorcist, by *William P. Blatty.* Harper & Row
3. The Passions of the Mind, by *Irving Stone.* Doubleday
4. The Day of the Jackal, by *Frederick Forsyth.* Viking Press
5. The Betsy, by *Harold Robbins.* Trident Press
6. Message from Malaga, by *Helen MacInnes.* Harcourt Brace Jovanovich
7. The Winds of War, by *Herman Wouk.* Little, Brown
8. The Drifters, by *James A. Michener.* Random House
9. The Other, by *Thomas Tryon.* Knopf
10. Rabbit Redux, by *John Updike.* Knopf

Nonfiction

1. The Sensuous Man, by *"M."* Lyle Stuart
2. Bury My Heart at Wounded Knee, by *Dee Brown.* Holt, Rinehart & Winston
3. Better Homes and Gardens Blender Cook Book. Meredith
4. I'm O.K., You're O.K., by *Thomas Harris.* Harper & Row
5. Any Woman Can! by *David Reuben, M.D.,* McKay
6. Inside the Third Reich, by *Albert Speer.* Macmillan
7. Eleanor and Franklin, by *Joseph P. Lash.* Norton
8. Wunnerful, Wunnerful! by *Lawrence Welk.* Prentice-Hall
9. Honor Thy Father, by *Gay Talese.* World
10. Fields of Wonder, by *Rod McKuen.* Random House

FOUR OF 1971's fiction leaders featured suspense in one way or another, three of them by writers new to the annual lists—William P. Blatty, Thomas Tryon, and Frederick Forsyth. Blatty's *The Exorcist,* gripping tale of demoniac possession, is well known to readers and film goers. *The Other,* work of the movie actor Thomas Tryon, was the story of a strange personality. First novelist Frederick Forsyth's *The Day of the Jackal* was also acclaimed as a movie and a television presentation. The fourth in this group was *Message from Malaga,* espionage story with a Spanish setting by Helen MacInnes.

Along with Helen MacInnes the other six best fiction sellers of 1971 represented the traditional best seller themes, titles selected by bookstore customers able to afford the high hardcover prices. Leader of fiction was *Wheels* by Arthur Hailey, which sold 238,766 copies. It was a novel based upon the automobile business in Detroit as was Harold Robbins' *The Betsy.* Irving Stone lengthened his shelf of biographical novels with one based upon the life of Sigmund Freud, *The Passions of the Mind.* Novels by Herman Wouk, James A. Michener, and John Updike, completed the list of first ten.

Though *The Sensuous Man* by "M." was the top-selling nonfiction hardcover title in 1971, its sales of 380,500 were just over half those of its counterpart *The Sensuous Woman* of the previous year. Again, in the case of sex, Dr. Reuben's reappearance with a new title *Any Woman Can!* was marked by a distinct falling off of total sales in comparison with his *Everything You Wanted to Know about Sex but Were Afraid to Ask* in 1970, only 170,729 copies versus the 1970's nearly a million.

Bury My Heart at Wounded Knee in which Dee Brown retold the history of the West from the viewpoint of the American Indian was second in 1971's nonfiction, selling 266,000 copies. It was a good example of the best kind of advertising, that is, word-of-mouth rather than newspaper advertising. Its sales started in the western states, then moved eastward as did those of another word-of-mouth best seller Thomas Harris' *I'm O.K., You're O.K.,* originally published with little fanfare in 1969 and not until 1971 piling up enough sales to reach the best seller lists. In 1971 it sold 210,038 copies. Still another Middle America favorite was television orchestra leader Lawrence Welk's autobiography, *Wunnerful, Wunnerful!* It was flanked by two biographies: *Eleanor and Franklin* by Joseph P. Lash, later the basis of a television special; and *Honor Thy Father,* Gay Talese's account of a Mafia family.

A notable historical work *Inside the Third Reich,* by Albert Speer, just missed making the first ten nonfiction list in 1970 with a sale of 160,000— in 1971 it sold 163,000 more copies to place sixth on that year's list.

Another Better Homes and Gardens cookbook was in third place on 1971's list and, winding it up, the usual Rod McKuen new book of verse.

Fiction

1. Jonathan Livingston Seagull, by *Richard Bach*. Macmillan
2. August, 1914, by *Alexander Solzhenitsyn*. Farrar, Straus & Giroux
3. The Odessa File, by *Frederick Forsyth*. Viking
4. The Day of the Jackal, by *Frederick Forsyth*. Viking
5. The Word, by *Irving Wallace*. Simon & Schuster
6. The Winds of War, by *Herman Wouk*. Little, Brown
7. Captains and the Kings, by *Taylor Caldwell*. Doubleday
8. Two from Galilee, by *Marjorie Holmes*. Revell
9. My Name Is Asher Lev, by *Chaim Potok*. Knopf
10. Semi-Tough, by *Dan Jenkins*. Atheneum

Nonfiction

1. The Living Bible, by *Kenneth Taylor*. Doubleday
2. I'm O.K., You're O.K., by *Thomas Harris*. Harper & Row
3. Open Marriage, by *Nena and George O'Neill*. M. Evans
4. Harry S. Truman, by *Margaret Truman*. Morrow
5. Dr. Atkins' Diet Revolution, by *Robert C. Atkins*. McKay
6. Better Homes and Gardens Menu Cook Book. Meredith
7. The Peter Prescription, by *Laurence J. Peter*. Morrow
8. A World Beyond, by *Ruth Montgomery*. Coward, McCann & Geoghegan
9. Journey to Ixtlan, by *Carlos Castaneda*. Simon & Schuster
10. Better Homes and Gardens Low-Calorie Desserts. Meredith

THIS WAS the year of the bird (*Jonathan Livingston Seagull*) and the Bible (*The Living Bible*), top sellers of 1972 in fiction and nonfiction. It was also the year of Richard Nixon's first trip to China, which he called "the week that changed the world." It was not until June 17 that burglars were caught breaking into Democratic Campaign Headquarters in the Watergate complex. "Those Were the Days, My Friend," was the most popular song of the year played in Russian and Armenian restaurants and nightclubs, according to author William Safire.

Though *Jonathan Livingston Seagull,* the inspirational story of a seagull by Richard Bach, illustrated with beautiful photographs by Russell Munson, had been published in 1970, it was not until 1972 that Macmillan put on one of its most concentrated publicity campaigns. For two years the bird had been selling steadily to readers who spread their interest by word-of-mouth. By the end of 1972 the little book had sold 1,815,000 copies. Alexander Solzhenitsyn, famous Russian novelist, made his first appearance on an annual American list in the number two spot, his *August, 1914* selling 152,300 copies in the last four months of the year. Frederick Forsyth was in the enviable position of claiming third and fourth places in one year with *The Odessa File* followed by *The Day of the Jackal,* holdover from 1971. The 1972 list is also remarkable for the appearance of four first novelists: they are Richard Bach; Frederick Forsyth (*The Day of the Jackal*); Marjorie Holmes with her *Two from Galilee,* the biblical "love story" of Mary and Joseph; and Dan Jenkins with *Semi-Tough,* story of pro-football players.

This might be called a year for religion in the bookstores. The new *Living Bible,* a paraphrase in modern English by Dr. Kenneth N. Taylor, reaffirmed the adage that the Bible is always the best seller. This one sold an enormous number of copies in 1972. Doubleday sold 757,216 copies to the trade and copublisher Tyndale House approximately five million through retail outlets not usually covered by trade publishers. Like *Jonathan Livingston Seagull,* the second semi-inspirational book on the nonfiction list *I'm O.K., You're O.K.,* by Thomas Harris was published long before it reached this annual list. For four years, word of the book was spread through the author's lecture tours, discussion and church groups. It sold 531,000 copies in 1972; its three-year sale was close to a million. Interesting in relation to the six "how-to" books that dominated most of the 1972 nonfiction list were Margaret Truman's biography of her father and two books of mystical-philosophical content, *A World Beyond* by Ruth Montgomery and *Journey to Ixtlan* by Carlos Castaneda.

1973

Fiction

1. Jonathan Livingston Seagull, by *Richard Bach*. Macmillan
2. Once Is Not Enough, by *Jacqueline Susann*. Morrow.
3. Breakfast of Champions, by *Kurt Vonnegut, Jr.* Delacorte/ Lawrence
4. The Odessa File, by *Frederick Forsyth*. Viking
5. Burr, by *Gore Vidal*. Random House
6. The Hollow Hills, by *Mary Stewart*. Morrow
7. Evening in Byzantium, by *Irwin Shaw*. Delacorte
8. The Matlock Paper, by *Robert Ludlum*. Dial Press
9. The Billion Dollar Sure Thing, by *Paul E. Erdman*. Scribner
10. The Honorary Consul, by *Graham Greene*. Simon & Schuster

Nonfiction

1. The Living Bible, by *Kenneth Taylor*. Doubleday and Tyndale House
2. Dr. Atkins' Diet Revolution, by *Robert C. Atkins*. McKay
3. I'm O.K., You're O.K., by *Thomas Harris*. Harper & Row
4. The Joy of Sex, by *Alex Comfort*. Crown
5. Weight Watchers Program Cookbook, by *Jean Nidetch*. Hearthside Press
6. How to Be Your Own Best Friend, by *Mildred Newman* et al. Random House
7. The Art of Walt Disney, by *Christopher Finch*. Harry N. Abrams
8. Better Homes and Gardens Home Canning Cook Book. Meredith
9. Alistair Cooke's America, by *Alistair Cooke*. Knopf
10. Sybil, by *Flora R. Schreiber*. Regnery

Again *Jonathan Livingston Seagull* and *The Living Bible* headed the list of ten best sellers of the year in fiction and nonfiction. Suspense was the dominant theme of the fiction list that represented the conservative taste of those who could afford to buy rather high-priced hardcover novels. The total sale of the ten best-selling novels was a bit larger than it had been the previous year—the Dow Jones average had reached a peak in January. The ragtime revival began. The last American troops left Vietnam on March 29. There was suspense in Washington, too, as the Senate Judiciary Committee held the Watergate hearings, the main feature of all the media, culminating in the "Saturday Night Massacre" on October 20.

Seagull added more than half-a-million copies to its 1,815,000 of the previous year despite its appearance in paperback in 1973. Jacqueline Susann's third novel *Once Is Not Enough* was second in fiction, selling 256,000 copies. Kurt Vonnegut, Jr., had his biggest hardcover success with his *Breakfast of Champions* in third place. One of the best-received novels of the year was Gore Vidal's *Burr,* based upon the life of Aaron Burr. A first novel was *The Billion Dollar Sure Thing,* written by Paul E. Erdman in his cell in a Swiss jail. It sold 90,000 copies and was a suspense story along with *The Matlock Paper* by Robert Ludlum, who made his first appearance on an annual list, and *The Odessa File* by Frederick Forsyth, continuing its success of 1972.

Doubleday and Tyndale House racked up 2,623,953 more copies of *The Living Bible* to add to its 5,757,216 of 1972. Again there were six "how-to" books among nonfiction best sellers if one includes *The Joy of Sex* by Alex Comfort among them. Published late in 1972, its two-year total was 715,000. The other three best-selling nonfiction were outstanding in their fields: *The Art of Walt Disney* by Christopher Finch, which sold 200,000 copies at $35 apiece; *Alistair Cooke's America,* one of the most popular of the Christmas season; and *Sybil* by Flora R. Schreiber, an account of the psychoanalytic treatment of a young woman, possessor of 16 distinct personalities.

1974

Fiction

1. Centennial, by *James A. Michener*. Random House
2. Watership Down, by *Richard Adams*. Macmillan
3. Jaws, by *Peter Benchley*. Doubleday
4. Tinker, Tailor, Soldier, Spy, by *John Le Carré*. Knopf
5. Something Happened, by *Joseph Heller*. Knopf
6. The Dogs of War, by *Frederick Forsyth*. Viking
7. The Pirate, by *Harold J. Robbins*. Simon & Schuster
8. I Heard the Owl Call My Name, by *Margaret Craven*. Doubleday
9. The Seven-Per-Cent Solution, by *John H. Watson, M.D.,* as edited by *Nicholas Meyer*. Dutton
10. The Fan Club, by *Irving Wallace*. Simon & Schuster

Nonfiction

1. The Total Woman, by *Marabel Morgan*. Revell
2. All the President's Men, by *Carl Bernstein* and *Bob Woodward*. Simon & Schuster
3. Plain Speaking: An Oral Biography of Harry S. Truman, by *Merle Miller*. Putnam.
4. More Joy: A Lovemaking Companion to The Joy of Sex, edited by *Alex Comfort*. Crown
5. Alistair Cooke's America, by *Alistair Cooke*. Knopf
6. Tales of Power, by *Carlos A. Castaneda*. Simon & Schuster
7. You Can Profit from a Monetary Crisis, by *Harry Browne*. Macmillan
8. All Things Bright and Beautiful, by *James Herriot*. St. Martin's
9. The Bermuda Triangle, by *Charles Berlitz* with *J. Manson Valentine*. Doubleday.
10. The Memory Book, by *Harry Lorayne* and *Jerry Lucas*. Stein & Day

1974 WAS a good year for first novelists: it also marked a first in American history—the resignation of the President of the United States on August 9. Among the three first novelists was Richard Adams with his *Watership Down,* second on the list of ten best sellers in fiction. His story of a band of rabbits who set out to find a new home in the English countryside sold more than 220,000 copies. In third place was Peter Benchley, who represented the third generation of a famous literary family. His *Jaws,* probably most widely known of all these ten titles, as a book and movie, is the story of the terrorization of a Long Island beach town by a great white shark. It sold 202,270 hardcover copies. Seventy-year-old Margaret Craven was the third first novelist. Her *I Heard the Owl Call My Name* was the story of a young minister among the Indians of British Columbia.

Topping 1974's best sellers was *Centennial* by James A. Michener; the price of this best seller also broke the record for a hardcover novel. After 175,000 copies were sold at $10.95, the price was raised to $12.50, and its total during the last four months of the year came to 330,289. The rest of the fiction best sellers were all by well-known novelists. The exception was editor Nicholas Meyer who did the Sherlock Holmes spoof, *The Seven-Per-Cent Solution* by John H. Watson, M.D.

Leader of nonfiction and leader of four "how-to" books of 1974 was *The Total Woman* by Marabel Morgan. The others were *More Joy: A Lovemaking Companion to The Joy of Sex* edited by Alex Comfort; *You Can Profit from a Monetary Crisis* by Harry Browne; and *The Memory Book* on which memory-training specialist Harry Lorayne and the New York Knicks' player Jerry Lucas collaborated.

Like its fiction counterpart *Jaws,* the best-known both as book and movie nonfiction title did not head the list. This was the famous *All the President's Men* by the two Pulitzer Prize winning *Washington Post* reporters, Carl Bernstein and Bob Woodward. Sales were more than 280,000 hardcover copies during 1974. Some interesting volumes, varied in appeal, filled the rest of the list: *Plain Speaking: An Oral Biography of Harry S. Truman* by Merle Miller; *Alistair Cooke's America,* which sold 240,182 additional copies in 1974; *Tales of Power,* the final volume of four in which Carlos A. Castaneda told of his tutelage by a Yaqui Indian sorcerer; *All Things Bright and Beautiful,* sequel to veterinarian James Herriot's previous best seller *All Creatures Great and Small;* and *The Bermuda Triangle* by Charles Berlitz with J. Manson Valentine, telling of the mysterious disappearance of ships and planes in that part of the Atlantic.

1975

Fiction

1. Ragtime, by *E. L. Doctorow*. Random House
2. The Moneychangers, by *Arthur Hailey*. Doubleday
3. Curtain, by *Agatha Christie*. Dodd, Mead
4. Looking for Mister Goodbar, by *Judith Rossner*. Simon & Schuster
5. The Choirboys, by *Joseph Wambaugh*. Delacorte
6. The Eagle Has Landed, by *Jack Higgins*. Holt, Rinehart and Winston
7. The Greek Treasure: A Biographical Novel of Henry and Sophia Schliemann, by *Irving Stone*. Doubleday
8. The Great Train Robbery, by *Michael Crichton*. Knopf
9. Shogun, by *James Clavell*. Atheneum
10. Humboldt's Gift, by *Saul Bellow*. Viking

Nonfiction

1. Angels: God's Secret Agents, by *Billy Graham*. Doubleday
2. Winning through Intimidation, by *Robert Ringer*. Funk & Wagnalls
3. TM: Discovering Energy and Overcoming Stress, by *Harold H. Bloomfield*. Delacorte
4. The Ascent of Man, by *Jacob Bronowski*. Little, Brown
5. Sylvia Porter's Money Book, by *Sylvia Porter*. Doubleday
6. Total Fitness in 30 Minutes a Week, by *Laurence E. Morehouse* and *Leonard Gross*. Simon & Schuster
7. The Bermuda Triangle, by *Charles Berlitz* with *J. Manson Valentine*. Doubleday
8. The Save-Your-Life Diet, by *David Reuben*. Random House
9. Bring on the Empty Horses, by *David Niven*. Putnam
10. Breach of Faith: The Fall of Richard Nixon, by *Theodore H. White*. Atheneum/Reader's Digest Press

IN THE YEAR the Big Apple went sour, hardcover fiction sales were down. There was not one first novelist among the top ten and, generally, sales for hardcover novels were lower than they had been. The leader was E. L. Doctorow's *Ragtime*. The author was new to the annual list, though he had previously written several well-reviewed books. *Ragtime* won the first National Book Critics Circle Fiction award and also set a record when Bantam Books bought the paperback reprint rights for $1,850,000. Only one other novel among the top ten in 1975 sold over 200,000 in hardcover, Arthur Hailey's *The Moneychangers*.

There were two more authors new to these annual lists, Judith Rossner, whose *Looking for Mister Goodbar* was based upon an actual New York City murder, and Jack Higgins with an adventure story, *The Eagle Has Landed,* about an attempt by German troops to kidnap Winston Churchill. Third in sales was the late Agatha Christie's mystery *Curtain* marking the final appearance of her famous detective, Hercule Poirot. The rest of the list was made up of writers well known to the fiction audience: *The Choirboys* by Joseph Wambaugh; *The Greek Treasure: A Biographical Novel of Henry and Sophia Schliemann* by Irving Stone; *The Great Train Robbery,* suspense story by Michael Crichton; *Shogun,* James Clavell's novel of early seventeenth-century Japan; and *Humboldt's Gift* by Saul Bellow.

The runaway top seller in 1975's nonfiction was evangelist Billy Graham's *Angels: God's Secret Agents*. Books on meditation, self-assertion, exercising and diet, and "how-to" books dominated most of the list. In second place, with its sale of close to 265,000 copies in 1975 was *Winning through Intimidation* by Robert Ringer. Then came *TM: Discovering Energy and Overcoming Stress,* by Harold H. Bloomfield; *The Ascent of Man,* by Jacob Bronowski; *Sylvia Porter's Money Book; Total Fitness in 30 Minutes a Week,* by Laurence E. Morehouse and Leonard Gross; and *The Save-Your-Life Diet,* by David Reuben, all hovering around 200,000 in sales. Among other nonfiction best sellers was *The Bermuda Triangle* by Charles Berlitz with J. Manson Valentine, in its second year, adding 191,182 copies to its 1974 sales. *Bring on the Empty Horses* was actor David Niven's account of the Hollywood scene from 1935 through 1960. In tenth place was *Breach of Faith: The Fall of Richard Nixon* by Theodore H. White, author of the popular "Making of the President" series.

Early Best Sellers

EARLY BEST SELLERS

THESE ARE the titles, published before 1895, when the systematic recording of best sellers began, which have without question sold a total of a million copies or more through the years. It is impossible to arrive at definite sales figures for most of these because each has been issued by a variety of publishers. Many of these firms are no longer in existence and few accurate sales records are obtainable now, especially for the earliest books.

Prayer books, hymn books, textbooks, and similar specialized volumes are not included in this list, although many of the titles that are included have appeared in school editions as well as in trade editions. The list is in chronological order according to American publication.

> The Holy Bible
>
> The Pilgrim's Progress, by *John Bunyan*
>
> Mother Goose
>
> Aesop's Fables
>
> The Vicar of Wakefield, by *Oliver Goldsmith*
>
> Robinson Crusoe, by *Daniel Defoe*
>
> Poems, by *Robert Burns*
>
> Gulliver's Travels, by *Jonathan Swift*
>
> Arabian Nights' Entertainment
>
> Autobiography, by *Benjamin Franklin*
>
> Plays, by *William Shakespeare*
>
> The Sketch Book of Geoffrey Crayon, Gent., by *Washington Irving*
>
> Ivanhoe, by *Sir Walter Scott*
>
> Kenilworth, by *Sir Walter Scott*
>
> The Spy, by *James Fenimore Cooper*
>
> The Last of the Mohicans, by *James Fenimore Cooper*
>
> The Swiss Family Robinson, by *Johann R. Wyss*
>
> American Dictionary of the English Language (in various editions), by *Noah Webster*
>
> The Last Days of Pompeii, by *Edward Bulwer-Lytton*
>
> Oliver Twist, by *Charles Dickens*

Tales, by *Edgar Allan Poe*

Two Years Before the Mast, by *Richard Henry Dana, Jr.*

The Deerslayer, by *James Fenimore Cooper*

The Old Curiosity Shop, by *Charles Dickens*

Essays, by *Ralph Waldo Emerson*

Poems, by *Alfred Tennyson*

A Christmas Carol, by *Charles Dickens*

The Three Musketeers, by *Alexandre Dumas*

The Count of Monte Cristo, by *Alexandre Dumas*

Poems, by *Henry Wadsworth Longfellow*

Fairy Tales, by *Hans Christian Andersen*

Jane Eyre, by *Charlotte Brontë*

Vanity Fair, by *William Makepeace Thackeray*

Wuthering Heights, by *Emily Brontë*

The Oregon Trail, by *Francis Parkman*

Poems, by *John Greenleaf Whittier*

David Copperfield, by *Charles Dickens*

Reveries of a Bachelor, by *Ik Marvell*

The Scarlet Letter, by *Nathaniel Hawthorne*

The Wide Wide World, by *Susan Warner*

The House of the Seven Gables, by *Nathaniel Hawthorne*

Moby-Dick, by *Herman Melville*

Bleak House, by *Charles Dickens*

Uncle Tom's Cabin, by *Harriet Beecher Stowe*

Hard Times, by *Charles Dickens*

Tempest and Sunshine, by *Mary Jane Holmes*

Walden, by *Henry David Thoreau*

The Age of Fable, by *Thomas Bulfinch*

Familiar Quotations, by *John Bartlett*

Leaves of Grass, by *Walt Whitman*

The Prince of the House of David, by *J. H. Ingraham*

Lena Rivers, by *Mary Janes Holmes*

John Halifax, Gentleman, by *Dinah Maria Mulock*

The Autocrat of the Breakfast Table, by *Oliver Wendell Holmes*

A Tale of Two Cities, by *Charles Dickens*

East Lynne, by *Mrs. Henry Wood*

Fairy Tales, by *Jakob and Wilhelm Grimm*

Silas Marner, by *George Eliot*

Les Misérables, by *Victor Hugo*

Lady Audley's Secret, by *Mary Elizabeth Braddon*

Ishmael, by *Mrs. E. D. E. N. Southworth*

Self-Raised, or, Out of the Depths, by *Mrs. E. D. E. N. Southworth*

Hans Brinker and His Silver Skates, by *Mary Mapes Dodge*

St. Elmo, by *Augusta J. Evans*

The Man Without a Country, by *Edward Everett Hale*

Alice's Adventures in Wonderland, by *Lewis Carroll*

Little Women, by *Louisa May Alcott*

The Rubaiyat of Omar Khayyam, Translated by *Edward Fitzgerald*

The Story of a Bad Boy, by *Thomas Bailey Aldrich*

Little Men, by *Louisa May Alcott*

Barriers Burned Away, by *E. P. Roe*

Science and Health with Key to the Scriptures, by *Mary Baker Eddy*

The Return of the Native, by *Thomas Hardy*

The Adventures of Tom Sawyer, by *Mark Twain*

The Faith of Our Fathers, by *Cardinal Gibbons*

Ben-Hur, by *Lew Wallace*

Nana, by *Emile Zola*

Madame Bovary, by *Gustave Flaubert*

Five Little Peppers and How They Grew, by *Margaret Sidney*

Poems, by *James Whitcomb Riley*

Heidi, by *Johanna Spyri*

Treasure Island, by *Robert Louis Stevenson*

A Child's Garden of Verses, by *Robert Louis Stevenson*

The Adventures of Huckleberry Finn, by *Mark Twain*

War and Peace, by *Leo Tolstoi*

The Birds' Christmas Carol, by *Kate Douglas Wiggin*

She, by *H. Rider Haggard*

Thelma, by *Marie Corelli*

Robert Elsmere, by *Mrs. Humphry Ward*

Stories, by *Guy de Maupassant*

Barrack-Room Ballads, by *Rudyard Kipling*

Black Beauty, by *Anna Sewell*

Plain Tales from the Hills, by *Rudyard Kipling*

Three Men in a Boat, by *Jerome K. Jerome*

The Adventures of Sherlock Holmes, by *A. Conan Doyle*
Steps to Christ, by *Ellen G. White*
Beautiful Joe, by *Marshall Saunders*
Coin's Financial School, by *William H. Harvey*
The Christian's Secret of a Happy Life, by *Hannah Whitall Smith*
Trilby, by *George du Maurier*
Memoirs of a Woman of Pleasure (Fanny Hill), by *John Cleland*

Books and Articles

about Best Sellers

BOOKS AND ARTICLES
ABOUT BEST SELLERS

America in Fiction: An Annotated List of Novels That Interpret Aspects of Life in the United States, rev. ed. by Otis W. Coan and Richard G. Lillard. Stanford University Press, 1945

America's Impact on the Arts: Literature, by Marcus Cunliffe. *Saturday Review,* Dec. 13, 1975
> "If American Writing has permeated the global consciousness, it is probably because of its distinctive and exhilarating low-mindedness."

America's Most Censored Author. *Publishers' Weekly,* May 14, 1949
> An interview with Erskine Caldwell.

Anthony Hits a Million! by Sanford Cobb. *Publishers' Weekly,* Aug. 24, 1935
> An account of the publication and sales of *Anthony Adverse* in the United States and in other countries.

April 1954—30th Birthday of Crossword Puzzle Books, by John J. Winterich. *Publishers' Weekly,* Apr. 17, 1954

Augusta Evans Wilson, 1833-1900, by William Perry Fidler. University of Alabama Press, 1954
> A biography of the author of *St. Elmo.*

The Bantam Story: Twenty-Five Years of Paperback Publishing, by Clarence Petersen. Bantam Books, 1970

Best Sellers: 1900-1935. The Trend of Popular Reading Taste Since the Turn of the Century, by Frederick Lewis Allen. *Saturday Review,* Dec. 7, 1935
> Analysis of American reading over an extended period. A similar analysis of the reading of the 1930's appears as a chapter in Mr. Allen's book, *Since Yesterday,* Harper, 1939.

Best Sellers in Fiction During the First Quarter of the Twentieth Century, by Irving Harlow Hart. *Publishers' Weekly,* Feb. 14, 1925

Best Sellers in Non-Fiction Since 1921, by Irving Harlow Hart. *Publishers' Weekly,* Feb. 4, 1933

Best Sellers of the Fifties, by Don C. Seitz. *Publishers' Weekly,* Feb. 28, 1931
> Discusses *A Prince of the House of David,* by Joseph Holt Ingraham.

Best Sellers of Yesterday. *The Bookman,* 1910
> Articles run throughout the year on such 19th-century best sellers as *St. Elmo, Innocents Abroad,* and *Mr. Barnes of New York.*

The Best Sellers Since 1875: Thirty-Five Books Have Had Sales of More Than 500,000 Copies Since 1875, by Edward A. Weeks. *Publishers' Weekly,* Apr. 4, 1934

Big Books: The Story of Best Sellers, by J. A. Goodman and Albert Rice. *Saturday Evening Post,* Nov. 17, 1934
> The sales and marketing of big best sellers of the 1930's.

The Book in America. A History of the Making and Selling of Books in the United States, by Hellmut Lehmann-Haupt and others. 2nd ed. R. R. Bowker Co., 1951

Book Publishing in America, by Charles A. Madison. McGraw-Hill, 1966
> Comprehensive coverage of the publishing scene from the Colonial beginnings through 1965, including a great deal of information on popular books.

Book Publishing: Inside Views, compiled by Jean Spealman Kujoth. Scarecrow Press, 1971
> Includes "Do You Remember? Popular Books, 1924–1964," by Alice P. Hackett.

The Book Trade in War Time, by Archibald G. Ogden. *Publishers' Weekly,* July 8, 1939
> Publishing and sales during World War I.

Books, Their Place in a Democracy, by R. L. Duffus. Houghton Mifflin, 1930

Books and Best Sellers, by Philip Van Doren Stern. *Virginia Quarterly Review,* Jan., 1942
> The making and importance of best sellers of the 1940's, with some historical background.

Bookselling in America and the World, Charles B. Anderson, ed. Quadrangle, 1975

The Case of Erle Stanley Gardner, by Alva Johnston. Morrow, 1947

Chronicles of Barabbas, 1884-1934: Further Chronicles and Comment, 1952, by George H. Doran. Rinehart, 1952
> A famous American publisher included background and anecdotal material about many best-selling authors, W. Somerset Maugham, H. G. Wells, Hugh Walpole, Mary Roberts Rinehart, Ralph Connor, among them.

Classics and Best-Sellers, by Malcolm Cowley. *New Republic,* Dec. 22, 1947

The Comics, by Coulton Waugh. Macmillan, 1947
> "From the Katzenjammer Kids to the Sad Sack."

The Content Characteristics of Best-Selling Novels, by John Harvey. *Public Opinion Quarterly,* v. 17, no. 1
> A statistical approach to "the puzzle of literary success."

The Critical Period in American Literature, by Grant C. Knight. University of North Carolina Press, 1951
> Writers and changing popular taste, 1890-1900.

Death's Fair-haired Boy, by Richard W. Johnston. *Life,* June 23, 1952
> Pictures and text about the success of the Mickey Spillane "sex and slaughter" novels.

The Devil with James Bond, by Ann S. Boyd. John Knox Press, 1966
> About the theological significance of the Ian Fleming spy stories.

The Extinction of the Dime Novel, by Firmin Dredd. *The Bookman,* March, 1900

The Fiction Factory, by Quentin Reynolds. Random House, 1956

The history of the magazine publishing firm of Street & Smith gives sidelights on such best-selling authors as Max Brand and Edgar Wallace.

Fiction Fashions from 1895 to 1926, by Irving Harlow Hart. *Publishers' Weekly,* Feb. 5, 1927

Fifty Years of Best Sellers, 1895–1945, by Alice Payne Hackett. R. R. Bowker Co., 1945

Forgotten Best Sellers That Influenced America. New York *Times Book Review,* 1944

>Ethan Allen, Author. (Ethan Allen's *A Narrative of Colonel Ethan Allen's Captivity.*) May 7

>A Southerner Who Maddened the South. (Hinton Rowland's *The Impending Crisis of the South.*) June 11

>Horatio Alger, Jr. and Ragged Dick. (Horatio Alger's *Ragged Dick.*) July 2

>An Outspoken Visitor. (Mrs. Trollope's *Domestic Manners of the Americans.*) July 9

>A Congressman Rediscovers Atlantis. (Ignatius Donnelly's *Atlantis.*) July 30

>Gen. Wallace and Ben Hur. (Lew Wallace's *Ben Hur.*) Aug. 6

>Professor Coin, Financial Wizard. (William Hope Harvey's *Coin's Financial School.*) Oct. 15

>Monk Hall, Shame of Philadelphia. (George Lippard's *The Quaker City, or the Monks of Monk Hall, a Romance of Philadelphia Life, Mystery and Crime.*) Oct. 22

>How to Drive the Sheriff from the Homestead Door. (Susan Warner's *The Wide, Wide World.*) Dec. 24

From Rags to Riches, by John Tebbel. Macmillan, 1963
>About Horatio Alger and the books he wrote.

Genteel Queen of Crime, by Nigel Dennis. *Life,* May 14, 1956
>Agatha Christie's life and writing.

Golden Multitudes, by Frank Luther Mott. R. R. Bowker Co., 1947
>A critical and anecdotal history of best sellers in this country from 1638 to 1947. The author evolved his own method of determining a best seller. The lists he made are based upon the formula of a book selling at least a number equal to "one per cent of the total population of continental United States for the decade in which the book was published."

"Heidi"—or the Story of a Juvenile Best Seller. *Publishers' Weekly,* July 25, 1953

The History of "In His Steps" by Its Author Charles M. Sheldon. Privately Printed. 1938
>The writing and the sales history of *In His Steps.*

Hoosiers Sell Best, by John H. Moriarty. *Indiana Quarterly for Bookmen.* Jan., 1947
>The most popular authors on the yearly lists, 1895-1944 in the first edition of this book, *Fifty Years of Best Sellers,* with statistics of their geographical origins, by States.

The House of Beadle and Adams and Its Dime and Nickel Novels; The Story of a Vanished Literature, by Albert Johannsen. University of Oklahoma Press, 1950

How a Best-Seller Happens, by E. M. D. Watson. *Cosmopolitan,* August, 1959

How Large Is Our Book-Reading Public? by Maxwell Aley. *Publishers' Weekly,* June 6, 1931

Ian Fleming: The Spy Who Came in with the Gold, by Henry A. Zeiger. Duell, Sloan & Pearce, 1966
> A biography of the creator of James Bond, Agent 007.

"In His Steps," the Story of a Best Seller. *Publishers' Weekly,* Mar. 2, 1946

"In Tune with the Infinite," Famous Best Seller, Now 50 Years Old. *Publishers' Weekly,* Feb. 22, 1947
> The author, Ralph Waldo Trine, the book, and its history.

The Inside Story of the World of Perry Mason, by Frank E. Robbins. Morrow, 1950
> About the chief characters created by Erle Stanley Gardner. Reprinted from the *Michigan Alumnus Quarterly Review.*

Irving to Irving: Author-Publisher Relations, 1800–1974, by Charles A. Madison. R. R. Bowker Co., 1974
> Many notable writers' relations with their publishers, from Washington Irving to Clifford Irving.

James Bond's World of Values, by Lycurgus M. Starkey, Jr. Abingdon, 1966
> A severe criticism, from the standpoint of Christian ethic, of the James Bond character in the Ian Fleming novels.

Lew Wallace's "Ben Hur" Gallops On, by Walter Moonfried. Milwaukee *Journal,* Feb. 27, 1955

The Life of Ian Fleming, by John Pearson. McGraw-Hill, 1966
> Biography of the author of the James Bond thrillers.

Lincoln's Doctor's Dog, by George Stevens. Lippincott, 1939
> Account of famous best sellers of the 1930's.

Margaret Mitchell of Atlanta, by Finis Farr. Morrow, 1965
> Authentic biography of Margaret Mitchell and a stimulating account of her writing of *Gone with the Wind.*

Mary Roberts Rinehart, by Geoffrey T. Hellman. *Life,* June 25, 1946

Miracle Books, by Leon Whipple. *Survey,* May 1, 1927
> Reasons for the sales of big nonfiction best sellers of the 1920's.

The Most Popular Authors of Fiction Between 1900 and 1925, by Irving Harlow Hart. *Publishers' Weekly,* Feb. 21, 1925

The Most Popular Authors of Fiction in the Post-War Period, 1919-1926, by Irving Harlow Hart. *Publishers' Weekly,* Mar. 12, 1927

The Nation's Appetite for Fiction, by Herbert F. Jenkins. *Publishers' Weekly,* Sept. 24, 1921
> Gives information and figures on the sale of many novels of the post-World War I period.

Nero Wolfe of West Thirty-Fifth Street, by William S. Baring-Gould. Viking Press, 1969
    Entertaining, imaginative biography.

Of Making Many Books: A Hundred Years of Reading, Writing and Publishing, by Roger Burlingame. Scribner, 1946
    A chapter on "Best-Sellers" is included in this 100th anniversary history of the publishing house of Charles Scribner's Sons as well as background material on such best-selling Scribner authors as Edith Wharton, F. Hopkinson Smith, S. S. Van Dine, Ernest Hemingway, John Galsworthy, James Boyd, Harold Frederic, and others.

The One Hundred "Best Sellers of the Last Quarter Century," by Irving Harlow Hart. *Publishers' Weekly,* Jan. 29, 1921

The One Hundred Leading Authors of Best Sellers in Fiction from 1895 to 1944, by Irving Harlow Hart. *Publishers' Weekly,* Jan. 19, 1946
    This, like all Professor Hart's studies of best sellers in *Publishers' Weekly,* is based upon his intensive analysis, over the years, of the monthly best seller geographical charts issued at one time by the *Publishers' Weekly* office. These charts are no longer published.

Over the Tops, by Gilbert Seldes. *Saturday Evening Post,* Apr. 25, 1936
    On the popularity of books, legitimate plays, musicals, road shows, moving pictures, sheet music, etc.

Paperback Books: A Pocket History, by John Tebbel. Pocket Books, 1964
    History of the paperback publishing firm, Pocket Books.

The Paperbound Book in America, by Frank L. Schick. R. R. Bowker Co., 1958
    The history of paperback publishing in the United States and its European background.

The Paper-Bound Book: Twentieth-Century Publishing Phenomenon, by Kurt Enoch. *Library Quarterly,* July, 1954

Paper-Bound Books in America, by Freeman Lewis. New York Public Library, 1952
    The history of paperbound publishing up to 1952.

Philo Vance: The Life and Times of S. S. Van Dine, by Jon Tuska. Bowling Green University Popular Press, 1971
    ". . . his commercial and literary influence on the entire genre of detective fiction."

The Popular Book, by James D. Hart. Oxford University Press, 1950
    Full of background material and facts about the popular and best-selling books from the beginning of American reading to 1950.

The Publisher, by Robert Sterling Yard. Houghton Mifflin, 1913
    A chapter on "What Makes a Book Sell."

70 Years of Best Sellers, 1895–1965, by Alice Payne Hackett. R. R. Bowker Co., 1967

60 Years of Best Sellers, 1895–1955, by Alice Payne Hackett. R. R. Bowker Co., 1956

Some "Best Sellers" of Other Days, by Michael Sadleir. *Publishers' Weekly,* Mar. 26, 1927

Subject matter and quality of best sellers and their chances for survival.

The Story of the McGuffeys, by Alice McGuffey Ruggles. American Book Co., 1950
> About the famous McGuffey readers.

The Strenuous Age in American Literature, by Grant C. Knight. University of North Carolina Press, 1954
> A critical history of the books of the years 1900-1910, against the social background of the period.

Ten Best Sellers, by W. Somerset Maugham. *Good Housekeeping,* Sept., 1948
> Discussion of the qualities that appealed to the public in ten famous 19th century novels.

There Were Giants in Those Days, by Mildred Catharine Smith. *Publishers' Weekly,* July 13, 1929
> *Quo Vadis* and its advertising campaign.

This Was Publishing, by Donald Sheehan. Indiana University Press, 1952
> The business, philosophy and problems of book publishing in the years from the close of the Civil War to the beginning of World War I. Information about many individual books and authors.

Twenty-five Years of Best-Sellers, by Harrison Smith. *The English Journal,* Oct., 1944
> Analysis of literature and reading tastes, 1914-1944.

Twenty Years of Post-War Best-Sellers—Part II: United States of America, by Alice P. Hackett. Publishers' World, 1965
> A survey of the hardbound best sellers in the years from the end of World War II through 1964.

What a New Englander Was Likely to Read in 1711, by John J. Winterich. *Publishers' Weekly,* Feb. 3, 1951

What Makes a Book Sell? by Robert Banker. *Publishers' Weekly,* Dec. 4, 1954

Why of the Best Seller, by William Lyon Phelps. *The Bookman,* Dec., 1921
> The quality of best sellers, chiefly *Main Street* and the novels of Harold Bell Wright and Gene Stratton Porter.

The Wonderful Career of the Wonderful Wizard. *Publishers' Weekly,* Feb. 13, 1961
> The publishing history of L. Frank Baum's *The Wonderful Wizard of Oz.*

Writing As a Career, by Thomas H. Uzzell. Harcourt, Brace, 1938
> The chapter on "The Popular Novel" analyzes the literary quality of some novels which sold over half a million copies between 1875 and 1938.

Title and Author Index

TITLE AND AUTHOR INDEX

ABC. 31
Abbe, Patience, Richard and Johnny. 121
Abbott, Eleanor. 74, 75
Abundant Living. 30
According to Hoyle. 18, 40, 55
Across the River and Into the Trees. 152, 153
Act One. 177, 179
Action at Aquila. 125
Adamic, Louis. 117, 118
Adams Family, The. 109
Adams, Henry. 87
Adams, James Truslow. 109–111, 113–115
Adams, Richard. 215, 216
Addams, Jane. 76, 77
Adler, Bill. 192
Adler, Mortimer. 129
Adler, Polly. 17, 40, 160, 162
Adventurer, The. 152, 153
Adventurers, The. 11, 35, 198, 199
Adventures and Letters of Richard Harding Davis. 85
Adventures of Captain Horn. 59
Adventures of François, The. 62
Adventures of Huckleberry Finn, The. 223
Adventures of Sherlock Holmes, The. 224
Adventures of Tom Sawyer, The. 223
Advise and Consent. 16, 41, 177, 178, 180, 187
Aeronautical Annual. 60
Aesop's Fables. 221
After Noon. 101
Age of Fable, The. 222
Age of Innocence, The. 91, 92
Agony and the Ecstasy, The. 14, 39, 183, 184, 186, 187
Airport. 11, 34, 203, 204
Aku-Aku. 174, 175
Alcott, Louisa May. 223
Aldrich, Bess Streeter. 111, 112, 115, 116
Aldrich, Thomas Bailey. 223
Alexander, Dan Dale. 169

Alice of Old Vincennes. 64, 65
Alice's Adventures in Wonderland. 223
Alistair Cooke's America. 213–216
Alive. 14, 37
All Creatures Great and Small. 216
All in the Family. 198, 199
All Kneeling. 105
All Quiet on the Western Front. 13, 25, 37, 107, 143
All the President's Men. 17, 39, 215, 216
All Things Bright and Beautiful. 19, 215, 216
All This, and Heaven Too. 125, 127
All This and Snoopy, Too. 13, 35
Allen, Frederick Lewis. 102, 113, 114
Allen, Hervey. 28, 115, 117, 125, 126, 135, 136
Allen, Ida Bailey. 15, 37
Allen, James Lane. 61, 64, 67
Allen, Robert S. 112–114
Alone. 125
Alsop, Joseph W., Jr. 129
Amateur Builder's Handbook. 30
Amateur Gentleman, The. 78
Amazing Interlude, The. 85
Ambassador, The. 195, 196
Ambler, Eric. 49
Amboy Dukes, The. 18, 40
American College Dictionary, The. 19, 23, 55
American Dictionary of the English Language. 221
American Doctor's Odyssey, An. 121, 123
American Everyday Dictionary, The. 24
American Heritage. 13, 37, 192, 194
American Heritage Book of Great Historic Places. 171
American Heritage Dictionary of the English Language. 10, 24, 34, 54, 205–208
American Idyll, An. 89
American Past, The. 144–146
American White Paper. 129, 130

American Woman's Cook Book, The. 13, 22, 48
Americanization of Edward Bok, The. 93, 95–97
Amy Vanderbilt's Complete Book of Etiquette, 24
Analysis of the Kinsey Report, An. 13, 36
Anatole France Himself. 99
Anatomy of a Murder. 14, 37, 174, 175
Anatomy of Peace, The. 142
And Now Tomorrow. 133
And So—Victoria. 123
And Tell of Time. 125, 126
Andersen, Hans Christian. 222
Andersonville. 166, 167, 169, 170
Andromeda Strain, The. 205, 206
Angel Pavement. 109, 110
Angel Unaware. 160, 161
Angela's Business. 81
Angels: God's Secret Agents. 217, 218
Anglund, Joan Walsh. 25, 47
Animal Farm. 10, 34
Animal Friends. 30
Ann Vickers. 115
Anna and the King of Siam. 137, 139, 156
Annie Jordan. 25
Another Country. 19, 41
Anthology of Robert Frost's Poems. 54
Anthony Adverse. 28, 115–117, 122, 126
Antin, Mary. 76, 78
Any Woman Can! 209, 210
Anything Can Happen. 140
Apostle, The. 135, 137, 138
Appleton, Everard J. 85
Appleton's English-Spanish, Spanish-English Dictionary. 27
Arabian Night's Entertainment. 221
Arch of Triumph. 142, 143
Arches of the Years, The. 115, 116
Ariel. 97, 99, 106
Arlen, Michael. 99, 100
Armageddon. 192, 194
Armour, Tommy. 160, 162
Armstrong, G. A. O. 160
Armstrong, Margaret. 125, 126
Armstrong, William. 47
Around the World in Eleven Years. 121
Around the World with Auntie Mame. 15, 174, 175
Arquette, Cliff. 177
Arrangement, The. 13, 36, 201, 202

Arrow of Gold, The. 87, 88
Arrowsmith. 99, 100
Art of Thinking, The. 107–109, 114
Art of Walt Disney, The. 213, 214
Artayeta de Viel, Josephine. 149, 150
Arthritis and Common Sense. 169, 170
Arthur, T. S. 4
Arts, The. 123
As He Saw It. 142
As I Remember Him. 129, 130
As the Earth Turns. 115
Ascent of Man, The. 217, 218
Asch, Sholem. 127, 129, 135–137, 149, 150, 155, 156
Ashe, Penelope. 205, 206
Ask Me Another. 98, 103, 104, 112
Asquith, Margot. 91
Atherton, Gertrude. 91, 92, 95, 96
Atkins, Robert C. 211, 213
Atlas Shrugged. 171
Auchincloss, Louis. 192, 194, 198
Auction Bridge Complete. 101
Auction Bridge To-Day. 78
Audrey. 66
August, 1914. 211, 212
Auntie Mame. 166, 167, 169, 170
Autobiography of Benjamin Franklin. 221
Autobiography of Margot Asquith, The. 91
Autobiography with Letters. 127
Autocrat of the Breakfast Table, The. 222
Awakening of Helena Ritchie, The. 70
Aylwin. 63

B. F.'s Daughter. 17, 28, 142, 143
Babbitt. 21, 26, 93, 95, 96, 100
Baby, The. 152, 153
Bach, Richard. 10, 23, 34, 211–213
Bacheller, Irving. 31, 64, 65, 83, 84, 89
Bachelor Belles. 72
Back Street. 111, 112
Bad Girl. 105
Bagnold, Enid. 18
Bailey, Charles S., II. 19, 52, 186, 187, 192, 194
Bailey, Temple. 87, 88, 95, 101
Baker, Samm Sinclair. 11, 34, 203, 204
Baldwin, James. 19, 41
Ball Four. 207, 208
Bangs, John Kendrick. 60, 61

Bankhead, Tallulah. 158
Bannerman, Helen. 28, 47
Barbusse, Henri. 86
Barclay, Florence. 27, 74, 75
Barnes, Clare, Jr. 98, 149, 150, 152, 154
Barnes, Margaret Ayer. 109, 111, 117
Barnhart, Clarence L. 19, 23, 55, 155
Barrack-Room Ballads, 223
Barrie, J. M. 60, 61, 72
Barrier, The. 72
Barriers Burned Away. 223
Barrington, E. 100
Bars of Iron. 82
Bartlett, John. 222
Barton, Bruce. 99–102, 114
Baruch, Bernard M. 171, 173
Baruch: My Own Story. 171, 173
Basic Carpentry. 53
Basso, Hamilton. 31, 163, 164
Battle Cry. 16, 38, 160, 161
Battle of the Strong, The. 62
Battle of the Villa Fiorita, The. 189
Baum, L. Frank. 11, 22, 41, 45, 46
Baum, Vicki, 111
Beach, Rex. 70, 72, 73, 76
Beamish, Richard J. 29
Beard, Charles and Mary. 109, 110
Beau Geste. 101, 102
Beau Sabreur. 101, 102
Beautiful Joe. 224
Beck, Mrs. L. Adams. 100
Becker, Marion Rombauer. 10, 22, 40,
    48, 186
Before the Sun Goes Down. 26
Begbie, Harold. 91, 93
Beim, Jerrold. 47
Belgium. 87
Believe It or Not. 98, 107, 108, 112
Bell for Adano, A. 137, 138
Bellamann, Henry. 133
Bellamann, Katherine. 31
Belles on Their Toes. 152, 153
Bellow, Saul. 192, 194–196, 217, 218
Beloved Vagabond. 73
Below the Salt. 171
Benchley, Peter. 10, 33, 215, 216
Benét, Stephen Vincent. 31, 53, 54, 107,
    112
Ben-Hur. 223
Benjamin Franklin. 125, 126
Benji. 18, 40, 46
Bennett, Arnold. 76–78

Bentley, Phyllis. 113, 116
Benton, Frances. 169, 170
Benton's Row. 163, 164
Bergson, Henri. 76
Berkowitz, Bernard. 18
Berlin Diary. 86, 131, 132, 138, 182
Berlitz, Charles. 215–218
Bermuda Triangle, The. 215–218
Berne, Eric. 13, 195, 197, 198, 201
Bernstein, Carl. 17, 32, 39, 215, 216
Bernstein, Morey. 169
Berolzheimer, Ruth. 13, 22, 48
Beside the Bonnie Briar Bush. 59, 60, 71
Best Loved Poems of the American Peo-
    ple. 54
Best of Everything, The. 15, 38
Bet It's a Boy. 129, 130
Betsy, The. 13, 36, 209, 210
Better Homes and Gardens Baby Book.
    14, 22, 189
Better Homes and Gardens Barbecue and
    Picnics. 26
Better Homes and Gardens Barbecue
    Book. 23, 48, 169
Better Homes and Gardens Best Buffets.
    26
Better Homes and Gardens Blender Cook
    Book. 26, 209
Better Homes and Gardens Bread Cook
    Book. 26, 189
Better Homes and Gardens Calorie
    Counter's Cook Book. 28
Better Homes and Gardens Casserole
    Cook Book. 16, 23, 48, 183
Better Homes and Gardens Cook Book.
    10, 21, 22, 48, 163, 164, 203, 204
Better Homes and Gardens Cooking for
    Two. 25
Better Homes and Gardens Cooking with
    Cheese. 29
Better Homes and Gardens Decorating
    Book. 26, 169
Better Homes and Gardens Decorating
    Ideas. 180
Better Homes and Gardens Dessert Cook
    Book. 25, 180
Better Homes and Gardens Diet Book.
    166, 167
Better Homes and Gardens Eat and Stay
    Slim. 25, 203, 204
Better Homes and Gardens Family Med-
    ical Guide. 14, 22

237

Better Homes and Gardens Favorite Ways with Chicken. 27, 201

Better Homes and Gardens First Aid for Your Family. 180

Better Homes and Gardens Flower Arranging. 27, 171, 172

Better Homes and Gardens Fondue and Tabletop Cooking. 19, 23, 49, 201

Better Homes and Gardens Garden Book. 155, 156

Better Homes and Gardens Gifts to Make Yourself. 53

Better Homes and Gardens Good Food on a Budget. 29

Better Homes and Gardens Handyman's Book. 16, 23, 155, 156

Better Homes and Gardens Holiday Cook Book. 24

Better Homes and Gardens Home Canning Cook Book. 25, 213

Better Homes and Gardens House Plants. 29

Better Homes and Gardens Jiffy Cooking. 24

Better Homes and Gardens Junior Cook Book. 27, 47

Better Homes and Gardens Low-Calorie Desserts. 211

Better Homes and Gardens Lunches and Brunches. 25

Better Homes and Gardens Make-Ahead Cook Book. 30

Better Homes and Gardens Meals in Minutes. 24

Better Homes and Gardens Meals with a Foreign Flair. 28

Better Homes and Gardens Meat Cook Book. 13, 22, 48

Better Homes and Gardens Menu Cook Book. 21

Better Homes and Gardens New Garden Book. 16, 23

Better Homes and Gardens Nutrition for Your Family. 183

Better Homes and Gardens Pies and Cakes. 26

Better Homes and Gardens Salad Book. 17, 23, 48, 174, 176

Better Homes and Gardens Sewing Book. 18, 23, 183

Better Homes and Gardens Snacks and Refreshments. 26

Better Homes and Gardens So Good Meals. 25

Better Homes and Gardens Story Book. 26, 47

Better Meals for Less Money. 83

Bettger, Frank. 152, 153

Betty Crocker's Cookbook. 10, 48

Betty Crocker's Good and Easy Cookbook. 17, 23, 48, 163, 164

Betty Crocker's New Picture Cookbook. 22, 169

Betty Crocker's Picture Cookbook. 152, 153, 155, 156

Between Parent and Child. 14, 38, 203, 204, 206

Between Parent and Teenager. 205, 206

Between You, Me and the Gatepost. 180, 182

Beverly of Graustark. 68, 71

Beyond This Place. 160

Bible Readings for the Home Circle. 19, 56

Bible: Revised Standard Version. 163, 167, 199

Big Book of Mother Goose. 25, 47

Big Fisherman, The. 30, 147, 149, 150

Big Kill, The. 11, 34, 50

Biggers, Earl Derr. 30

Billion Dollar Sure Thing, The. 213, 214

Birds, The. 190

Birds' Christmas Carol, The. 223

Birmingham, Stephen. 201, 202

Bishop, Jim. 28, 171, 173, 192, 194

Bishop, Joseph B. 89

Bishop Murder Case, The. 107, 108

Bishop's Mantle, The. 147, 148

Black Bag, The. 72

Black Beauty. 223

Black Boy. 140, 141

Black Like Me. 11, 35

Black Oxen. 95, 96

Black Rose, The. 18, 23, 140, 142, 143, 145

Blanton, Smiley. 169

Blatty, William P. 10, 33, 209

Bleak House. 222

Blood, Sweat and Tears. 131

Bloomfield, Harold H. 217, 218

Blue Camellia. 171

Blue Flower, The. 66

Blue Window, The. 101

Blunt, Betty B. 129

Body Language. 18, 41, 207, 208
Bok, Edward. 93–97, 99
Bolshevism. 87
Bond, Otto F. 10, 33, 54
Boners. 98, 111, 112
Boni, Margaret B. 144
Bonjour Tristesse. 166, 167, 170
Bonsai. 52
Book Nobody Knows, The. 101
Book of Etiquette, The. 31
Boon Island. 169
Boone, Pat. 174, 176–178, 180, 182
Border Legion, The. 31
Boston Cooking School Cook Book, The.
    12, 22, 48, 97–102
Boston Strangler, The. 19, 41
Bottome, Phyllis. 117, 118, 125
Boulle, Pierre. 19, 41
Bouton, Jim. 207, 208
Bowen, Catherine Drinker. 137
Bowers, Claude G. 101, 107
Boy Scouts Handbook. 46
Bracken, Peg. 14, 38, 48
Braddon, Mary Elizabeth. 223
Bramble Bush, The. 19, 41
Brand, Max. 17, 39
Brande, Dorothea. 121
Brass Bowl, The. 71
Brave Men. 28, 137, 140, 141
Brave New World. 15, 38
Brazilian Adventure. 117
Breach of Faith. 217, 218
Breakfast of Champions. 213, 214
Breaking Point, The. 93, 95
Breslin, Jimmy. 207, 208
Bride of Fortune. 30
Bridge of Desire, The. 111
Bridge of San Luis Rey, The. 105, 106
Bridge Over the River Kwai. 19, 41
Brieux, Eugène. 76, 78
Briffault, Robert. 119
Brimming Cup, The. 91, 92
Bring on the Empty Horses. 217, 218
Brinkley, William. 169, 170
Bristow, Gwen. 152, 153
British Agent. 115
Broad Highway, The. 75
Bromfield, Louis. 103–105, 109, 115,
    116, 123–126, 129, 135, 140
Bronowski, Jacob. 217, 218
Brontë, Charlotte. 222
Brontë, Emily. 222

Brooks, Van Wyck. 123, 129, 130
Brousson, J. J. 99
Brown, Dee. 209, 210
Brown, Helen Gurley. 186
Browne, Harry. 215, 216
Brush, Katharine. 109
Bryant, Thomas A. 20, 55, 56
Bryce, James. 76, 78
Buck, Pearl S. 12, 17, 27, 29, 36, 111,
    113, 114, 133, 134
Bugliosi, Vincent. 12, 36, 49, 50
Bulfinch, Thomas. 222
Bulwer-Lytton, Edward. 221
Bunyan, John. 211
Buranelli, Prosper. 97, 99
Burdick, Eugene L. 12, 16, 35, 39, 52,
    177, 178, 186, 187
Burma Surgeon. 135, 136
Burnett, Frances Hodgson. 60, 71, 72, 78,
    80, 93, 94
Burns, Robert. 221
Burr. 213, 214
Burroughs, Edgar Rice. 31
Bury My Heart at Wounded Knee. 209,
    210
Busch, Niven. 13, 36
But We Were Born Free. 163, 165
Butterfield 8. 13, 36
Butterfield, Roger. 144, 145, 163
By Love Possessed. 171, 172
Byrd, Richard E. 105, 106, 125, 126
Byrnes, James F. 144, 145
Byron. 109, 110

Caine, Hall. 59, 61, 78
Caine Mutiny, The. 19, 24, 155, 156, 158,
    159, 167
Caldwell, Erskine. 10–14, 16, 18, 33, 35–
    38
Caldwell, Taylor. 14, 25, 28, 37, 142, 143,
    163, 177, 178, 180, 189, 190, 203,
    207, 208, 211
Caleb West. 62
Call of the Canyon, The. 97
Call of the Wild, The. 24
Calling of Dan Matthews, The. 29
Calories Don't Count. 28, 183, 186, 188
Came a Cavalier. 25
Cameron, Margaret. 87
Campus Zoo. 152, 154

Camus, Albert. 18, 172

Canasta. 149, 150

Canasta, the Argentine Rummy Game. 149, 150

Canby, Henry Seidel. 18, 40

Candy. 192, 193

Canfield, Dorothy. 91, 92

Cannery Row. 17, 39

Capable of Honor. 198, 199

Capote, Truman. 12, 35, 49, 50, 198, 199

Capp, Al. 147, 148

Captain from Castile. 140

Captains and the Kings. 14, 37, 211

Caravans. 179, 180

Cardinal, The. 14, 152, 153, 155, 156

Carey, Ernestine Gilbreth. 149, 151–153

Carlson, C. C. 10, 34

Carlson, John Roy. 135, 137

Carmer, Carl. 117, 118

Carnegie, Dale. 10, 16, 24, 26, 34, 123, 125, 147, 148

Carolinian, The. 99

Carpetbaggers, The. 10, 33, 183, 184

Carrel, Alexis. 121

Carroll, Gladys Hasty. 115, 116

Carroll, Lewis. 223

Carry On. 83, 86

Carson, Johnny. 195, 196, 201, 202

Carson, Rachel L. 155, 156, 158

Cartland, Barbara. 49

Case of the Baited Hook, The. 15, 39, 51

Case of the Black-Eyed Blonde, The. 16, 51

Case of the Borrowed Brunette, The. 20, 52

Case of the Careless Kitten, The. 17, 41, 52

Case of the Caretaker's Cat, The. 15, 38, 51

Case of the Cautious Coquette, The. 18, 31, 52

Case of the Counterfeit Eye, The. 15, 38, 51

Case of the Crooked Candle, The. 19, 52

Case of the Curious Bride, The. 14, 37, 50

Case of the Dangerous Dowager, The. 16, 41, 51

Case of the Empty Tin, The. 17, 40, 52

Case of the Golddigger's Purse, The. 19, 52

Case of the Half-Wakened Wife, The. 16, 39, 51

Case of the Haunted Husband, The. 14, 36, 50

Case of the Lame Canary, The. 16, 39, 51

Case of the Lucky Legs, The. 13, 37, 50

Case of the Rolling Bones, The. 14, 37, 51

Case of the Silent Partner, The. 14, 37, 51

Case of the Sleepwalker's Niece, The. 15, 39, 51

Case of the Stuttering Bishop, The. 15, 38, 51

Case of the Substitute Face, The. 15, 38, 51

Case of the Sulky Girl, The. 13, 36, 50

Case of the Velvet Claws, The. 14, 38, 51

Casino Royale. 14, 37, 50

Cass Timberlane. 140

Casserole Cook Book. 183

Castaneda, Carlos A. 211, 212, 215, 216

Castillo, Carlos. 10, 33, 54

Castle, Agnes. 62

Castle, Egerton. 62

Castle, Marian. 29

Cat in the Hat, The. 11, 22, 46

Cat in the Hat Beginner Book Dictionary, The. 29

Cat in the Hat Comes Back, The. 13, 22, 46

Catch-22. 11, 34

Catcher in the Rye, The. 11, 34, 80, 184

Cather, Willa. 111, 112

Caught in the Quiet. 207

Centennial. 13, 37, 215, 216

Ceramics, Techniques and Projects. 53

Cerf, Bennett. 140

Certain Smile, A. 169, 170

Chain, The. 30

Chambers, Robert W. 70, 71, 75, 87

Chambers, Whittaker. 158

Chances. 109

Chandler, Raymond. 49

Chapman Report, The. 15, 37, 180, 181, 187

Chariots of the Gods? 11, 34

Charley Weaver's Letters from Mamma. 177, 179

Charlie Brown's All-Stars. 16, 38

Charlotte's Web. 12, 26, 36, 46

Charrière, Henri. 16, 39

Chase, Ilka. 133

Chase, Mary Ellen. 117, 118, 131
Chase, Stuart. 111
Cheaper by the Dozen. 149, 151
Chesser, Eustace. 13, 35
Child's Garden of Verses, A. 223
Chinese Parrot, The. 30
Chinese Room, The. 14, 36
Choir Invisible, The. 61
Choirboys, The. 217, 218
Cholmondeley, Alice. 83
Cholmondeley, Mary. 64
Chosen, The. 17, 39, 201, 202
Christian, The. 61
Christian's Secret of a Happy Life, The. 206, 224
Christie, Agatha. 49, 217, 218
Christine. 83
Christmas Carol, A. 222
Christmas Is Together-Time. 192, 194
Christopher and Columbus. 89
Christy. 12, 35, 201, 203
Churchill, Sir Winston. 28, 30, 63, 131, 132, 147, 148, 155, 160, 168, 218
Churchill, Winston. 9, 26, 31, 61, 63, 65, 68, 70, 72, 74, 78, 80, 81
Cimarron. 109, 110
Circular Staircase, The. 30
Citadel, The. 123–126, 132
City of Night. 189, 190
Claire Ambler. 105, 106
Clansman, The. 69, 81
Clark, G. H. 85
Clarke, Arthur C. 18, 40
Clarke, Donald Henderson. 30
Clavell, James. 217, 218
Cleaver, Eldridge. 19
Cleft Rock, The. 30
Cleland, John. 224
Closing the Ring. 30
Clue of the Forgotten Murder, The. 18, 41, 52
Coast of Folly, The. 97
Cobb, Hubbard. 25, 27, 30, 152, 154
Cobb, Irvin S. 131, 132
Coin's Financial School. 60, 224
Collier, Price. 78
Color in Your Garden. 53
Columbia Viking Desk Encyclopedia. 16, 23, 55
Come and Get It. 119
Comfort, Alex. 28, 213, 214–216
Common Law, The. 75

Comparative World Atlas. 15, 38, 55
Complete Book of Interior Decorating, The. 53
Complete Book of Sewing, The. 53
Complete Home Handyman's Guide. 27
Compulsion. 171, 172
Confessions of Nat Turner, The. 201, 202
Coniston, 70
Connell, Vivian. 14, 36
Connolly, Mike. 17, 163
Connor, Ralph. 71, 85, 87, 104
Conrad, Joseph. 87, 88
Conscience of a Conservative, The. 14, 38, 182
Constant Image, The. 180
Constant Nymph, The. 99
Contract Bridge Blue Book. 111, 115
Convention. 192, 194
Cook, R. J. 11, 28, 34, 53
Cooke, Alistair. 213, 215
Cooper, James Fenimore. 221, 222
Corelli, Marie. 223
Costain, Thomas B. 18, 23, 28, 30, 140, 142–145, 149, 150, 158, 160, 166, 171
Coué, Emile. 95, 96
Coulson, Zoe. 22, 48
Count Luckner, The Sea Devil. 105
Count of Monte Christo, The. 222
Country Lawyer. 127, 128
Country Squire in the White House. 129, 130
Couples. 13, 36, 203, 204
Coward, Noel. 123, 124
Cowman, Mrs. Charles E. 20, 24, 56
Cozzens, James Gould. 171, 172
Cradle of the Deep, The. 107, 108
Crafts for Children. 53
Craig, Marjorie. 205
Crane, Stephen. 14, 41, 60
Craven, Margaret. 215, 216
Crazy Ladies, The. 17, 39
Creative Evolution. 76
Crewel Embroidery. 53
Crichton, Michael. 205, 206, 217, 218
Crichton, Robert. 198, 199
Crisis, The. 26, 65, 70
Cronin, A. J. 25, 27, 113, 114, 123–125, 131–133, 137, 147, 160
Cross Creek. 133

241

Cross Word Puzzle Books, The. 97, 99, 108, 112
Crossing, The. 68, 70
Crowds. 78
Cruel Sea, The. 155, 156
Crusade in Europe. 27, 147, 148
Crystal Cave, The. 207, 208
Culbertson, Ely. 29, 79, 111–113, 115, 116
Culbertson's Summary. 29, 111, 113
Cummins, Maria. 4
Curie, Eve. 125, 126, 135, 136
Currie, Enid. 13, 36
Curtain. 217, 218
Curtain Rises, The. 137, 138
Curtin, D. Thomas. 84
Curwood, James Oliver. 89–91, 97
Cutlass Empire. 149, 150
Cuyas, Arturo. 27

Dacey, Norman F. 198, 199
Daddy Long Legs. 82
Daily Strength for Daily Needs. 26
Dalrymple, Leona. 80
Damnation of Theron Ware, The. 60
Damned, The. 17, 39, 51
Dana, Richard Henry, Jr. 222
Dangerous Days. 87
Dark Fires. 18, 40
Dark Hester. 107
Darrow, Clarence. 113, 114
Daughter of Anderson Crow, The. 71
Daughter of Silence. 183
Daughter of the Land, A. 85
Davenport, Marcia. 135, 144, 145, 180
David Copperfield. 222
David Harum. 26, 63, 64
Davies, Joseph E. 86, 133, 134
Daviess, Maria Thompson. 76
Davis, Adelle. 12, 15, 31, 35, 41
Davis, Elmer. 163, 165
Davis, Gwen. 205, 206
Davis, Richard Harding. 59, 61, 85
Dawn. 87
Dawson, Coningsby. 83, 85, 86, 91, 92, 97
Day Christ Died, The. 28, 171, 173
Day, Clarence. 119, 121, 123, 124
Day in the Life of President Kennedy, A. 192, 194

Day Lincoln Was Shot, The. 173
Day of the Jackal, The. 17, 41, 49, 51, 209, 211, 212
Days of Auld Lang Syne. 59
Days of Our Years. 127, 129, 130
Day's Work, The. 62, 63
Dear Abby. 174, 176
Dear and Glorious Physician. 177, 178
Dear Enemy. 82
Dear Sir. 140, 141
Dearly Beloved. 186, 187
Death of a President. 201, 202
Death of a Salesman. 53
de Beauvoir, Simone. 169, 170
Deep, The. 19, 41, 52
Deeping, Warwick. 101–105, 107, 109, 111, 113
Deerslayer, The. 222
Definite Object, The. 83
Defoe, Daniel. 221
De Gouy, Louis P. 31
de la Roche, Mazo. 103–105, 111, 115
Deland, Margaret. 60, 70, 75
Deliverance. 18, 41
Deliverance, The. 68
Dell Crossword Dictionary, The. 10, 33, 54
Dell, Ethel M. 82, 83, 85, 89
Delmar, Vina. 105
Dennis, Patrick. 15, 166, 167, 169, 174, 175
Dennis the Menace: Household Hurricane. 17, 39
Dennis the Menace Rides Again. 18, 40
Dere Mable. 85, 86, 134, 150
Derieux, Mary. 53
Desert Gold. 29
Desert of Wheat, The. 87
Désirée. 26, 160, 161
Devil's Garden, The. 80
Diamonds Are Forever. 15, 38, 51
Diane of the Green Van. 80
Diary of a Young Girl. 11, 34
Dickens, Charles. 117, 118, 221, 222
Dickey, James. 18, 41
Diet and Health. 30, 93, 95–102
Diet Watcher's Guide. 25
Diller, Phyllis. 198, 201, 202
Dim Lantern, The. 95
Dimnet, Ernest. 107, 109, 113, 114
Dinesen, Isak. 117
Dinner at Antoine's. 24, 147–150

Diplomatic Days. 85
Disenchanted, The. 152, 153
Disputed Passage. 127
Disraeli. 105, 106
Dixon, Jeane. 205, 206
Dixon, Thomas, Jr. 67, 69
Doctor, The. 71, 121
Dr. Atkins' Diet Revolution. 211, 213
Dr. No. 13, 36, 50, 190
Dr. Seuss's ABC. 11, 22, 45
Doctor Zhivago. 11, 28, 36, 174, 175, 177, 178
Doctorow, E. L. 32, 217, 218
Doctor's Quick Weight Loss Diet, The. 11, 34, 203, 204
Dodge, Mary Mapes. 223
Dodsworth. 107, 108
Dogs of War, The. 215
Don't Go Near the Water. 169, 170
Don't Stop the Carnival. 195, 196
Doomsday. 103
Door, The. 109
Dorothy Vernon of Haddon Hall. 66
Dorsey, George A. 101–104
Double-Crostics. 98
Double Image, The. 198, 199
Douglas, Lloyd C. 12, 14, 22, 30, 39, 113–116, 119–121, 127, 133, 135, 137, 138, 147, 149, 160
Doyle, Sir Arthur Conan. 49, 66, 224
Dragon Seed. 133, 134
Dream Merchants, The. 13, 36
Dream of Fair Women, A. 71
D'ri and I. 65
Drifters, The. 16, 19, 39, 209
Drivin' Woman. 133
Drum. 16, 38
Drums Along the Mohawk. 121, 123
Drury, Allen. 16, 41, 177, 178, 180, 186, 198, 203
Duel in the Sun. 13, 36
Dumas, Alexandre. 222
du Maurier, Daphne. 15, 25–27, 30, 49, 125–127, 135, 136, 142, 152, 153, 158, 163, 171, 189, 205
du Maurier, George. 59, 224
Dunne, Finley Peter. 63
Durant, Will. 29, 101–103, 107–110
Duranty, Walter. 121
Duvall, Evelyn. 17, 39, 46
Duvall, Sylvanus. 17, 39, 46

Eagle Has Landed, The. 217, 218
Earth and High Heaven. 140
East Lynne. 222
East of Eden. 158, 159
East Side, West Side. 144
Eastman, Nicholson J. 19, 23
Eastman, P. D. 29
Eben Holden. 31, 64, 65
Economic Consequences of the Peace, The. 89, 90
Eddy, Mary Baker. 223
Edgar Cayce—The Sleeping Prophet. 201, 202
Edge of Sadness, The. 183, 184
Edmonds, Walter D. 121–123
Education of a Princess. 111
Education of Henry Adams, The. 87, 88
Egermeier, Elsie E. 17, 23, 39, 46, 56
Egermeier's Bible Story Book. 17, 23, 39, 46, 56
Egg and I, The. 26, 140, 142–144, 146
Egyptian, The. 149, 150, 153, 163, 164
Eichler, Lillian. 31
Eighth Day, The. 201, 202
Eisenhower, Dwight D. 147, 148, 168, 169
Elbert, Joyce. 17, 39
Eleanor and Franklin. 209, 210
Elements of Style. 20, 177, 178
Eliot, George. 223
"Elizabeth." 87, 95
Elizabeth and Essex. 107, 108
Elizabeth Appleton. 189, 190
Ellis, J. Breckenridge. 76
Ellis, O. O. 83
Elmer Gantry. 100, 103, 104
Eloise. 169, 170
Eloise at Christmastime. 174
Eloise in Paris. 171, 172
Embezzler, The. 198, 200
Emerson, Ralph Waldo. 222
Empey, Arthur Guy. 83, 85
Enchanted April, The. 95
Encyclopedia Cookbook. 24
Enemy Camp, The. 174, 175
English-Spanish, Spanish-English Dictionary, The. 10, 33, 54
English through Pictures. 17, 39, 55
Epic of America, The. 111, 113
Erdman, Paul E. 213, 214
Erskine, John. 30, 101, 102
Ertz, Susan. 101, 107
Escape. 127, 128

243

Essays. 222
Esty, Lucien. 103
Etiquette. 25, 95–98, 169, 170
Europa. 119
Evans, Augusta J. 223
Evening in Byzantium. 213
Everything but Money. 198, 201
Everything You Always Wanted to Know about Sex but Were Afraid to Ask. 10, 34, 207, 208, 210
Exhibitionist, The. 201
Exile. 109
Exit Laughing. 131
Exodus. 11, 34, 177, 178, 184
Exorcist, The. 10, 33, 209
Expectant Motherhood. 19, 23
Ex-Wife. 73
Eyeless in Gaza. 121
Eyes of the World, The. 80

FBI Story, The. 171, 172
Face to Face with Kaiserism. 86
Fadiman, Clifton. 126, 131, 132
Fail-Safe. 16, 39, 52, 186, 187, 190
Fairbanks, Douglas. 83–85
Fairy Tales. 222
Faith of Our Fathers, The. 223
Fallada, Hans. 115, 116
Familiar Quotations. 222
Family, The. 129
Family of Man, The. 166, 167
Family Reference Atlas. 18, 40, 55
Fan Club, The. 18, 41, 215
Fanny Hill. 224
Fanny Kemble. 125, 126
Far Country, A. 81
Farm, The. 115
Farmer, Fannie. 12, 22, 97, 99, 101
Farnol, Jeffery. 75, 78, 83
Farson, Negley. 121
Fast, Julius. 18, 41, 207, 208
Fatal Interview. 111, 112
Father of the Bride. 86, 149, 150
Faulkner, William. 19, 41, 186, 187
Fear of Flying. 11, 35
Federal Aviation Regulations and Flight Standards for Pilots. 24
Fedorova, Nina. 129
Felix O'Day. 81
Felleman, Hazel. 54

Feminine Mystique, The. 20
Ferber, Edna. 97, 98, 101, 102, 104, 109, 110, 119, 127, 128, 131, 132, 158, 174, 175
Field Guide to the Birds, A. 26
Field, Rachel. 119, 120, 125–127, 133
Fields of Wonder. 209
54-40 or Fight. 73
Fighting Chance, The. 70, 71
Final Days, The. 32, 185
Finch, Christopher. 213, 214
Finch's Fortune. 111
Finley, Martha. 45
Fireside Book of Folk Songs, The. 144
First Hundred Thousand, The. 83
Fishbein, Morris. 27
Fisher, Dorothy Canfield. 97
Fitzgerald, Edward. 223
Fitzgerald, F. Scott. 11, 34
Five Acres and Independence. 28
Five Little Peppers. 45, 64
Five Little Peppers and How They Grew. 223
Fixer, The. 198, 200
Flaming Youth. 89
Flaubert, Gustave. 223
Fleischer, Leonore. 18, 40, 46
Fleming, Ian. 12–15, 35–38, 49–51, 190–193, 195, 196
Fleming, Peter. 117
Flesch, Rudolf. 166
Fletcher, Inglis. 27
Flight to Arras. 133, 134
Floodtide. 28, 152, 153
Flowering of New England, The. 123, 124
Flynn, John T. 129
Folk Medicine. 12, 35, 177, 178, 180, 181
Fondue Cookbook. 31
For the Love of Peanuts. 16, 38
For 2¢ Plain. 177, 179
For Whom the Bell Tolls. 30, 129–132
For Your Eyes Only. 15, 37, 51
Ford, Paul Leicester. 61, 63, 64
Forest and the Fort, The. 135
Forever Amber. 14, 24, 137, 138, 140, 153
Forgive Us Our Trespasses. 115
Forsyte Saga, The. 102, 110
Forsyth, Frederick. 15, 17, 39, 41, 49, 51, 209, 211–215
Fortunate Youth, The. 80
Fortune to Share, A. 113

Forty Days of Musa Dagh, The. 119
Forty-Two Years in the White House. 117
Fosdick, Harry Emerson. 135, 136
Foster, Robert F. 102
Foundling, The. 155, 156
Fountain, The. 113, 114
Fountainhead, The. 14, 37
Four Days. 13, 37, 192, 194
Four Horsemen of the Apocalypse, The. 87, 88
Fowler, Gene. 137, 142
Fowles, John. 15, 38, 207, 208
Fox, John, Jr. 25, 27, 67, 68, 72, 73, 78
Foxes of Harrow, The. 15, 24, 142, 143
Fran. 76
Francis the First. 119
Franck, Harry A. 78
Frank, Anne. 11, 34
Frank, Gerold. 17, 19, 41, 163
Franklin, Benjamin. 221
Franny and Zooey. 183, 184, 186, 187, 190
Freckles. 19, 23, 45, 46, 75
Frederic, Harold. 60, 63
Freeman, Douglas Southall. 119, 120
Freeman, H. W. 107
French Lieutenant's Woman, The. 15, 38, 207, 208
Frey, Richard L. 18, 40, 55
Friedan, Betty. 20
Friend Is Someone Who Likes You, A. 25, 47
From Here to Eternity. 12, 36, 155, 156, 160, 161
From Russia with Love. 13, 36, 50
From the Terrace. 174, 175
Frost, Robert. 53, 188
Fun with Peanuts. 15, 37
Funk, Wilfred J. 11, 24, 35, 55
Furniture Finishing and Refinishing. 53
Furniture Upholstery and Repair. 53
Furniture You Can Make. 52
Future Shock. 12, 35

Gabriel Hounds, The. 201, 202
Galaxy, The. 107
Gallico, Paul. 177, 178
Galsworthy, John. 101, 102, 105, 110, 111, 115, 116
Gambler, The. 69

Games People Play. 13, 195, 197–199, 201
Gang That Couldn't Shoot Straight, The. 207, 208
Gann, Ernest K. 160, 161
Garden and Patio Building. 52
Garden of Allah, The. 69
Gardening in Containers. 52
Gardner, Erle Stanley. 13–20, 31, 36–41, 49–52
Garey, E. B. 83
Gathering Storm, The. 30, 147, 148
Geddes, Donald P. 13, 36
General Foods Kitchen Cookbook, The. 177, 179, 180, 182
General Marshall's Report. 140, 141
Gentle Julia. 93
Gentleman from Indiana, The. 66
Gentleman of Courage, A. 97
Gentleman with a Duster. 91, 93
Gentleman's Agreement. 26, 144, 145
Gentlemen Prefer Blondes. 101
Gentry, Curt. 12, 36, 49, 50
Georgia Boy. 13, 37
Gerard, James W. 85, 86
Germany and the Germans. 78
Getting Together. 83
Giant. 158, 159
Giants in the Earth. 108
Gibbons, Cardinal. 223
Gibbs, A. Hamilton. 99, 109
Gibbs, Philip. 89, 90, 97
Gibran, Kahlil. 10, 22, 53
Gibson, C. M. 17, 39, 55
Gift from the Sea. 166, 167
Gift of Prophecy, A. 195, 197
Gilbert, Clinton W. 93
Gilbreth, Frank B., Jr. 149, 151, 152
Ginott, Dr. Haim G. 14, 38, 203–206
Girl of the Limberlost, The. 19, 23, 47
Girl Scouts Handbook. 46
Glasgow, Ellen. 68, 70, 82, 113, 114, 119, 120
Glass-Blowers, The. 189
Glorious Adventure, The. 103
Glorious Apollo. 99, 100
Glorious Pool, The. 16
Glory of the Trenches, The. 85
Glyn, Elinor. 4, 65
Go Ask Alice. 18, 40, 46
God the Invisible King. 83
Godden, Rumer. 189

Godfather, The. 10, 33, 49, 50, 205, 206
Gods from Outer Space. 18, 40
God's Little Acre. 10, 33
Goethe. 105, 106
Gold Cook Book, The. 31
Golden Dictionary, The. 47
Golden Fury, The. 29
Golden, Harry. 174, 175, 177, 179, 181, 182
Golden Hawk, The. 24, 147, 148
Goldfinger. 12, 35, 50
Golding, Louis. 113
Golding, William. 18, 41
Goldsmith, Oliver. 221
Goldwater, Barry. 14, 38, 180
Gone with the Wind. 10, 22, 36, 116, 121–123, 136
Good-Bye, Mr. Chips. 117–120
Good Companions, The. 110
Good Earth, The. 12, 27, 36, 111, 113, 114
Good Grief, Charlie Brown. 15, 37
Good Housekeeping Cookbook, The. 22, 48
Good Night, Sweet Prince. 137, 138
Good Ol' Snoopy. 12, 35
Good Woman, A. 103, 104
Goodman, George. 204
Goodman, Linda. 205
Goose Girl, The. 73
Gordon Keith. 67
Goren, Charles. 79, 112
Goss, Charles Frederic. 64
Goudge, Elizabeth. 25, 30, 137, 138, 147
Gown of Glory, The. 158, 159
Graham, Billy. 56, 166, 195, 197, 217, 218
Graham, Gwethalyn. 140, 141
Graham Kerr Cookbook, The. 205
Grand Alliance. 29
Grand Hotel. 111, 112
Grandmother and the Priests. 189, 190
Grant, Robert. 64
Grapes of Wrath, The. 19, 127, 129
Graustark. 65
Great Controversy. 28
Great Gatsby, The. 11, 34
Great Impersonation, The. 29, 89
Great Lion of God. 207, 208
Great Train Robbery, The. 217, 218
Greatest Book Ever Written, The. 17, 26, 56

Greatest Faith Ever Known, The. 160, 162
Greatest Story Ever Told, The. 12, 24, 39, 56, 149, 150
Greatheart. 85
Greek Treasure, The. 217, 218
Green, Anna Katherine. 49
Green Berets, The. 13, 36, 195, 196
Green Dolphin Street. 25, 137, 138
Green Eggs and Ham. 11, 22, 46
Green Hat, The. 99, 100
Green Light. 30, 119
Green, Mary. 83
Green Years, The. 137
Greenberg, Joanne. 11, 34
Greenburg, Dan. 195, 196
Greene, Graham. 207
Greene Murder Case, The. 105, 106, 108
Greening of America, The. 16, 40
Grew, Joseph E. 86, 137, 138
Grey, Lord. 99, 100
Grey, Zane. 4, 19, 26, 27, 29–31, 81, 83–91, 93, 95, 97
Griffin, John. 11, 35
Grimm, Jakob and Wilhelm. 222
Gross, Leonard. 217, 218
Grosset Webster Dictionary. 14, 22, 55
Group, The. 13, 36, 189, 190
Guadalcanal Diary. 135, 136
Guard of Honor. 172
Guest, Edgar. 28, 54, 85, 86
Guide to Confident Living, A. 147–150
Guinness Book of World Records, The. 10, 23, 33, 54
Gulag Archipelago I, The. 15, 38
Gulliver's Travels. 221
Guns of August, The. 92
Gunther, John. 121, 122, 127, 128, 131–133, 144, 145, 166, 174, 176
Guralnik, David B. 169

H. M. Pulham, Esquire. 131
Hackett, Francis. 107, 119, 120
Haggard, H. Rider. 223
Hailey, Arthur. 11, 16, 34, 39, 195, 196, 203, 204, 209, 210, 217, 218
Hale, Edward Everett. 223
Half a Rogue. 71
Hall, James Norman. 13, 26, 121, 122
Halley, Henry H. 14, 22, 55, 56

Halley's Bible Handbook. 14, 22, 55, 56
Halliburton, Richard. 31, 103, 104
Halsey, Margaret. 125, 126
Hamilton, Edith. 10, 33
Hammarskjöld, Dag. 195, 197
Hammett, Dashiell. 49
Hankey, Donald. 83
Hans Brinker and His Silver Skates. 223
Happiness Is a Dry Martini. 195, 196
Happiness Is a Warm Puppy. 28, 186,
    188, 189, 191
Happy Hooker, The. 10, 33
Harbor, The. 81
Hard Times. 222
Hardy, Thomas. 223
Hargrove, Marion. 15, 40, 133, 135
Harland, Henry. 68
Harlow. 19, 42
Harriet and the Piper. 89
Harris, Thomas. 11, 27, 34, 209–213
Harrison, Henry Sydnor. 75, 78, 81
Harry S. Truman. 211
Harry, the Dirty Dog. 47
Hart, James D. 4
Hart, Moss. 177, 179
Harvester, The. 24, 75, 76
Harvey, William H. 224
Hauser, Gayelord. 152, 153, 155, 156
Hawaii. 12, 35, 177, 178, 180
Hawthorne, Nathaniel. 222
Hay, Ian. 83
Head of the House of Coombe, The. 93,
    94
Heap O'Livin', A. 28, 54
Heart of Rachael, The. 82
Heart of the Hills. 78
Heaven's My Destination. 119
Hegan, Alice Caldwell. 66
Heggen, Thomas. 18, 41
Heidi. 223
Heilbroner, Robert. 25
Heirs Apparent, The. 97
Heiser, Victor. 121, 123
Helbeck of Bannisdale. 62
Helen of the Old House. 93
Heller, Joseph, 11, 34, 215
Helmet of Navarre, The. 65
Heloise's Housekeeping Hints. 189
Helter Skelter. 12, 36, 49, 50
Hemingway, Ernest. 30, 129–131, 152,
    153, 158, 192, 194, 207, 208
Hémon, Louis. 93, 104

Hendrick, Burton J. 95
Henry the Eighth. 107, 108
Her Father's Daughter. 91
Here Comes Charlie Brown. 15, 38
Here Comes Snoopy. 12, 35
Here Is Your War. 29, 135–137
Herries Chronicle. 110
Herriot, James. 19, 215, 216
Hersey, John. 18, 42, 137, 138, 152, 153
Hertzler, Arthur E. 125
Herzog. 192, 194, 195, 196
Hewlett, Maurice. 65
Hey, Peanuts. 14, 37
Heyerdahl, Thor. 18, 28, 152, 153, 155,
    156, 174, 175
Heyward, DuBose. 107, 108, 119
Hichens, Robert S. 69, 83, 84
Hicks, Wilson. 158
Hidden Persuaders, The. 14, 37
Higgins, Jack. 217, 218
High and the Mighty, The. 160, 161
High Towers. 28, 149, 150
Hillis, Marjorie. 121, 123, 124
Hillman, William. 158
Hilton, James. 12, 17, 27, 37, 117–120,
    123, 131, 132, 140, 160, 181
Hinge of Fate. 29
Hiroshima. 18, 42
His Children's Children. 95
His Family. 83
History of the Standard Oil Company.
    68
History of the World War. 29
Hitler, Adolf. 127
Hobart, Alice Tisdale. 30, 31, 117, 118
Hobson, Laura Z. 26, 144, 145
Hoffenberg, Mason. 192, 193
Hogben, Lancelot. 123
Hollander, Xaviera. 10, 13, 33, 35
Hollow Hills, The. 213
Holmes, Marjorie. 211, 212
Holmes, Mary Jane. 222
Holmes, Oliver Wendell. 138, 222
Holt, Victoria. 207, 208
Holy Bible, The. 221
Holy Bible: Revised Standard Version.
    158–161, 163, 164, 167, 199
Home Sweet Zoo. 149, 150
Homemaker, The. 97
Honor Thy Father. 16, 40, 209, 210
Honorable Peter Stirling, The. 61
Honorary Consul, The. 213

247

Hoosier Chronicle, A. 76
Hoover, Ike. 117
Hoover, J. Edgar. 18, 174
Hop on Pop. 11, 22, 46
Hope, Anthony. 59, 61, 62
Hope, Bob. 137, 138, 189, 191
Horn, Alfred Aloysius. 103, 105
Horse and Buggy Doctor, The. 125
Hotel. 195, 196
Hough, Emerson. 66, 73
Hound of the Baskervilles, The. 66
Hounds of Spring, The. 101
House-Boat on the Styx, A. 60
House Divided. 144, 145
House in the Uplands, A. 13, 36
House Is Not a Home, A. 17, 40, 160, 162
House of a Thousand Candles, The. 70
House of Exile, The. 115
House of Mirth, The. 69, 70
House of the Seven Gables, The. 222
House on the Strand, The. 205
House Plants. 16, 38, 52
Houses in Between, The. 158
How Green Was My Valley. 129, 130
How I Raised Myself from Failure to Success in Selling. 152, 153
How to Avoid Probate. 198, 199
How to Be a Jewish Mother. 195, 196
How to Be Your Own Best Friend. 18, 213
How to Live on Twenty-Fours Hours a Day. 76
How to Live 365 Days a Year. 166, 167, 169
How to Play Your Best Golf. 160, 162
How to Prepare Your Income Tax. 20, 42
How to Read a Book. 129, 130
How to Stop Worrying and Start Living. 147, 148
How to Win at Canasta. 149, 150
How to Win Friends and Influence People. 10, 24, 34, 123–125, 148
Howard, Elizabeth M. 26
Huard, Frances W. 83
Hubbard, Elbert. 12, 28, 37
Hucksters, The. 142, 143
Hudson, Virginia Cary. 186, 188, 189
Hugh Wynne. 62
Hugo, Victor. 223
Huie, William Bradford. 19, 41
Hull, Edith M. 26, 91–93

Hull, Raymond, 205, 206
Hulme, Kathryn. 16, 40, 56, 169, 170
Human Comedy, The. 135
Human Destiny. 144, 146
Human Sexual Response. 198, 199
Humboldt's Gift. 217, 218
Hundredth Chance, The. 83
Hungry Hill. 27, 135, 142
Hurlbut, Jesse Lyman. 14, 22, 55, 56
Hurricane, The. 121
Hurst, Fannie. 111, 112
Hutchinson, A. S. M. 93–95, 99
Huxley, Aldous. 15, 38, 121, 122
Hyman, Mac. 17, 40, 163, 164, 166, 167

I Chose Freedom. 142
I Hate to Cook Book, The. 14, 38, 48
I Heard the Owl Call My Name. 215, 216
I Kid You Not. 180
I Married Adventure. 129, 130
I Need All the Friends I Can Get. 192, 194
I Never Left Home. 137
I Never Promised You a Rose Garden. 11, 34
I Owe Russia $1200. 189, 191
I, the Jury. 11, 34, 50
I Write As I Please. 121
Ibañez, V. Blasco. 87
Ice Palace. 174, 175
If Winter Comes. 93, 94
Ilin, M. 111, 112
I'll Cry Tomorrow. 17, 40, 163, 165
I'm a Stranger Here Myself. 125, 126
Immortal Poems of the English Language. 54
Immortal Wife. 140
I'm O.K., You're O.K. 11, 21, 27, 34, 209–213
Impatient Virgin. 30
Importance of Living, The. 125
In Cold Blood. 12, 35, 49, 50, 198, 199
In Flanders Fields, 87, 88
In His Own Write. 192
In His Steps. 10, 24, 34
In Secret. 87
In Someone's Shadow. 205–207
In the Bishop's Carriage. 68
In the Clearing. 188
In the Wilderness. 83

In Tune with the Infinite. 24
Information Please Almanac. 144, 145
Ingersoll, Ralph. 142
Ingraham, J. H. 222
Inheritance. 113, 114, 116
Inheritors, The. 16, 39, 205, 206
Inner Shrine, The. 73
Inside Africa. 166, 167
Inside Asia. 127, 128, 132
Inside Europe. 121, 122, 132
Inside Latin America. 131, 133, 134
Inside of the Cup, The. 78, 80
Inside Russia Today. 174, 176
Inside the Third Reich. 209, 210
Inside U.S.A. 144, 145
Intelligent Woman's Guide to Socialism
    and Capitalism, The. 105
Iron Woman, The. 75
Irving, Washington. 221
Ishmael. 223
Islands in the Stream. 207, 208
It Can't Happen Here. 121
Italy, France and Britain at War. 84
It's for You, Snoopy. 13, 36
Ivanhoe. 221

"J." 10, 33, 207, 208
J. F. K.: The Man and the Myth. 189,
    191
Jackson, Josephine A. 93
Jacobson, Edmund. 117
Jacoby, Oswald. 149, 150
Jaffe, Rona. 15, 38
Jaffery. 81
Jalna. 103–105
James, Will. 109, 110
Jane Cable. 70
Jane Eyre. 222
Janice Meredith. 63, 64
Janney, Russell. 31, 142–145
Jarvis, D. C. 12, 35, 177, 180
Jaws. 10, 33, 215, 216
Jefferson and Hamilton. 101
Jenkins, Dan. 211, 212
Jerome, Jerome K. 223
Jogging. 25
John Brown's Body. 54, 107, 108
John F. Kennedys, The. 192, 194
John Halifax, Gentleman. 222
John Ward, Preacher. 60

Johnson, Osa. 129, 130
Johnson, Owen. 80
Johnston, Annie Fellows. 45
Johnston, Mary. 61, 64, 66, 68, 72, 75
Johnston, Virginia E. 198, 199
Jonathan Livingston Seagull, 10, 21, 23,
    34, 211, 212–214
Jones, E. Stanley. 30
Jones, James. 12, 36, 155, 156, 160
Jones, Mary Alice. 30
Jong, Erica. 11, 35
Joseph and His Brethren. 107
Joseph, David. 20, 42
Journey among Warriors. 135
Journey to Ixtlan. 211, 212
Journeyman. 12, 35
Joy of Cooking, The. 10, 22, 32, 40, 48,
    186
Joy of Sex, The. 21, 28, 213, 214
Joy Street. 25, 152, 153
Jubilee Trail. 152, 153
Judgment House, The. 78
Jungle, The. 17, 41
Just and the Unjust, The. 76
Just David. 82
Just So Stories. 30

K. 81
Kains, M. G. 28
Kallet, Arthur. 115, 116, 117
Kander, Mrs. Simon. 24
Kane, Harnett. 30
Kantor, MacKinlay. 169, 170
Karen. 19, 41
Kate Carnegie. 60
Katrine. 73
Kaufman, Bel. 12, 35, 195, 196
Kavanaugh, Father James. 201, 202
Kazan, Elia. 13, 36, 201, 202
Keable, Robert. 93
Keeper of the Bees, The. 99
Keith, Agnes Newton. 129
Kelly, Walt. 155
Kenilworth. 221
Kennedy. 195, 197
Kennedy, John F. 12, 29, 35, 181, 189–
    192, 194, 197, 199, 202
Kennedy, Margaret. 99
Kennedy Wit, The. 192, 194

Kerr, Graham. 205
Kerr, Jean. 15, 38, 171, 172, 174
Kester, Vaughan. 75, 76
Ketcham, Hank. 16–19, 39–41
Keyes, Frances Parkinson. 13, 24–27, 142, 143, 147–149, 152, 153, 158, 163, 171, 174
Keynes, John Maynard. 89, 90
Keys of the Kingdom, The. 25, 131–133
Kids Say the Darndest Things! 12, 27, 38, 171, 172, 174, 176
Kieran, John. 144
Killilea, Marie. 19, 41
Kim, Richard E. 192, 193
Kimbrough, Emily. 31, 135, 136
Kindred of the Dust. 89
King, Alexander. 177, 179, 180, 182
King, Basil. 73, 74, 76
Kingdom of Slender Swords, The. 74
Kingdom Round the Corner, The. 91
King's General, The. 25, 142, 143
Kings Row. 133, 142
Kingsblood Royal. 144, 145
Kinsey, Alfred C. 147, 160
Kinsey Reports. 162, 199
Kintnor, Robert. 129
Kipling, Rudyard. 30, 62, 63, 87, 88, 223
Kiplinger, W. M. 133
Kiss Me, Deadly. 11, 34, 50
Kitty. 17
Kitty Foyle. 127–129
Knebel, Fletcher. 19, 52, 186, 187, 192, 194, 203
Knight, Eric. 131, 132
Knight, William Allen. 19, 23, 56
Kon-Tiki. 18, 28, 152, 153, 155, 156
Kravchenko, Victor. 142
Krey, Laura. 125
Kyne, Peter B. 89, 90

Laddie. 24, 47, 78
Lady Audley's Secret. 223
Lady Baltimore. 70
Lady Chatterley's Lover. 11, 34, 177, 178
Lady of Quality, A. 60
Lady of the Decoration, The. 67, 71
Lady Rose's Daughter. 67
Lait, Jack. 155, 156, 158

Lamb in His Bosom. 117, 118
Lamp in the Desert, The. 89
Lampedusa, Guiseppe di. 180, 181
Lamplighter, The. 4
Land Below the Wind. 129, 130
Land Birds East of the Rockies. 29
Land of Deepening Shadow, The. 84
Landon, Margaret. 137
Lane, Elinor Macartney. 73
Lane, Mark. 198, 199
Langenscheidt's German-English, English-German Dictionary. 13, 36, 55
Langley, Adria Locke. 140, 141
Lansing, Robert. 91
Lantern in Her Hand, A. 112
Larousse French-English, English-French Dictionary. 10, 33, 54
Lash, Joseph P. 209, 210
Lasky, Victor. 189, 191
Lasser, J. K. 157
Lassie Come-Home. 132
Last Battle, The. 198
Last Chapter. 142
Last Days of Pompeii, The. 221
Last Hurrah, The. 169
Last of the Mohicans, The. 221
Last Puritan, The. 122
Last Time I Saw Paris, The. 133, 134
Late George Apley, The. 128, 150
Late Great Planet Earth, The. 10, 34
Lauder, Harry. 85
Laugh and Live. 83, 85
Lawrence, D. H. 11, 34, 177, 178
Lawrence, T. E. 103, 104, 119, 120
Leave Her to Heaven. 19, 23, 137
Leavenworth Case, The. 49
Leaves of Grass. 222
Le Carré, John. 192, 195, 196, 203, 215
Lecomte du Noüy, Pierre. 146
Lederer, William. 12, 35, 177, 178, 183, 185
Lee, Edna L. 28
Lee, Gerald Stanley. 78
Lee, Harper. 10, 33, 183, 184
Leech, Margaret. 131
Lena Rivers. 222
Lenard, Alexander. 183, 184
Lennon, John. 192, 194
Leopard, The. 180, 181, 190
Le Petit Prince. 47
Let's Cook It Right. 15, 41, 49

Let's Eat Right to Keep Fit. 12, 31, 35
Let's Face It, Charlie Brown. 14, 36
Let's Get Well. 15, 41
Letters from a Self-Made Merchant to His Son. 67
Levant, Oscar. 129, 130
Levenson, Sam. 198, 201
Levin, Ira. 12, 35, 201, 202
Levin, Meyer. 171, 172
Lewis, Ethelreda. 103, 105
Lewis, Norman. 11, 24, 35, 55
Lewis Rand. 72
Lewis, Sinclair. 21, 26, 29, 55, 91–93, 95, 99, 100, 103, 104, 107, 108, 115–117, 121, 140, 144, 145, 155
Liebman, Joshua L. 27, 142–145, 147, 148, 150
Life and Death of a Spanish Town. 134
Life and Gabriella. 82
Life and Letters of Walter H. Page, The. 95
Life and Times of the Shmoo, The. 147, 148
Life Begins at Forty. 115–118
Life Is Worth Living. 160, 161
Life of Christ, The. 95–100
Life of Our Lord, The. 117
Life with Father. 119–121
Life with Mother. 123, 124
Light in the Clearing, The. 83, 84
Light of Faith, The. 101
Light of Western Stars. 27
Lincoln. 109
Lincoln, Joseph C. 89, 90
Linda Goodman's Sun Signs. 205, 206
Lindbergh, Anne Morrow. 119–122, 125–127, 166, 186, 187
Lindbergh, Charles A. 103, 105, 106
Lindsey, Hal. 10, 34
Link, Henry C. 123
Linkletter, Art. 12, 27, 38, 171, 172, 174, 176
Lion Is in the Streets, A. 140
Lippmann, Walter. 107, 108, 135, 136
Listen! The Wind. 125–127
Listen to the Warm. 19, 23, 53, 203, 204
Listener, The. 180
Little Black Sambo. 28, 47
Little Colonel, The. 45, 120
Little Engine That Could, The. 18, 23, 46
Little, Frances. 71

Little French Girl, The. 97, 99
Little Golden Book. 45
Little House in the Big Woods, The. 16, 41, 46
Little House on the Prairie, The. 15, 39, 46
Little Lord Fauntleroy. 72
Little Man, What Now? 115
Little Men. 223
Little Prince, The. 15, 40, 46
Little Shepherd of Kingdom Come, The. 27, 67, 68
Little Women. 223
Live Alone and Like It. 121, 122, 124
Live and Let Die. 14, 37, 51
Living Bible, The. 55, 211–214
Llewellyn, Richard. 129
Locke, William J. 73, 74, 80, 81, 83, 84
Lockhart, R. H. Bruce. 115
Lockridge, Ross, Jr. 147, 148
Lodge, Sir Oliver. 83, 84
Lofting, Hugh. 45
Lolita. 12, 36, 174, 175, 177, 178
Lolly Willowes. 102
London, Jack. 24
Lone Cowboy. 109
Lone Star Ranger. 29, 81
Lonesome Cities. 203, 204
Long Roll, The. 75
Long Wait, The. 11, 34, 50
Longfellow, Henry Wadsworth. 222
Look Homeward, Angel. 120
Look Younger, Live Longer. 152, 153, 155, 156
Looking for Mister Goodbar. 217, 218
Looking Forward. 115
Looking Glass War, The. 195, 196
Loos, Anita. 101
Lorayne, Harry. 215, 216
Lord Loveland Discovers America. 74
Lord of the Flies. 18, 41
Lord Vanity. 160
Lorimer, George Horace. 67
Lost Ecstasy. 103
Lost Horizon. 12, 37, 119, 120
Love and the Facts of Life. 17, 39, 46
Love Is a Special Way of Feeling. 25, 47
Love Is Eternal. 27, 163, 164
Love Machine, The. 12, 35, 205, 206
Love or Perish. 169
Love Story. 10, 33, 207, 208

Love without Fear. 13, 35
Lovely Ambition, The. 180
Lovey Mary. 67
Low Carbohydrate Diet. 29
Lowell, Joan. 107
Lowell, Juliet. 140
Lucas, Jerry. 215, 216
Ludlum, Robert. 213, 214
Ludwig, Emil. 103–106, 109, 110, 123, 124
Lure of the Mask, The. 72
Lusty Wind for Carolina. 27
Lydia Bailey. 25, 145

"M." 12, 35, 209, 210
Maartens, Maarten. 59
Maas, Peter. 17, 40
MacArthur, General Douglas. 192, 194
McCarthy, Mary. 13, 36, 189, 190
McCrae, John. 87, 88
McCutcheon, George Barr. 65, 68–73, 80
MacDonald, Betty. 26, 140, 142, 144, 146, 148
MacDonald, John D. 17, 39, 49, 51
MacDonald, Ross. 49
McDonnald, A. H. 26
McGinniss, Joe. 205, 206
MacGrath, Harold. 65, 71–73
MacInnes, Helen. 44, 190, 198, 203, 209, 210
McKenna, Stephen. 85, 189, 190
McKuen, Rod. 19, 23, 25, 53, 201–210
Maclaren, Ian. 59, 60, 71
Macramé. 52
McWhirter, Norris and Ross. 10, 23, 33, 54
Madame Bovary. 223
Madame Curie. 125
Magnificent Obsession. 14, 39, 113, 115, 116
Magnolia Street. 113, 114
Maid in Waiting. 111
Mailer, Norman. 15, 39, 147, 148
Main Street. 29, 91
Major, The. 85
Major, Charles. 61, 63, 64, 66
Making of the President, 1960, The. 183, 185, 195, 197
Malamud, Bernard. 198, 200

Malet, Lucas. 66
Maltz, Maxwell. 12, 35
Mamba's Daughters. 107
Man, The. 19, 192, 194
Man Called Peter, A. 28, 158–161, 166, 167
Man for the Ages, A. 89
Man from Brodney's, The. 72
Man from Maine, A. 95
Man in Lower Ten. 73, 110
Man in the Gray Flannel Suit, The. 166, 167
Man Nobody Knows, The. 99, 101, 102
Man of the Forest, The. 31, 89, 90
Man the Unknown. 121
Man with the Golden Gun, The. 195, 196
Man without a Country, The. 223
Manchester, William. 201, 202
Mandarins, The. 169, 170
Mandingo. 11, 34
Mansions of Philosophy, The. 107, 108
Manxman, The. 59
March, F. A. 29
March of Democracy, The. 113, 115
Margaret Ogilvy. 61
Maria Chapdelaine. 93, 94
Marie Antoinette. 115
Marie, Grand Duchess. 111
Marjorie Morningstar. 166, 167
Mark Twain. 76, 223
Mark Twain's Autobiography. 97
Mark Twain's Letters. 85, 86
Market Place, The. 63
Markings. 195, 197
Marks, Percy. 97, 98
Marquand, John P. 17, 28, 127, 128, 130–132, 135, 136, 142, 143, 149, 150, 155, 156
Marriage of William Ashe, The. 69
Marshall, Catherine. 12, 28, 35, 160, 163, 166, 171, 172
Marshall, Edison. 28
Marshall, Katharine T. 144, 201, 203
Marshall, Peter. 152–154, 172
Marshall, Rosamond. 17
Martyred, The. 192–194
Marvell, Ik. 222
Mary. 149, 150
Mary Anne. 163, 164
Mary-Marie. 89
Mary Peters. 117, 118

252

Mary Poppins. 47
Mary Queen of Scotland and the Isles. 119
Mary's Neck. 123
Mason, F. van Wyck. 129, 130, 149, 150
Masquerader, The. 68, 69, 73
Master, The. 59
Master of Jalna. 115
Masters of Deceit. 18, 174, 175
Masters, William Howard. 198, 199
Mathematics for the Millions. 123, 124
Matlock Paper, The. 213, 214
Mature Mind, The. 152, 154
Maugham, W. Somerset. 13, 16, 24, 123, 124, 137
Mauldin, Bill. 140
Maupassant, Guy de. 223
Maurois, André. 97–99, 105, 106, 109, 110
Max. 74
Maxwell, Gavin. 183, 185
Maxwell, W. B. 80
May This House Be Safe from Tigers. 180, 182
Mayo, Katherine. 103–105
Means, Gaston B. 109
Mein Kampf. 101, 127, 128
Melting of Molly, The. 76
Melville Goodwin, U.S.A. 155, 156
Melville, Herman. 222
Memoirs of a Woman of Pleasure. 224
Memory Book, The. 215, 216
Mergendahl, Charles. 19, 41
Merton, Thomas. 149, 150
Message from Malaga. 209, 210
Message to Garcia, A. 12, 28, 37
Metalious, Grace. 10, 12, 20, 33, 35, 42, 169, 171
Mettle of the Pasture, The. 67
Mexico. 111
Meyer, Nicholas. 215, 216
Michael O'Halloran. 26, 81
Michael, Ralph. 149, 150
Michelson, Miriam. 68
Michener, James. 12, 13, 15, 35, 37–39, 155, 156, 177, 178, 189, 190, 195, 196, 209, 210, 215, 216
Midlander, The. 97
Mila 18. 183, 184
Millay, Edna St. Vincent. 111
Miller, Alice Duer. 131

Miller, Caroline. 117, 118
Miller, Douglas S. 131
Miller, Henry. 14, 38
Miller, Merle. 215, 216
Milne, A. A. 28, 30, 47, 99, 100, 184
Mind in the Making, The. 93–95
Mine Enemy Grows Older. 177, 179
Mine with the Iron Door, The. 95
Minstrel in France, A. 85
Miracle of the Bells, The. 31, 142–144
Mirrors of Downing Street, The. 91, 92, 94
Mirrors of Washington. 93, 94, 112
Misérables, Les. 223
Misery Is a Blind Date. 201, 202
Miss Bishop. 115
Miss Craig's 21-Day Shape-Up Program for Men and Women. 205
Mrs. 'Arris Goes to Paris. 177, 178
Mrs. Miniver. 129, 130
Mrs. Parkington. 135
Mrs. Wiggs of the Cabbage Patch. 66, 67, 71
Mission to Moscow. 86, 133
Mississippi Bubble, The. 66
Mr. and Mrs. Cugat. 131, 132
Mr. Britling Sees It Through. 82–84, 88
Mr. Crewe's Career. 72
Mr. Dooley in Peace and War. 63
Mr. Jones, Meet the Master. 152, 153
Mr. President. 158, 159
Mr. Roberts. 18, 41
Mistress Wilding. 97
Mitchell, Margaret. 10, 22, 36, 131, 133
Mitchell, S. Weir. 62
Moby-Dick. 222
Modern Chronicle, A. 74
Modern Comedy, A. 102
Modern Encyclopedia. 26
Modern Home Medical Advisor. 27
Modern Home Physician. 27
Modern Priest Looks at His Outdated Church. 201, 202
Modern World Atlas. 11, 34, 55
Molly Make-Believe. 74, 75
Money Game, The. 203, 204
Moneychangers, The. 217, 218
Moneyman, The. 30, 144
Monsarrat, Nicholas. 155, 156, 169
Montessori, Maria. 76, 77

Montessori Method, The. 76, 77
Montgomery, Ruth. 195, 197, 211, 212
Moon Is Down, The. 133, 134
Moonraker. 14, 37, 51
Moore, Robin. 13, 36, 195, 196
More Dennis the Menace. 16
More Joy. 215, 216
More Merry-Go-Round. 113, 114
Morehouse, Laurence E. 217, 218
Morgan, Charles. 113, 121
Morgan, Edward P. 158, 160
Morgan, Marabel. 15, 40, 215, 216
Morley, Christopher. 127–129
Morley, Viscount. 85, 86
Morris, Desmond. 17, 40
Morris, William. 205, 207
Mortal Storm, The. 125
Mortimer, Lee. 155, 156, 158
Morton, Frederic. 186, 188
Moses. 155, 156
Mother. 24
Mother Goose. 221
Mother India. 113–116
Moveable Feast, A. 192, 194
Mulock, Dinah Maria. 222
Munsterberg, Hugo. 78
Munthe, Axel. 109–111
Murrow, Edward R. 158, 160
Mutiny on the Bounty. 13, 26, 122
My Cousin Rachel. 27, 158, 159
My First Atlas. 17, 39, 46, 55
My First Book About Jesus. 30
My First Dictionary. 31
My Four Years in Germany. 85
My Friend Flicka. 29
My Friend Prospero. 68
My Gun Is Quick. 11, 34, 50
My Home in the Field of Honor. 83
My Lady Nobody. 59
My Life and Prophecies. 205, 206
My Life in Court. 186, 188
My Name Is Asher Lev. 211
My Second Year of the War. 83
My Shadow Ran Fast. 195, 197
My Sister and I. 131, 132
My Son, My Son! 125
Myra Breckinridge. 18, 41, 203, 204
Mysterious Rider, The. 29, 91
Mystic Isles of the South Seas. 91
Mythology. 10, 33

Nabokov, Vladimir. 12, 36, 174, 177, 178
Naked and the Dead, The. 15, 39, 147, 148
Naked Ape, The. 17, 40
Naked Came the Stranger. 205, 206
Nan of Music Mountain. 82
Nana. 223
Napoleon. 103, 105, 106
Nash, Ogden. 53, 125, 126
Nation of Sheep, A. 183, 185
National Velvet. 18
Native's Return, The. 117
Nazarene, The. 127–129
Nedra. 69
Needlepoint. 53
Net, The. 76
Nevada. 19
Never Leave Me. 15, 37
Never Love a Stranger. 11, 35
Never Victorious, Never Defeated. 163, 164
New American Roget's College Thesaurus in Dictionary Form. 10, 33, 54
New American Webster Handy Dictionary, The. 10, 34, 55
New Centurions, The. 17, 39, 51
New Century Dictionary of the English Language, The. 26
New Compact Bible Dictionary, The. 20, 55, 56
New Conscience and an Ancient Evil, A. 76
New Decalogue of Science, The. 97
New England: Indian Summer. 129, 130
New English Bible, The. 183, 185, 186, 207, 208
New Freedom, The. 78
New Russia's Primer. 111, 112
New Testament, The. 185, 188
New Testament in Modern English, The. 176, 177
New Yorker Twenty-Fifth Anniversary Album, The. 155–157
Newman, Mildred. 18, 213
Nicholson, Meredith. 70, 71, 76
Nidetch, Jean. 16, 23, 48, 203, 204, 213
Night in Bombay. 129
Nijinsky, Romola. 117
Nile, The. 123
1984. 10, 33
90 Minutes at Entebbe. 32

Niven, David. 217, 218
Nizer, Louis. 186, 188
No Time for Sergeants. 17, 40, 163, 164, 166, 167
Noorbergen, René. 205
Nordau, Max. 59
Nordhoff, Charles. 13, 26, 121, 122
Norris, Frank. 67
Norris, Kathleen. 24, 82, 88, 89
North to the Orient. 119, 121, 126
Northwest Passage. 123–126
Not As a Stranger. 15, 24, 163, 164, 166, 167
Not Peace But a Sword. 127
Now It Can Be Told. 89, 90
No. 5 John Street. 63
Nun's Story, The. 16, 40, 56, 169, 170
Nygaard, Norman F. 27

O Ye Jigs & Juleps. 186, 188, 189, 191
O'Brien, Frederick. 89–92, 104
O'Brien, Lieut. Pat. 86
O'Brien, Patrick J. 28
O'Connor, Edwin. 169, 183, 184, 198
Odessa File, The. 15, 39, 49, 51, 211–214
Of Human Bondage. 16
Of Lena Geyer. 136
Of Mice and Men. 123, 124
Of Time and the River. 119, 120
Oh, Money! Money! 85
O'Hara, John. 13, 36, 149, 150, 166, 174, 175, 180, 181, 189, 190
O'Hara, Mary. 29, 30
Oil for the Lamps of China. 117
Old Countess, The. 103
Old Curiosity Shop, The. 222
Old Farmer's Almanac. 54
Old Man and the Sea, The. 158
Old Pybus. 105
Old Wine and New. 113
Oliver Twist. 221
Oliver Wiswell. 129–132
On Being a Real Person. 135, 136
On Her Majesty's Secret Service. 13, 36, 50, 190
On the Beach. 15, 171, 172
On the Face of the Waters. 61
Once Is Not Enough. 12, 35, 213, 214

One Fish, Two Fish, Red Fish, Blue Fish. 11, 22, 46
101 Famous Poems. 11, 2ô, 34, 53
One Increasing Purpose. 99
One Lonely Night. 11, 34, 50
100,000,000 Guinea Pigs. 115–117, 120
One More River. 115
One Woman, The. 67
One World. 135, 136, 138
O'Neill, Eugene. 105, 106, 160, 172
O'Neill, Nena and George. 211
Only in America. 174, 175, 177, 179
Only Yesterday. 102, 113
Onstott, Kyle. 11, 16, 34, 38
Open Marriage. 211
Oppenheim, E. Phillips. 29, 85, 86, 89
Orchids on Your Budget. 123
Oregon Trail, The. 222
Orwell, George. 10, 33, 34
O'Shaughnessy, Edith. 85
Other, The. 13, 36, 209
Other Side of Midnight, The. 12, 35
Our Crowd. 201, 202
Our Hearts Were Young and Gay. 31, 135
Our Times, Vol. 1. 101, 102
Ourselves to Know. 180
Oursler, Fulton. 12, 17, 26, 39, 56, 149, 150, 160
Out of the Night. 131, 132
Outline of History, The. 19, 23
Outline of Science, The. 77, 91–95, 109
Outwitting Our Nerves. 93
Outwitting the Hun. 86
Over the Top. 83–85
Overstreet, H. A. 152–154

Paar, Jack. 180, 182
Packard, Vance. 14, 37, 177, 179
Page, Elizabeth. 127
Page, Thomas Nelson. 63, 67
Page, Walter H. 96
Paine, Albert Bigelow. 76, 85, 86
Painted Windows. 93, 94
Palmer, Frederick. 83
Papashvily, George and Helen. 140
Papillon. 16, 39
Papini, Giovanni. 95–100
Parasites, The. 30, 152, 153
Parker, Cornelia Stratton. 89

Parker, Sir Gilbert. 60, 62, 64–66, 71, 72, 78, 104
Parkman, Francis. 222
Parris Mitchell of Kings Row. 31
Parrish, Anne. 99, 100, 103, 105
Parrott, Ursula. 73
Partridge, Bellamy. 127
Passionate Witch, The. 17, 40
Passions of the Mind, The. 209, 210
Past Imperfect. 133
Pasternak, Boris. 11, 28, 36, 174, 177, 178
Paul, Elliot. 133, 134
Pavilion of Women. 17, 29
Pawns Count, The. 85
Peace Negotiations. 91
Peace of Mind. 27, 142–144, 146–148, 150
Peace of Soul. 149, 150
Peace with God. 56
Peacock Sheds His Tail, The. 31
Peale, Norman Vincent. 11, 23, 38, 56, 147–149, 158, 160, 161, 163, 166, 171, 172
Pearl, The. 17, 40
Pearson, Drew. 111–114
Peat, Harold R. 86
Peculiar Treasure, A. 127, 128
Peder Victorious, 107, 108
Pelo, W. J. 19, 41, 55
Penelope's Progress. 62
Penrod. 30, 80, 82
Perennial Bachelor, The. 99
Perkins, Frances. 142
Personal History. 119, 120
Peter. 72, 73
Peter, Laurence J. 205, 206, 211
Peter Prescription, The. 211
Peter Principle, The. 205, 206
Peterkin, Julia. 28, 107, 108
Peters, Lulu Hunt. 30, 93, 95–97, 99, 101
Peterson, Roger Tory. 26
Peyton Place. 10, 33, 169–171
Phelps, William Lyon. 127, 128
Phillips, J. B. 174, 175
Phillips, M. C. 119
Phroso. 61
Phyllis Diller's Housekeeping Hints. 198
Phyllis Diller's Marriage Manual. 201
Pickett, Elizabeth. 133
Pictorial History World War II. 30
Pigman, The. 47
Pilgrim's Inn. 30, 147

Pilgrim's Progress, The. 221
Pillsbury Family Cookbook, The. 189
Piper, Watty. 18, 23, 46
Pirate, The. 14, 37, 215
Pit, The. 67
Pitkin, Walter B. 115, 117
Plague and I, The. 147, 148
Plain Speaking. 215, 216
Plain Tales from the Hills. 223
Plastic Age, The. 189, 197, 198
Plattsburg Manual, The. 83, 84
Plays of William Shakespeare. 221
Pleasant Valley. 140
Please Don't Eat the Daisies. 15, 38, 171, 172, 174, 175
Plot, The. 201, 202
Plutocrat, The. 103
Pocket Atlas. 10, 33
Pocket Book of Baby and Child Care. 10, 33
Pocket Book of Erskine Caldwell Stories. 18, 40
Pocket Book of Ogden Nash. 53
Pocket Book of Short Stories. 13, 36
Pocket Book of Verse, The. 15, 38, 53
Pocket Cook Book, The. 11, 35, 48
Pocket Dictionary, The. 19, 41, 55
Poe, Edgar Allan. 222
Poems of Alan Seeger. 83, 85, 88
Poems of Alfred Tennyson. 222
Poems of Henry Wadsworth Longfellow. 222
Poems of James Whitcomb Riley. 223
Poems of John Greenleaf Whittier. 222
Poems of Robert Burns. 221
Pogo. 155, 156
Point of No Return. 149, 150
Pollyanna. 27, 47, 78, 80
Pollyanna Grows Up. 28, 47, 81
Poor No More. 81, 83, 91, 177, 178
Popular Book, The. 4
Porgy. 108, 119
Port of Missing Men, The. 71
Porter, Eleanor H. 27, 28, 47, 80–83, 85, 89
Porter, Gene Stratton, 9, 19, 23, 26, 46, 47, 75–78, 81, 85, 87, 91, 99
Porter, Katherine Anne. 186, 187
Porter, Sylvia. 217
Portnoy's Complaint. 12, 36, 205, 206
Portygee, The. 89, 90

Post, Emily. 25, 95–97
Post, Mary Brinker. 25
Potok, Chaim. 17, 39, 201, 202, 205, 211
Power of Positive Thinking, The. 11, 23, 38, 56, 158–161, 163, 164, 166, 167
Prayers of Peter Marshall, The. 163, 164
Preface to Morals, A. 107, 136
Pregnancy, Birth and Family Planning. 19, 41
Present Indicative. 123
Preserve and Protect. 203, 204
President's Daughter, The. 110
Pretenders, The. 205, 206
Pride of Jennico, The. 62
Pride's Castle. 18, 27, 149, 150, 153
Priestley, J. B. 109, 110
Prince of Foxes. 18, 29, 144
Prince of Graustark, The. 80
Prince of the House of David, The. 222
Princess Aline. 59
Princess Passes, The. 69
Prisoner of Zenda, The. 59, 61
Private Life of Helen of Troy, The. 30, 101, 102
Private Peat. 86
Private Worlds. 117
Prize, The. 186, 187
Prodigal Judge, The. 75
Profiles in Courage. 12, 29, 35
Promise, The. 205
Promised Land, The. 76, 78
Prophet, The. 11, 22, 53
Psycho-Cybernetics. 12, 35
Psychology and Industrial Efficiency. 78
Puppet Crown, The. 65
Pursuit of the House-Boat, The. 61
Puzo, Mario. 10, 33, 49, 50, 205, 206
Pyle, Ernie. 28, 29, 135–138, 140, 142

QB VII. 207
Queed. 75
Queen, Ellery. 49
Queen Victoria. 93
Quo Vadis. 61, 62

RCAF Exercise Book. 12, 35
R. E. Lee. 119

Rabbit Redux. 209
Rafferty, Kathleen. 10, 33, 54
Rage to Live, A. 149, 150
Ragtime. 32, 217, 218
Rainbow Trail. 30
Rains Came, The. 123, 125, 126
Raintree County. 147, 148
Raise High the Roof Beam, Carpenters, and Seymour—An Introduction. 189, 190
Rally Round the Flag, Boys! 18, 42, 171, 172
Rand, Ayn. 14, 37, 171
Rand McNally Dollar World Atlas. 27
Random Harvest. 131, 132
Random House Dictionary of the English Language, The. 27, 198, 199, 203, 204
Rats, Lice and History. 119, 130
Raucher, Herman. 14, 37
Rawlings, Marjorie Kinnan. 125, 127, 133, 134
Raymond. 83
Razor's Edge, The. 13, 24, 137, 138
Reaching for the Stars. 127, 128
Read, Piers Paul. 14, 37
Reading I've Liked. 131, 132
Real Adventure, The. 82
Real Mother Goose, The. 25, 45, 47
Rebecca. 15, 26, 125–127, 136, 142
Rebecca of Sunnybrook Farm. 25, 47, 68
Rechy, John. 189, 190
Recollections. 85, 86
Re-Creation of Brian Kent, The. 31, 87, 89
Rector of Justin, The. 192, 194
Red Badge of Courage, The. 14, 41, 60
Red Planet, The. 83
Red Pottage. 64
Red Rock. 63
Redemption of David Corson, The. 64
Reed, Chester A. 29
Regeneration. 59
Reich, Charles. 16, 40
Reign of Law, The. 64
Reilly, Ottilie H. 149
Reivers, The. 186, 187
Remarque, Erich Maria. 13, 25, 107, 111, 142, 143
Reminiscences. 192, 194
Report of the Warren Commission. 199

Return of the Native, The. 223
Return to Paradise. 155, 156
Return to Peyton Place. 12, 35
Return to Religion, The. 123, 124
Reuben, David. 10, 34, 207–210, 217, 218
Reveille in Washington. 131, 132
Reveries of a Bachelor. 222
Reves, Emery. 142
Revolt in the Desert. 103, 104, 120
Revolt of Mamie Stover, The. 19, 41
Reynolds, Quentin. 137, 138
Rhymes of a Red Cross Man. 83, 85
Rice, Alice Hegan. 67, 69
Rice, Grantland. 163, 164
Rich Man, Poor Man. 11, 207, 208
Richard Carvel. 31, 63, 64
Richard Yea-and-Nay. 64
Richards, I. A. 17, 39, 55
Riders of the Purple Sage, The. 26
Right of Way, The. 65, 66
Riley, James Whitcomb. 86, 223
Rinehart, Mary Roberts. 30, 49, 73, 74,
    81, 85, 87, 91, 93, 95, 103, 106, 109,
    110, 119
Ring of Bright Water. 183, 185
Ringer, Robert. 217, 218
Ripley, Robert L. 107, 108
Rise and Fall of the Third Reich, The.
    14, 40, 180, 182, 183, 185
Rise of American Civilization, The. 109
River Road, The. 27, 142, 143
River's End, The. 89
Rives, Hallie Erminie. 71, 74
Road Back, The. 111
Road to Understanding, The. 83
Robbins, Harold. 10–16, 33, 35–37, 39,
    183, 184, 198, 199, 205, 206, 209,
    210
Robe, The. 12, 22, 133–135, 137, 138,
    140, 141, 148, 160, 161
Robert Elsmere. 60, 223
Roberts, Kenneth. 25, 123–125, 129–
    131, 144, 169
Robinson Crusoe. 221
Robinson, Henry Morton. 14, 152, 153,
    155, 156
Robinson, James Harvey. 93–96
Robinson, Victor. 27
Roe, E. P. 223
Rogers, Dale Evans. 160
Rogers, Rosemary. 18, 40

Roget's International Thesaurus. 28
Roget's Pocket Thesaurus. 10, 34, 54
Rogue Herries. 109
Rölvaag, O. E. 107, 108
Rombauer, Irma S. 10, 22, 40, 186
Roosevelt and Hopkins. 147, 148
Roosevelt, Elliott. 142
Roosevelt, Franklin D. 115, 116
Roosevelt I Knew, The. 142
Roosevelt's Letters to His Children. 89
Roper's Row. 107
Rorick, Isabel Scott. 131
Rosary, The. 27, 74, 75
Rose, Billy. 147, 148
Rose o' the River. 69
Rosemary's Baby. 12, 35, 201, 202
Rossner, Judith. 217, 218
Roth, Lillian. 17, 40, 163, 164
Roth, Philip. 12, 36, 205, 206
Rothschilds, The. 186, 188
Royal Box, The. 14, 27, 163, 164
Royal Road to Romance, The. 31, 103
Ruark, Robert. 166, 177, 178
Rubaiyat of Omar Khayyam, The. 223
Runkle, Bertha. 65
Rush to Judgment. 198, 199
Ryan, Cornelius. 198

Sabatini, Rafael. 30, 95–97, 99
Sagan, Françoise. 166, 167, 169, 170
St. Elmo. 223
Saint-Exupery, Antoine de. 15, 40, 46, 47
Saint Joan. 97, 98
St. Johns, Adela Rogers. 198
Salamander, The. 80
Sale, Chic. 25, 107, 108
Salinger, J. D. 11, 34, 80, 183, 184, 186,
    187, 189, 190
Salisbury, Helen M. 93
Salzburg, Connection, The. 203, 204
Sanctuary. 19, 41
Sand Pebbles. The. 189, 190
Sands, Bill. 195, 197
Sandy, 69
Santa Mouse. 30
Santayana, George. 121, 122
Saracen Blade, The. 158, 159
Saratoga Trunk. 131
Saroyan, William. 135, 136

Satan Sanderson. 71
Saturday Evening Post Treasury, The. 163, 165
Saunders, Marshall. 224
Save-Your-Life Diet, The. 217, 218
Scapegoat, The. 171
Scaramouche. 30
Scarlet Letter, The. 222
Scarlet Sister Mary. 28
Schindler, John A. 166, 169
Schlesinger, Arthur M., Jr. 195, 197, 198
Schlink, F. J. 115–117
Scholastic World Atlas. 17, 39, 55
Schreiber, Flora R. 13, 36, 213, 214
Schreiner, Olive. 76
Schulberg, Budd. 152, 153
Schulz, Charles M. 12–18, 28, 35, 36, 38–40
Science and Health with Key to the Scriptures. 223
Scott, Sir Walter. 221
Scrabble Word Guide. 26
Sea Around Us, The. 155, 156, 158
Sea-Hawk, The. 95
Seagrave, Lt. Col. Gordon. 135
Search for Bridey Murphy, The. 169, 170
Seats of the Mighty, The. 60
Secret of Happiness, The. 166, 167
Secret of Santa Vittoria, The. 198, 199
Secret Woman, The. 207, 208
Security Is a Thumb and a Blanket. 189, 191
Sedgwick, Anne Douglas. 76, 77, 97–99, 103, 107
See Here, Private Hargrove. 15, 40, 86, 133–136
Seeger, Alan. 83–85, 88
Segal, Erich. 10, 33, 207, 208
Self-Mastery Through Conscious Auto-Suggestion. 95
Self-Raised, or, Out of the Depths. 223
Selinko, Annemarie. 26, 160
Selling of the President 1968, The. 205, 206
Semi-Tough. 211, 212
Sendak, Maurice. 47
Sensuous Man, The. 12, 35, 209, 210
Sensuous Woman, The. 10, 33, 207, 208, 210
Sentimental Tommy. 60, 61
Septimus. 73

Sermons and Soda-Water. 180
Serpico. 17, 40
Service Cook Book, The. 15, 37
Service, Robert W. 83–85
Seton, Anya. 12, 22, 174, 175
Settlement Cook Book, The. 24
Seuss, Dr. 11, 13, 22, 46
Seven Days in May. 19, 52, 186, 187
Seven Gothic Tales. 117, 118
Seven Minutes, The. 18, 41, 205, 206
Seven-Per-Cent Solution, The. 215, 216
Seven Pillars of Wisdom. 119, 120
Seven Purposes, The. 187
Seven Storey Mountain, The. 149, 150
Seventeen. 45, 47, 182
79 Park Ave. 12, 35
Seversky, Major Alexander P. de. 133
Sewell, Anna. 223
Sex and the Single Girl. 186
Sexual Behavior in the Human Female. 160, 162
Sexual Behavior in the Human Male. 147, 148
Seymour, E. L. D. 26
Shade of Difference, A. 186, 187
Shadows on the Rock. 111, 112
Shakespeare, William. 221
Shannon's Way. 27, 147
Shaw, George Bernard. 97, 98, 105, 106
Shaw, Irwin. 11, 18, 34, 41, 147, 148, 207, 208, 213
Shaw, Mark. 192
She. 223
Sheean, Vincent. 119, 120, 127, 128
Sheen, Fulton J. 149, 150, 160
Sheik, The. 26, 91–94
Sheldon, Charles Monroe. 10, 24, 34
Sheldon, Sidney. 12, 35
Shellabarger, Samuel. 18, 29, 140, 144, 160
Sheltered Life, The. 113
Shepherd of the Hills, The. 26
Sherwood, Margaret. 84
Sherwood, Robert E. 147, 148
Ship of Fools. 186, 187
Shirer, William L. 14, 40, 86, 131, 132, 180, 182, 183
Shoes of the Fisherman, The. 189, 190
Shogun. 217, 218
Show Boat. 101, 102
Shrewsbury. 62

Shulman, Irving. 18, 19, 40, 42
Shulman, Max. 18, 42, 171, 172
Shute, Nevil. 15, 38, 171, 172, 180
Shuttle, The. 71, 72
Sidney, Margaret. 223
Sienkiewicz, Henryk. 61, 62
Silas Marner. 223
Silent Places, The. 68
Silver Chalice, The. 18, 23, 158–161
Silver Horde, The. 73
Silver Spoon, The. 101
Simon Called Peter. 93, 94
Simon Dale. 62
Simon the Jester. 74
Simple Life, The. 28
Since Yesterday. 102
Sinclair, May. 85
Sinclair, Upton. 17, 41, 70
Singing Guns. 17, 39
Singular Life, A. 60
Sir Mortimer. 68
Sir Richard Calmady. 66
Sisters-In-Law, The. 91
Six Weeks to Words of Power. 29
Sixty Years of Best Sellers. 32
Sketch Book of Geoffrey Crayon, Gent., The. 221
Skin Deep. 119, 120
Skinner, Cornelia Otis. 31, 135, 136
Sky Pilot in No Man's Land, The. 87
Skyward. 105
Small Town in Germany, A. 203, 204
Smattering of Ignorance, A. 129, 130
Smith, Adam. 203, 204
Smith, Betty. 16, 23, 135–137, 147, 148
Smith, F. Hopkinson. 60, 62, 72, 73, 81
Smith, Hannah Whitall. 224
Smith, Lillian. 17, 137
Smith, Robert Paul. 171, 172
Smith, Thorne. 16, 17, 28, 40
Snake Pit, The. 142, 143
So Big. 97, 98, 102
So Little Time. 135, 136
So Red the Rose. 117, 118
So Well Remembered. 17, 27, 140
Soldiers of Fortune. 61
Solo in Tom-Toms, A. 142
Solzhenitsyn, Alexander. 15, 38, 211, 212
Something Happened. 215
Something of Value. 166, 167, 178
Song of Bernadette, The. 18, 133–136

Song of Our Syrian Guest, The. 19, 23, 56
Sonia. 85
Sons. 113
Sorensen, Theodore C. 195, 197
Sorrell and Son. 101–104
Soul on Ice. 19
Sounder. 47
Soundings. 99
Source, The. 15, 39, 195, 196
South America. 76, 78
Southern, Terry. 192, 193
Southworth, Mrs. E. D. E. N. 223
Spafford, Julian. 103
Spargo, John. 87
Sparkenbroke. 121
Speaking Frankly. 144, 145
Speare, M. E. 13, 15, 36, 38, 53
Spearman, Frank H. 82
Specialist, The. 25, 107
Speer, Albert. 209, 210
Spellman, Cardinal. 155, 156
Spillane, Mickey. 11, 19, 34, 50, 52
Spock, Benjamin. 10, 33
Spoilers, The. 70
Spring, Howard. 125, 126, 158
Spy, The. 221
Spy Who Came in from the Cold, The. 192, 193
Spy Who Loved Me, The. 15, 37, 51
Spyri, Johanna. 223
Standish, Burt L. 45
Stanyan Street and Other Sorrows. 25, 53, 201–204
Star Money. 152, 153
Starling, Col. Edmund. 142
Starling of the White House. 142
Stars Fell on Alabama. 117
Stars on the Sea. 129, 130
Status Seekers, The. 177, 179
Stay Alive All Your Life. 171, 172
Steamboat Gothic. 26, 158, 159
Stearn, Jess. 201, 202
Steel, Flora Annie. 61
Steen, Marguerite. 28
Steichen, Edward. 166, 167
Stein, Jess. 24, 27
Steinbeck, John. 17, 19, 39, 40, 123, 124, 127, 129, 133, 134, 144, 145, 158, 163, 183, 184, 186, 188
Steps to Christ. 224

Stevenson, Isabelle. 53
Stevenson, Robert Louis. 223
Stewart, Mary. 49, 192, 193, 201, 202, 207, 208, 213
Stillman, Erwin M. 11, 34, 203, 204
Stockton, Frank R. 59
Stone for Danny Fisher, A. 13, 36
Stone, Grace Zaring. 128
Stone, Irving. 14, 27, 39, 140, 163, 183, 184, 186, 195, 196, 209, 210, 217, 218
Stories of Guy de Maupassant. 223
Story of a Bad Boy, The. 223
Story of Mankind, The. 93–95
Story of My Life, The. 113
Story of Philosophy, The. 29, 94, 101–104, 108–110
Story of San Michele, The. 109–111
Story of the Bible, The. 14, 22, 56
Story of the Other Wise Man, The. 28
Stowe, Harriet Beecher. 222
Strachey, Lytton. 93, 94, 107
Strange Case of Miss Annie Spragg, The. 105
Strange Death of President Harding, The. 109, 110
Strange Fruit. 17, 137, 138
Strange Interlude. 105
Strange Woman. 25
Stranger, The. 18
Streams in the Desert. 20, 24, 56
Street Called Straight, The. 76
Streeter, Edward. 85, 86, 149, 150
Strength for Service to God and Country. 27
Strunk, William, Jr. 20, 177, 178
Struther, Jan. 129, 130
Stuart Little. 18, 46
Student in Arms, A. 83
Study of History, A. 144, 145
Styron, William. 201, 202
Sugrue, Thomas. 142
Sullivan, Mark. 101, 102, 114
Summer of '42, The. 14, 37
Sun Is My Undoing, The. 28, 131, 133
Sunset Editors. 16, 19, 38, 41, 52, 53
Sure Hand of God, The. 14, 37
Susann, Jacqueline. 10, 12, 35, 198, 199, 205, 206, 213, 214
Sutherland, Halliday. 115
Sutton, Henry. 201

Swan Song. 105
Sweet Thursday. 163, 164
Swift, Jonathan. 221
Swing, Raymond. 163
Swiss Family Robinson, The. 221
Sybil. 13, 36, 213, 214
Sylvia Porter's Money Book. 217, 218

TM: Discovering Energy and Overcoming Stress. 217, 218
T. Tembarom. 78, 80
Tai-Pan. 198, 200
Talbot, Constance. 53
Tale of Two Cities, A. 222
Tales by Edgar Allan Poe. 222
Tales of Power. 215, 216
Tales of the South Pacific. 15, 38, 156
Talese, Gay. 16, 40, 209, 210
Taller, Dr. Herman. 28, 183, 186, 188
Tallulah. 158, 159
Tante. 76, 77
Tarbell, Ida. 68
Tarkington, Booth. 30, 47, 66, 80–82, 93, 97, 103–106, 113, 114
Tarzan of the Apes. 31
Taylor, Kenneth. 211–213
Tell No Man. 198, 200
Tempest and Sunshine. 222
Ten Nights in a Bar-Room. 4
Ten North Frederick. 166, 167
Ten Years in Japan. 86, 137
Tennyson, Alfred. 222
Terrariums. 52
Testimony of Two Men. 205
Thacker, May Dixon. 109
Thackeray, William Makepeace. 222
Thayer, William Roscoe. 189, 190
Theatre. 123
Their Finest Hour. 28
Their Yesterdays. 76
Thelma. 223
Theodore Roosevelt. 89
They Were Expendable. 133, 134
Thin Man, The. 49
Thinking Reed, The. 121
30 Days to a More Powerful Vocabulary. 11, 24, 35, 55
This Above All. 131
This Freedom. 93, 95, 96

This I Believe. 158–161, 163, 164
This Is Ike. 158, 159
This Is Murder. 17, 41, 52
This Rough Magic. 192, 193
This Side of Innocence. 25, 142, 143
This Side of Paradise. 189, 198
This Very Earth. 16, 38
Thomas, Lowell. 105, 106
Thompson, Kay. 169, 171, 174
Thompson, Maurice. 64, 65
Thompson, Morton. 15, 24, 163, 164
Thompson, Sylvia. 101
Thomson, J. Arthur. 93, 94
Thoreau, Henry David. 4, 222
Those Who Love. 195, 196
Thousand Days, A. 195, 197–199
Three Harbours. 130
Three Loves. 113, 114
Three Men in a Boat. 223
Three Musketeers, The. 222
Three Plays. 76, 78
Three Weeks. 4
Thunderball. 12, 35
Thunderhead. 30
Thurber Carnival, The. 140
Thurber, James. 140
Thurston, Katherine Cecil. 68, 69, 73, 74
Tight White Collar, The. 20, 42
Tileston, Mary W. 26
Time and Time Again. 160
Time for Decision, The. 137
Time Out of Mind. 119
Tin Soldier, The. 187
Tinker, Tailor, Soldier, Spy. 215
To Have and To Hold. 64
To Kill a Mockingbird. 10, 33, 183, 184
To Live Again. 171, 172
To the Last Man. 30, 93
Tobacco Road. 12, 35
Toffler, Alvin. 12, 35
Together. 144, 146
Tolstoi, Leo. 223
Tom Grogan. 60
Tom Jones. 190
Tomorrow Morning. 103
Tomorrow Will Be Better. 147, 148
Tontine, The. 166, 167
Top Secret. 142
Topaz. 19, 201, 202
Topper. 16, 28
Torres, Tereska. 16, 38

Tortilla Flat. 124
Total Fitness in 30 Minutes a Week. 217, 218
Total Woman, The. 15, 40, 215, 216
Touch Typing. 25
Tower of Babel, The. 203, 204
Townsend, Robert. 207, 208
Toynbee, Arnold J. 144, 145
Trader Horn. 103–105, 108
Tragic Era, The. 107
Tragic Ground. 11, 35
Trail of the Lonesome Pine, The. 25, 72, 73
Train, Arthur. 95, 96
Travels with Charley. 186, 188
Travels with My Aunt. 207
Traver, Robert. 14, 37, 50, 174
Travers, Pamlea L. 47
Treasure Island. 223
Treasury of War Poetry. 85
Tree Grows in Brooklyn, A. 16, 23, 135, 137, 138, 148
Tree of Heaven, The. 85, 86
Tree of Liberty, The. 127, 128
Tregaskis, Richard. 135
Tribe That Lost Its Head, The. 169
Trilby. 59, 224
Trine, Ralph Waldo. 24
Triumph and Tragedy. 29
Tropic of Cancer. 14, 38, 183, 184
Trouble after School. 47
Trouble in July. 13, 35
Truman, Harry S. 166
Truman, Margaret. 211, 212
Trustee from the Toolroom. 180
Truxton King. 73
Try and Stop Me. 140
Tryon, Thomas. 13, 36, 209
Tuchman, Barbara. 92
Tumult and the Shouting, The. 163, 164
Turmoil, The. 81
Turnbull, Agnes Sligh. 147, 148
Twain, Mark. 97, 223
Twelve Years of Christmas. 205, 206
Twenty-Five Years. 99
Twenty-Four Hours. 109
Twice Thirty. 99
Twilight Sleep. 103
Twixt Twelve and Twenty. 174, 176–178, 182
Two from Galilee. 211, 212

2001: A Space Odyssey. 18, 40
Two Vanrevels, The. 66
Two Years Before the Mast. 222

U. P. Trail, The. 31, 85, 86
U.S.A. Confidential. 158, 159
U. S. Foreign Policy. 135
Ugly American, The. 12, 35, 177, 178, 185, 187
Ullman, James Ramsey. 140, 141
Uncle Tom's Cabin. 222
Unconquered, The. 160
Under Cover. 135–137
Under Fire. 86
United Press International. 192, 194
Unleavened Bread. 64
Untermeyer, Louis. 54
Up Front. 140
Up the Down Staircase. 12, 35, 195, 196
Up the Organization. 207, 208
Updike, John. 13, 36, 203, 204, 209, 210
Urdang, Laurence. 27, 203
Uris, Leon. 11, 16, 19, 34, 38, 160, 161, 177, 178, 183, 184, 192, 194, 201, 202, 207

V. V.'s Eyes. 78
Valentine, J. Manson. 215, 216, 217, 218
Valiants of Virginia, The. 78
Valley of Decision, The. 135, 136
Valley of Silent Men, The. 91
Valley of the Dolls. 10, 33, 198, 199
Valtin, Jan. 131, 132
Van Buren, Abigail. 174, 176
van der Heide, Dirk. 131
van Dine, S. S. 105–108
van Doren, Carl. 125, 126
van Dyke, Henry. 66
Van Loon, Hendrik Willem. 93–96, 113–115, 123, 124
Van Loon's Geography. 113, 115
van Paassen, Pierre. 127–129
Vance, Ethel. 127, 128
Vance, Louis J. 71, 72
Vanderbilt, Amy. 24
Vanished. 203, 204
Vanity Fair. 222

Vein of Iron. 119
Venetian Affair, The. 190
Vengeance Is Mine. 11, 34, 50
Very Funny, Charlie Brown. 15, 37
Vicar of Wakefield, The. 221
Victorine. 174
Victory Through Air Power. 133, 134
Vidal, Gore. 18, 41, 203, 204, 213, 214
View from Pompey's Head, The. 31, 163, 164
Virginian, The. 24, 66, 67
Visits of Elizabeth, The. 65
Vixens, The. 14, 24, 144
Von Daniken, Erich. 11, 18, 34, 40
Vonnegut, Kurt, Jr. 213, 214

Wagner, Charles. 28
Wake Up and Live! 121
Wakeman, Frederic. 142, 143
Walden. 4, 222
Wall, The. 152, 153
Wallace, Irving. 15, 18, 19, 37, 41, 180, 181, 186, 187, 192, 194, 201, 202, 205, 206, 211, 215
Wallace, Lew. 223
Waln, Nora. 115, 127, 128
Walpole, Ellen Wales. 47
Walpole, Hugh. 105, 109, 110
Waltari, Mika. 149, 150, 152, 153, 155, 156, 163
Wambaugh, Joseph. 17, 39, 51, 217, 218
Wanderer, The. 155, 156
Wanderer of the Wasteland, The. 95
Wanted: Dennis the Menace. 19, 41
War and Peace. 223
Ward, Elizabeth Stuart Phelps. 60
Ward, Mary Jane. 142, 143
Ward, Mrs. Humphry. 60, 62, 67, 69, 223
Warner, Susan. 222
Washington Confidential. 155, 156
Washington Is Like That. 133
Washington Merry-Go-Round. 111–113
Watership Down. 215, 216
Watts-Dunton, Theodore. 63
Way of a Transgressor, The. 121
Wayward Bus, The. 144, 145
We. 103, 105, 106

We Are Not Alone. 123
We Love You, Snoopy. 14
Weavers, The. 71, 72
Web of Days, The. 28
Webster, Henry Kitchell. 82
Webster, Jean. 82
Webster, Noah. 221
Webster's New School and Office Dictionary. 20, 42
Webster's New World Dictionary of the American Language. 10, 33, 169
Weidman, Jerome. 174, 175
Weight Watcher's Cook Book, The. 203, 204
Weight Watchers Program Cookbook, The. 16, 23, 48, 213
Welk, Lawrence. 209, 210
Welles, Sumner. 137, 138
Wellman, Paul. 30
Wells, H. G. 19, 23, 77, 82–84, 91–93, 95, 96, 109, 110
We're on Your Side, Charlie Brown. 17, 40
Werfel, Franz. 28, 119, 133, 135, 136
West, Morris L. 183, 184, 189, 190, 195, 196, 203
West, Rebecca. 121, 122
Westcott, Edward Noyes. 26, 63
Western Garden Book. 19, 41, 52
Weyman, Stanley. 62
Wharton, Edith. 69, 70, 91, 92, 103
What Next, Charlie Brown. 16, 38
What We Live By. 113
Wheel of Life, The. 70
Wheeler, Harvey. 16, 39, 52, 186, 187
Wheels. 16, 39, 209, 210
When a Man Marries. 74
When a Man's a Man. 82
When Knighthood Was in Flower. 63, 64
When We Were Very Young. 30, 99, 100
Where Did You Go? Out. What Did You Do? Nothing. 171, 172
Where Love Has Gone. 12, 35
Where the Wild Things Are. 47
While Rome Burns. 117–120
White Banners. 121
White Bird Flying, A. 111, 112
White Cliffs, The. 131, 132
White Collar Zoo. 149, 150
White, E. B. 12, 18, 20, 26, 36, 46, 177, 178

White, Ellen G. 28, 224
White Shadows in the South Seas. 89–92, 104
White, Stewart Edward. 68, 71
White, Theodore H. 183, 185, 195, 197, 217, 218
White Tower, The. 140
White, W. L. 133, 134
Whitehead, Don. 171
Whiteing, Richard. 63
Whitlock, Brand. 87
Whitman, Walt. 222
Whittier, John Greenleaf. 222
Why Johnny Can't Read. 166, 167
Why We Behave Like Human Beings. 101–103
Wickford Point. 127
Wide Wide World, The. 222
Wiggam, Albert E. 97
Wiggin, Kate Douglas. 25, 47, 62, 68, 69, 223
Wild Olive, The. 73, 74
Wilder, Laura Ingalls. 15, 16, 39, 41, 46
Wilder, Thornton. 105, 106, 109, 110, 119, 201, 202
Wildfire. 27, 83
Wilkins, Vaughan. 123, 124
Will Rogers. 28
Williams, Ben Ames. 19, 23, 25, 137, 138, 144, 160
Williams, Oscar. 54
Williamson, A. M. 69, 74
Williamson, C. N. 69, 74
Willkie, Wendell L. 135, 136, 138
Wilson, Erica. 53
Wilson, Sloan. 166, 167
Wilson, Woodrow. 78, 116
Wind, Sand and Stars. 127, 128, 134
Window at the White Cat, The. 74, 106
Winds of War, The. 209, 211
Windswept. 131, 133
Wine, Women and Words. 147, 148
Winnie Ille Pu. 45, 183, 184
Winnie-the-Pooh. 28, 45, 47, 184
Winning of Barbara Worth, The. 29, 75, 76
Winning through Intimidation. 217, 218
Winsor, Kathleen. 14, 24, 137, 138, 140, 152, 153
Winter of Our Discontent, The. 183
Wintersmoon. 105

Winthrop Woman, The. 12, 22, 174, 175
Wise Garden Encyclopedia. 26
Wister, Owen. 24, 66, 67, 70
With Malice Toward Some. 125, 126
With the Colors. 85
Within This Present. 117
Witness. 158, 159
Wolfe, Thomas. 119, 120
Woman and Labor. 76
Woman Called Fancy, A. 155, 156
Woman of Andros, The. 109
Woman Thou Gavest Me, The. 78
Women's Barracks. 16, 38
Wonderful Wizard of Oz, The. 11, 22, 41, 46
Wonderful World of Peanuts, The. 18, 40
Wood, Mrs. Henry. 222
Woodcarving Techniques and Projects. 53
Woodward, Bob. 17, 32, 40, 215, 216
Woodworking Projects. 53
Woody, Elizabeth. 11, 35
Woolf, Virginia. 123, 124
Woollcott, Alexander. 117–120
Word, The. 211
Work, Milton C. 78, 79, 101, 102, 112
Work of Art. 117
World Aflame. 195, 197
World Almanac. 54, 157
World Beyond, A, 211, 212
Worldly Philosophers, The. 25
Worn Doorstep, The. 84
Wouk, Herman. 19, 24, 155, 156, 159, 166, 167, 186, 187, 195, 196, 209, 211
Wren, P. C. 101, 102
Wright, Harold Bell. 9, 26, 29, 31, 75–77, 80, 82, 87, 89, 93, 95
Wright, Richard. 140
Wright, Willard Huntington. 106
Wunnerful, Wunnerful! 209
Wuthering Heights. 222
Wyss, Johann R. 221

Xaviera. 13, 35

Yankee from Olympus. 137, 138
Yankee Pasha. 28
Year of Decision. 166, 167
Yearling, The. 125–127, 134
Years, The. 123
Years Between, The. 87, 88
Years of Grace. 109–111
Yerby, Frank. 14, 15, 18, 24, 27, 28, 142–144, 147–150, 152, 153, 155, 156, 158, 163
You Are Too Much, Charlie Brown. 16
You Can Profit from a Monetary Crisis. 215
You Can't Do Business with Hitler. 131, 132
You Must Relax. 117, 118
You Only Live Twice. 13, 36, 50, 192
Young Lions, The. 18, 41, 147, 148
Young Man of Manhattan. 109, 110
Young, Stark. 117, 118
Young, Vash. 113, 114
Youngblood Hawke. 186, 187
Younger Set, The. 71
Your Dream Home. 25, 152, 154
Your Income Tax. 157
Your United States. 76, 78
You're a Winner, Charlie Brown. 17, 39
Yutang, Lin. 125

Zangwill, Israel. 59
Zindel, Paul. 47
Zinsser, Hans. 119, 120, 129, 130
Zion, Gene. 47
Zola, Emile. 223
Zone Policeman. 78
Zweig, Stefan. 115, 119, 120